The AUTOBIOGRAPHY *of*

LEVERETT SALTONSTALL

The AUTOBIOGRAPHY *of* LEVERETT SALTONSTALL

Massachusetts Governor, U.S. Senator, and Yankee Icon

LEVERETT SALTONSTALL,
AS TOLD TO EDWARD WEEKS

Introduction by Richard E. Byrd III

LYONS PRESS

Essex, Connecticut

LP
LYONS
PRESS

An imprint of The Globe Pequot Publishing Group, Inc.
64 South Main Street
Essex, CT 06426
www.globepequot.com

First published by Rowman & Littlefield 2015

British Library Cataloguing in Publication Information Available

Library of Congress Cataloging-in-Publication Data available

ISBN 978-1-4930-9897-2 (paperback)
ISBN 978-1-4930-1309-8 (ebook)

CONTENTS

FOREWORD

Leverett Saltonstall retired to Dover, Massachusetts. He used to talk about blisters in the pines which make them worthless for commercial use. He pointed to the half mile swath of grazing land to the Charles River which he and his sons cleared with two-man saws and axes on weekends. He showed off his daughter's ponies and the water and land conservation work which "the government" had done on his land. "'Course we pay 50 percent."

But one could not look at him and not call him "Senator," "Governor." His was a lifetime of public service. If there is a word that marks it, it is integrity. That great Yankee face—if there is a description for it—is the "Mayflower compact."

Life was different for him in retirement. There were no breakfasts at the White House, long tortuous hearings on spending programs for the Pentagon, emergency flights to Washington for crisis briefings.

He became Leverett Saltonstall, Dover Town Meeting Member.

He was a gentleman farmer with fifteen head of cattle, two pigs, a stable full of horses and ponies and, as a personal luxury for himself and a few friends, a coop full of guinea hens.

Next to his rambling old home on the knoll there was a pond where he floated his duck decoys.

He talked about his pines: "We're still cleaning up from the 1938 hurricane." And about his land: "I have about 150 acres. I'll want to hold onto it. Someday it'll probably be worth some money." The land is beautiful.

His dress: Well on the day I visited it was a blue poplin jacket, khaki trousers, a checked tweed hat and rubber soled shoes.

But behind him were 21 years in the Senate, three terms as governor of Massachusetts (the state's only three-term governor) and four terms as Speaker of the Massachusetts House of Representatives.

In Washington, he knew them all. He got advice from Calvin Coolidge; Harry Truman asked him to pray for him when he learned of Roosevelt's death; he was close to Lyndon Johnson. He was the only man in the capital who called John F. Kennedy "Johnny." If Senator Kennedy in the 1950s was up for re-election it would be known as the Kennedy-Saltonstall bill; and if Saltonstall was up for re-election it would be known as the Saltonstall-Kennedy bill. They had that kind of relationship which other Democrats or Republicans in Massachusetts could never crack. Only rarely did he and Kennedy vote differently in the Senate. The St. Lawrence Seaway was one such occasion. Kennedy supported it and Saltonstall fought down the line for the New England interest.

Senator Saltonstall was known as "Mr. Fish" on Capitol Hill for all his legislative activity in support of New England fishermen. And he relished the seafood that resulted. A special feature of the Senate restaurant was the Saltonstall-sponsored "shore dinners" complete with New England clam chowder and lobsters. He was the epitome of the frugal New England Yankee. House Majority Leader Thomas P. O'Neill, Jr. tells the story of helping "Lev" carry to the airport empty egg cartons tied together which would be taken back to Dover over the weekend, filled with eggs and brought back to Washington on Monday to be sold to the Senator's customers. He also played golf at Burning Tree in Maryland with wooden shaft golf clubs.

Senator Saltonstall was much more than a charming character. He was one of those men who make the United States Senate work. He was not flashy. He made few speeches on the floor or outside of his home state. He was the ranking Republican on the Armed Services and Appropriation Committees, and he would sit in the mark-up sessions for bills or on the conference committees between the House and Senate to settle differences in House and Senate versions of bills by the hour. Here was where the real Senate decisions were made. He worked earnestly at making the regional conferences work, not an easy task given the New England Congressional membership.

Senator Saltonstall also had his legislative landmarks. First was the Unification Act for Armed Services, passed in 1957 and consolidated by the Congress and the executive through the administration of President Kennedy. He played a major role in this bill through these years. He also sponsored and maintained an active interest in the National Science Foundation established in 1950, through which the government supported scholarship in the sciences.

His interests extended far beyond New England. He was invited to the Mackinac Conference in Michigan by Senator Arthur Vandenberg in 1944. It was here that Vandenberg broke with Republican isolationist traditions, and thereby helped make bipartisan foreign policy for such things as the Marshall Plan possible. The man from Massachusetts followed Vandenberg's lead, supporting most of what evolved into the internationalist, one-world policies of Roosevelt and Truman.

Finally, Leverett Saltonstall had the good sense to know when to leave public life. One day in January 1966, just after he announced his retirement, I met with him for several hours on his farm in Dover. He showed me a letter he had received from a friend: "Dear Lev: Some 30 years ago your mother and I served on the Board of Trustee of the Chestnut Hill School. At that time she said to me, 'One of the troubles of growing old is that you don't have the sense to know when the time has come to get off committees'. . . . I feel sure she would have approved of your very difficult decision." The senator looked up and said, "I guess I simply followed my mother's advice."

—ROBERT L. HEALY

Former Executive Editor
The Boston Globe

PREFACE

On an auspicious day in June 1971, Leverett Saltonstall came to my office on Arlington Street to discuss his memoir which his family had been urging him to write, but about which he had his doubts. He had told me he was working on it when we talked at the Tavern Club. I had heard that another Boston publisher had considered and dismissed the book. There was a challenge in the idea we might succeed with a different approach.

Saltonstall brought with him a bare chronology of the high points of his forty years in public office, copies of speeches, a series of lectures on public service which he delivered at Penn State, and a sheaf of short anecdotes. So we began that morning: the Senator drew up a chair at the right of my desk; I introduced him to my secretary, Virginia Albee, and then started questioning him about his family traditions. His answers were taken down in shorthand. I was surprised when he told me that he came from a long line of Yankee Democrats, and that his great grandfather, also a Leverett, had served as the first Mayor of Salem, and then as President of the Massachusetts Senate in 1830. Leverett blushed as he added parenthetically that it had been his ambition to be elected the Speaker of the Massachusetts House a hundred years later—and so he had. His father's life-long friendship with Theodore Roosevelt that began when they were classmates at Harvard had swung Saltonstall Senior and son to the Republican Party.

These morning meetings were to continue each week for the ensuing three and a half years, with time off for Saltonstall's summer cruising at North Haven. His memory was fresh and his speaking style was colloquial, candid, colorful, and very emphatic when he was aroused. He was punctual to the minute and about two hours was our limit. The routine never varied: we went over the notes of the previous meeting, clearing up the confusion when both of us had been talking too fast, and when those points were clarified, I resumed questioning him on the next phase of his career. Once when I was out of the room Lev paid me a compliment when he said to Miss Albee, "Your boss asks the right questions." This was the first time in a rather long career that I ever attempted to edit a book by asking questions.

There was one exception to our office routine when we went out to the Saltonstall farm in Dover to select from the score of albums the pictures we wanted for the book. This stirred up some old embers, especially Lev's love of parades. From his first year as a Newton alderman he had never missed one, striding along in top hat and cutaway, or in his uniform astride a white horse, or marching through South Boston on Evacuation Day, grinning as the crowd shouted, "Hi, Salty!"

I knew nothing about parliamentary procedure or of how a senatorial committee does its work, and my ingenuous questions sometimes made him laugh, but they also made him spell things out; they reminded him of the opposition he had put out of mind, and occasionally sent him home to look up at the record. As our talks continued, I grew aware of Saltonstall's modesty, of his reluctance to criticize people but not policies—except when he had been doublecrossed—and of his intense loyalty to his family, to Harvard, and to the nation.

Tears came to his eyes when he told how during the war, and even today, people would stop him on the street to thank him for what he had done for a son in the service. His wife Alice he usually referred to as "My Missus." He was very proud of her and he would smile guiltily when he spoke of something that he had done which landed him in the doghouse. When the magnificent battleship *Massachusetts* was to be christened, Secretary of the Navy Knox telephoned him from Washington to say that it was customary for a governor to designate the person who was to christen a ship named for his state. "The rather formal way which he said this made me hesitate to name my own good wife, though I wanted her to do it. Instead I suggested that Mrs. Charles Francis Adams, the wife of the former Secretary of the Navy and a member of a most distinguished family, would be a happy choice, and Knox agreed." When Lev told Mrs. Saltonstall of the suggestion, she agreed it was a good choice but was naturally disappointed and felt hurt.

I knew I had an ally in Mrs. Saltonstall, and a check point. I wanted an amusing account of their marriage in Jaffrey, New Hampshire, when Alice had refused to ride in the old Saltonstall coach, and when no amount of poking would get the true story from Lev, I turned to her, and she told it with glee.

I interviewed Leverett's aides, beginning with Dan Lynch who had served him so loyally during his days in the State House, then Jimmy Reynolds who followed him from Boston to Washington, and those younger assistants who cut their teeth in his senatorial office—Jonathan Moore, Tom Winship, Bill Saltonstall, and Elliot Richardson. I wish I might've consulted Henry Minot who figured so often in Lev's remembrance. Al Larivee, Lev's driver, told the touching account of how Lev received the news of his second son's death. On the evening of August 13, 1944, the Boston manager of Western Union personally delivered a cable from the Commandant of the Marines, stating that Peter had been ambushed and killed while on patrol in Guam. Lev insisted on driving himself back to Dover, planning what to say to Alice. But Al followed him out in S-1 (Saltonstall's official car) to see if he could be of help. Lev thanked him, gave him some fresh eggs, and asked Larivee to pick him up early the next morning. The following day he spoke at a memorial service on the Boston Common honoring a young marine who was missing in combat and whose mother was presented with her boy's decoration. Lev had prepared his remarks in advance and they were underscored with personal grief, though without any direct reference to Peter.

As we proceeded the "anecdotes" began to fit into their proper places, but now they became episodes, filled out with lively detail. For instance, when Saltonstall ran against James Michael Curley for the governorship, Curley made a disparaging reference to him as "a man with a Harvard accent and a South Boston face." Actually that description had appeared years earlier in the *Boston Evening Transcript,* and Curley's revival of it was a real blunder, for Lev quoted it repeatedly and added his retort, "I'll have the same face *after* election that I have before election," meaning that he would live up to his campaign promises—and in this good natured way he won the respect of the Boston Irish.

It is a measure of a politician in Washington to name the men he most admired (and who in turn admired him). Saltonstall's list was topped by President Eisenhower, and General George C. Marshall; it included Admiral Rickover, whom Leverett pushed through for rank of admiral when the submariner would otherwise have been "plucked" by the Navy Board; it included "Vinegar" Joe Stilwell, with whom Saltonstall paced the deck in the dawn hours before the atom bomb tests at Bikini; it included Senator Richard Russell of Georgia, Saltonstall's opposite number on the Armed Services Committee (Russell, returning after a long illness, as he scanned the Appropriations Bill, exclaimed, "Damn it, Lev, you got just the bill you wanted and you had only one third of the votes."); and Senatir Lyndon B. Johnson who, in a trying conference, said in an aside to one of Saltonstall's aides, "Tell Lev he wouldn't know how to doublecross anyone."

Saltonstall's account of these men and of the admiration he felt for them gives us an insight on American integrity, theirs and his.

—EDWARD WEEKS

Former Senior Editor
Atlantic Monthly

INTRODUCTION TO THE 2015 EDITION

When the publisher of this autobiography of my grandfather, Leverett Saltonstall, asked me to write an Introduction to it, I reached out to other family members and asked for their recollections of him. I will get to their stories in a moment, but let me begin with my earliest memory of Grandpa. He was about my age now, mid-60s, and he's carrying my three brothers and me up the stairs to bed at our home in Chestnut Hill outside of Boston, bouncing us up and down on the beds, much to our delight, but to the dismay of my mother who knew we would be wide awake a little longer. He was 6 feet tall and still in great shape from a lifetime of exercise and swimming, at that time in the U.S. Senate pool in Washington where he was serving as the senior Senator from Massachusetts.

Grandpa loved spending time with his grandchildren. We saw him mostly up in Maine in the summer on North Haven. The other place where we gathered often was Grandpa's farm in Dover, Massachusetts, about 45 minutes from Boston. There we enjoyed many family Thanksgiving and Christmas holidays together. Grandpa loved the farm and did his best to play the role of "Gentleman Farmer" when he could. He raised animals, rode horses, and even had a small cart pulled by a donkey that we children loved to ride in with him. Our grandmother, Alice, was a good sport about all these activities and supported Grandpa, the ringleader. One thing we children knew was that both of them loved and supported us unconditionally.

My favorite time with Grandpa was at breakfast in Maine. He always ate his meals at the same time every day. Breakfast at 7:15 was a bowl of Special K cereal ("K ration" he called it), cream from the farm, two poached eggs, bacon, orange juice, and coffee. Then it was time for "chores" or boat "business" until lunch at 12:45.

Lunch was a sandwich, usually grilled cheese and bacon, desert, and a glass of "Shandygaff" (half Ginger Ale and half beer). Next a nap, and at 2 p.m. or whenever the Sou'west wind would come up, a sailboat race or a sail in the *Fish Hawk*, a 63-foot sloop he owned with his brother Dick and his sister Muriel. He kept her moored off the dock when it was his turn to have her every other week. Often he'd bring us along for a sail and a picnic on one of the many uninhabited, rocky islands nearby. We'd delight in one of his favorites, hash with an egg dropped into it, served below in the main cabin.

My brother, Leverett Byrd, remembers that Monday and Saturday afternoons were the dinghy races in the waters of North Haven and it was mandatory that our dinghy, the *Kedogo*, be raced. "When Grandpa raced we would accompany him as the crew which was a thrill and, when he became too old to race, it was our job to race the boat. Racing was 'serious' business, and it was important that we do well. He came out in our launch, the *Useful*, to observe the start and part of the race. Later on at cocktails on the porch or at dinner after the race there was always a brief discussion about the results which quite often were favorable. However, we would always be surprised because Grandpa would make some observation about the race: how we had strayed too close to the shore and lost our wind or tacked too late and let another boat sneak by us at the windward mark. I think he was a little more competitive than we thought. I know he was proud of us when we did win a race."

Once Grandpa had a visitor in Maine named Clarence Birdseye, the founder of the now famous frozen food company. He had come to pitch Grandpa's brother Dick to become an investor in his new business. They took him out on the *Fish Hawk* where Mr. Birdseye served them warmed-up frozen peas. Being gentleman farmers back in Dover, they were used to fresh peas, especially in the summer. They turned him down, much to their later regret!

He was away in Washington so much that he rarely had time to attend our sports events in Boston. Back in those days, they went to Washington to work and stayed there like everyone else, coming home only on holidays. But if it was holiday time and the Senate was out of session, he would come home and all of us were thrilled when he did. We loved attending Harvard football games with him. One year he was the speaker at my seventh-grade graduation at Dexter School and I remember how proud I was. I introduced him, myself and, after saying all these wonderful things about him, I concluded by saying, "and he is MY grandfather!" which caused much applause and laughter.

The truth is we kids had no idea how prominent he was in the political life of the state or the nation. To us, he was just Grandpa.

He would often remind us of what was important in life: "Country, Family, and Harvard College!" We would most often hear about the latter. One of his favorite stories that he tells in his book is the time he outskated legendary Princeton hockey star, Hobey Baker, to score the winning goal for Harvard in the national championship game of 1914. Grandma, sitting at the other end of the table, would remind him that in those days the starting players like Baker usually played the entire game and Grandpa had just come off the bench fresh and ready to go. Years later, wearing the same old ice skates and wielding his college hockey stick, he taught my brothers and me to skate on the ice at Hammond's Pond near where we grew up.

The other big Harvard victory he enjoyed describing came at the end of his senior year when he and some of his classmates took an eight-man shell to Henley in England and were the first American crew team to win there. That entire eight-man team remained fast friends into their 80s, including Grandpa's great friend Bobby Cobb, who was a substitute. In 1964, fifty years after their victory, they returned to Henley for a reunion row. One by one, they stepped into the shell, took their seats, and off they went! Their families and friends were there, of course, and I remember getting a glimpse of the Queen Mother herself after the races concluded. I still have the old Kodak snapshot I took that day, although all that's visible of the Queen is her pink bonnet. Grandpa, still a sitting U.S. Senator, met the Queen at the ceremonies afterward.

Grandpa had a wonderful sense of humor and a way of always looking for the best in people. He was well off, but never ostentatious. He didn't judge people on the basis of their position in society or how much money they had. Old Yankee that he was, he was usually trying to save money himself. My cousin Tim Saltonstall remembers Grandpa arranging for Tim to drive Grandpa, Grandma, and Senator and Mrs. Prescott Bush to a White House State dinner for the poet Robert Frost. They piled into Grandpa's old Studebaker Lark, maybe one of the ugliest cars ever built, all four of them in the small back seat which caused the rear end to noisily bump against the raised pavement as they pulled into the White House driveway. As other Senators and dignitaries pulled up in their limousines, Grandpa's Lark with the Massachusetts license plate "USS 1" was quite a sight. Tim says that all the other chauffeurs got a big kick out of it.

Another cousin, Lily Russell Heiliger, remembers a visit to Washington at Eastertime in 1959 to see Grandpa and Grandma. She writes, "That evening we had dinner with them at home. I remember Aunt Alice explaining to us that when she departed for the summer holiday in Maine ahead of Uncle Lev, she roasted a large leg of lamb. This would be the base of Uncle Lev's meals for the next two weeks until he could join the family for the summer Senate break. Aunt Alice explained that cooked meat keeps in the icebox for at least three weeks. What a wonderful example of Yankee thrift in someone who was extremely generous and caring."

My cousin, Susan Lawrence, remembers how supportive Grandma was of Grandpa's political endeavors. She frequently hosted election night gatherings at their home in Washington for friends, political supporters, and reporters as they listened for the returns. She also worked alongside other Senate wives on Red Cross volunteer efforts. Grandma stayed out of the limelight, but she had "quiet power." When Susan's grandmother, Susan Russell, who was Grandma's sister, lost her husband Renouf Russell unexpectedly, Grandma took in the whole family which included four children. The children were given Christmas presents as if they had been her own children. She was generous and kind.

My brother, Ames Byrd, tells the story of Grandpa, now a former Governor and former U.S. Senator, entertaining family and friends at his annual September 1 birthday party in North Haven, Maine, with his favorite hors d' oeuvres, Ritz crackers with cheese. All three of my brothers and I delight in imitating Grandpa's distinctive forms of expression in those days, especially when he was getting ready to go for a swim before lunch in the chilly Maine water. My brother, Harry Byrd, does it best. At that point, Grandpa was too old to jump in, so he would climb down the short dock ladder with many "Oh's" and huffs and puffs, slowly sinking into the water which might reach 55 degrees during a hot summer.

After he retired from the Senate, he rarely discussed his political life. He preferred to talk about his old friends and their sports exploits. His early childhood friend, James Hale Lowell, was born in 1892, the same year as Grandpa, in Chestnut Hill. They were distantly related through the Amos Lawrence family and graduated from Harvard together. Jimmy was a lawyer, his best friend, his regular companion at Red Sox opening day, and one of his favorite subjects for old stories. In fact, whenever we came up with some story of our own to share with Grandpa, he'd always say, "Is that so, Jim Lowell!"

His favorite Jimmy Lowell story is about the time that former President Theodore Roosevelt came to Boston to attend a dinner to which Grandpa had also been invited. Roosevelt had gone to Harvard with Grandpa's father and he courted his first wife, Alice Lee, at the Lee house next door to my Great Grandfather's house in Chestnut Hill. My cousin, Westy Saltonstall, lives in that house now. Anyway, Grandpa waited all night for a chance to speak to the President alone and, just when he had his chance, along came Jimmy Lowell who interrupted them and spoiled his opportunity. They loved to tell that story on each other.

My cousin, Alice Saltonstall, reminded me of how much Grandpa loved working on his farm during his retirement, tidying the woods and firing the hayfields and wood pile. She writes, "I remember a day when he was quite old and had a hankering to go up the hill in Dover and cut some dead tree limbs. Aunt Sus did not want him handling a chain saw so she gave him a little hand saw that would only cut a skinny little branch. He had me come along and bring a bigger saw. She caught us and took the saw away to Grandpa's great dismay. I had enjoyed being his accomplice."

As Grandpa grew older, he and I would take walks at the farm together. Once, he pointed to a very old Maple tree, a live tree along the road, and said, "I'm going to last about as long as that tree there." Sometimes he spoke about how some of his forebears passed away and that they deliberately let go to save their families the burden of having to care for them as they became frail and old. I remember well the last time I saw him and when he said goodbye to me. I had no inkling of how sick he really was and was sadly surprised when he died just four or five days later on June 17, 1979, at Lone Oak Farm in Dover. He had decided not to use his oxygen anymore and was determined to let go. The day after he died, it was very still in Dover, one of those hot days in June, and I was out on the terrace listening to the dull click clack of the lawnmower and other farm equipment. There wasn't a hint of wind in the air yet suddenly I heard a cracking sound and turned to see that old Maple tree slowly fall over on its side. I thought, well, ok Grandpa, you knew.

During Grandpa's time in the Senate, our Grandmother was very much a part of his life there. She always maintained that one of the reasons that Grandpa got along so well with the other legislators is that he never said a bad word about any of them. When he was Chairman of the Senate Armed Services Committee, he deflected credit onto others and was known for his ability to find consensus on tough issues across both aisles. When a young Jack Kennedy was elected as the junior Senator from Massachusetts, Grandpa, the senior Republican Senator, welcomed him heartily and they got along very well. A bill proposed by Kennedy would be a Saltonstall-Kennedy bill and a bill proposed by Saltonstall would be a Kennedy-Saltonstall bill.

Grandpa was known as a moderate Republican in an era when that was not a contradiction in terms. He was conservative on economic and national security issues and more moderate on social issues. Some might remember the expression, a "Rockefeller Republican." I prefer a "Saltonstall Republican." We could use more Senators like him today.

—Richard E. Byrd III
April 2015

I. Growing up in politics

My father always expected me to become a lawyer, and after I graduated from Harvard Law School it looked as if I would follow in his footsteps. But my uncle, Endicott Peabody Saltonstall, himself an able trial lawyer, changed the pattern when he asked me to stand as an alderman-at-large from Ward 6 in Newton. My unopposed election started me in public office, and for most of the forty-five years that followed I strove to be a responsible politician. People often ask me if I have enjoyed politics. I reply, yes, I have, because I love people and the contacts that come from close association with men and women serving in the common cause of government.

I come from a long line of Yankee Democrats. My great-grandfather, Leverett Saltonstall, was president of the Massachusetts Senate in 1830, was elected the first mayor of Salem in 1836, and then served in the U.S. House of Representatives in the twenty-fifth and twenty-seventh Congresses. His son, my grandfather, another Leverett, served as collector of the Port of Boston in the first Cleveland administration and gave John F. Fitzgerald, the future mayor of Boston and grandfather of John F. Kennedy, his first job as a customs inspector. Honey Fitz himself told me this one day while I was governor when he was urging me to take a greater interest in the Port of Boston, for which he had an inexhaustible enthusiasm.

By my grandfather's time the Saltonstall money had pretty much run out, and after finishing Harvard Law School my father had to work hard. He was one of the founding partners of Gaston, Snow, Saltonstall and Hunt, the law firm that I eventually joined, and was in his office five days a week and every Saturday until his last years. It was my mother's side of the family — she was a Brooks, a descendant of Peter Chardon Brooks, a wealthy New Englander at the time of his death in 1849 — that helped to make it easier for me to enter politics.

My parents lived on one of the lots on Chestnut Hill Road in Newton given by my grandfather to his four children and there, near my future home, I was born on Sept. 1, 1892. Late in that afternoon the nurse placed me in a blanket on a large rocking chair while she turned her back to care for mother. Father, who weighed over 200 pounds, entered at that moment, stood looking down at mother, and was about to lower himself into his favorite rocker when the nurse screamed and I was saved for better things.

During the spring and fall we lived in Chestnut Hill, and for the winters, after 1901, we moved intown to Bay State Road. Chestnut Hill in those days was a neighborly community with winding dirt roads, shaded by elms, oaks, and maples. There were few fences; horses, not cars, were in the stables, and the azalea, rhododendrons, peonies, lilacs, and dogwood were a familiar part of our spring. We had boardwalks instead of pavements on the principal street, Hammond Street; our house was lit by kerosene lamps, and a showerbath was such a novelty when my father had one installed that I bribed my friend Bobby Cobb to come and try it out for twenty-five cents. He did so, and then enjoyed a hearty breakfast; I paid him out of my allowance.

I was the eldest of four children and the eldest is commonly thought to acquire an early sense of responsibility; I wonder if I did. But it was my sister, Eleanor, thirteen months younger than I, who always went riding with father on weekends. After Nora, as we called her, came Muriel, now Mrs. George Lewis, and then my younger brother, Dick, five years my junior, with whom I shared a room and the shower. We were a loyal family, in and out of each other's lives, and never more so than during our summers together in North Haven, Maine, where I was taught to sail by an old-timer, Zene Burgess, who knew every rock and current in the Fox Island Thoroughfare.

My father, who came down for the weekends and his vacation in August, sailed the *Dragon,* a 37-foot sloop that he bought with my cousin, George West. But the boat I loved was a 14-foot dinghy, the *Kedogo,* a member of one of the oldest racing classes still in existence. Thirty to forty such dinghies competed against each other twice each week in July and August. If the southwest puffs up Seal Cove were strong enough, there was always the chance that one would capsize, though with little risk because air tanks would keep the dinghy afloat until a launch could rescue the crew and pump her out. I loved to cross the finish line first and did so occasionally, and while we often shipped water, I can honestly say that I have yet to tip over a dinghy. My grandchildren still successfully race the *Kedogo,* now in her seventy-third year, and sometimes I take their grandmother out for an afternoon sail up Seal Cove.

My father was a friend of Theodore Roosevelt. They were classmates at Harvard, members of the same dining table in the Commons — along with Robert Bacon, Gorham Peters, ten in all — and fellow members of the Porcellian and A.D. clubs. In 1905, when I was twelve, my parents took Nora and me on our first visit to Washington. Shortly before noon we presented ourselves at the White House. Roosevelt made it a practice to be accessible at midday to those who wanted to see him, and on this occasion, punctually at twelve o'clock, he burst into the reception room with his characteristic velocity to shake hands with the score or more who were lined up. His aides had seen to it that my father and his offspring were at the head of the line and he came straight to us with, "Hello, Dick." "How are you, Mr. President?" asked my father, and then solemnly we each shook hands with the Chief Executive. It was of course a matter of pride when he asked father to stay on for luncheon.

Call it aura or inclination, that turned my allegiance toward the Republican camp and led me to cast my first vote for William Howard Taft in the election of 1912. It was a tough vote for my father because of his friendship with T. R. Roosevelt, but he was not happy about Teddy's campaign to have the judges to the Supreme Court elected rather than nominated, and therefore he put the Republican Party first.

* * *

Several years before I entered Noble and Greenough School, there was an epidemic of measles. My sisters and brother each came down with it in turn, and during the three months of quarantine, I was kept home and tutored by mother to such good effect that I was able to skip a grade when I began my six and a half years at Noble. For most of that time I either led my class or was in second place, and when I took my entrance examinations for Harvard, I received credit for elementary or advanced French, Greek, Latin, and German. (I wish I could honestly say that French and German had stayed with me, for they would have been such a help during my years in Washington, but in those days we were not taught to speak, merely to translate, a foreign tongue.)

I would have graduated from Noble when I was sixteen, so my family decided that it might be sensible to postpone my graduation and hold me out of school for a year. Early in the autumn of 1909, with nine other boys of my age — including my close friends Jimmy Lowell, George Aspinwall, and Bobby Cobb — I went west to spend the autumn and winter at the Evans School in Mesa, Arizona. It was my first long stay away from New England, and everything was exciting.

We changed trains in Chicago, had a swim at the University Club, and then boarded the California Limited, the Santa Fe's crack train, the like of which does not exist today. The ten of us certainly had our fill in the deluxe diner before we arrived at Ashfork Junction, Arizona, where we changed to the local that took us on to Phoenix, and at last, in a Toonerville Trolley, we reached Mesa after dark.

The driver of the school carryall who met the train and helped us with our baggage was a loquacious cuss, and as he drove the team through the unlighted streets and out into the prairie, he kept talking about some local bandits who had pulled off a couple of holdups and were still on the loose. We had gone some distance when suddenly he jammed on the brakes, pulled in the horses, and hollered, "My God, boys, it's a holdup! Get your hands up!"

In the dim light stood two masked men, one with a pistol, the other with a shotgun aimed directly at us. We were ordered to hold up our hands and get out. Then they stripped us of all our money, American Express checks, and watches, everything of value we had, and off they rode with two bags of booty.

When we arrived at the school, we poured out our story to Professor Evans, who seemed disturbed and told us he would immediately get in touch with the sheriff. Then we were given supper and shown to the tenthouses with open sides and canvas roofs where we were to live. But sleep that night was difficult; in fact, the holdup kept coming back to me in my dreams all year.

At breakfast next morning, there, by each of our plates, were our valuables as far as they could be sorted out. The holdup was a hoax originated by Jimmy Lowell's oldest brother, Jack, and a friend. It made a great story in the local newspaper, all about the fright of "those Eastern dudes," but our families back home were not amused.

Riding was one of the daily disciplines at the Evans School. We went on long camping trips, and while in the saddle we saw a good deal of the cattle and cactus country with its big irrigation ditches. At school my day began early. I would be up at 6:30 a.m., water my horse and muck out his stall, and then go on to milk three of the school cows, all so that I could have a little free time to practice punts and drop kicks after breakfast. I bought two ponies off the desert and broke them. I paid $20 for the first one and rode him a lot before selling him for half that price. The second one cost me $10. I sold him for $5 to some gypsies — not good trading.

On the weekends we played baseball. I was captain and played first base on the school team. Carl Hayden, later my colleague in Washington, was then sheriff of Maricopa County and watched several games to "preserve order." Many years later, when I made my first appearance in the United States Senate, there he was with a welcoming grin. In 1912, when Arizona became a state, Carl was its first congressman and later moved up to be the senior senator from Arizona and one of the Senate's most beloved members as well as a great friend of mine.

Mesa was the nearest town to the Evans School, and I remember the day when a group of us rode our ponies to town to hear William Jennings Bryan orate. He spoke in the late afternoon and at some length (I wish I could remember whether it was his famous "Cross of Gold" speech), after which his audience, we boys included, sat down to have dinner with him. It was impossible not to notice his large belly with the gold watch chain stretched across it. After dinner he spoke again, this time seated. Bryan never seemed to tire. When he finished, we shook his hand and rode home under the stars.

* * *

My last spring at Noble, following that winter in Arizona, was a happy one. I had passed most of my exams, was required to take only three courses, and was let out of school as soon as I had finished the day's work. Ever since I was eleven, at dancing school, I had kept an eye on Alice Wesselhoeft, who was now studying at Miss Winsor's School only a few doors away from us at Noble. When she passed by on her way home for lunch, I would occasionally hurry out to carry her books and once or twice stayed for lunch before leaving for baseball practice. Her grandmother was present once and asked Alice's mother in no uncertain terms how it was that I could get out of school so early. Alice's mother referred the question to me, but I was so embarrassed that I simply blurted out, "They let me out," which did not satisfy her. But our parents were kind to us, without putting it into words; my father invited Alice to go abroad with my sister, Nora, and Alice's parents used to invite me to their summer place in Jaffrey, N.H.

Our friendship lasted over the years. Because she was an excellent dancer, she was cut in on often at dancing school and parties, and I had to work hard to get my share. My friends never recognized that I had any prior right; they wanted a good dance and she gave them one. But I retaliated by inviting Alice to be my partner for the "German," generally the closing event, where I had first call.

In those days we were awarded sweaters and hatbands in the school colors for sports. The girls came to our games wearing straw hats with wide brims, known as boaters, and it made me proud to see Alice sporting the hatband that I had given her.

My grandfather, Peter C. Brooks, had a one-cylinder Cadillac; on it I learned to drive. In the early 1900s, anyone who had driven a hundred miles could get a license, and when I had done so, Grandmother Brooks, on my sixteenth birthday, presented me with a two-cylinder Autocar of my own. It had a kerosene sidelight, a Presto searchlight, no windshield, and a maximum speed of 28 miles an hour. There were no demountable rims in those days; we changed tires with tire irons, and after the first one hundred miles the punctures came often and always when you least expected them.

I was the first of our crowd to have a car of my own. But Alice never rode with me. It was not done in those days. That Autocar was the apple of my eye, but father did not want me to have it at Harvard, so the summer before I entered I sold it. However, in my college days Alice did drive with me on the front seat of my mother's Packard landaulet. She was two years older, so it was au fait.

* * *

It was on the old Chestnut Hill Club field that Bobby Cobb and I, both in short pants, had our first encounter with a member of the Harvard football varsity, "Hooks" Burr. He was practicing by himself, kicking punts, and Cobb and I stationed ourselves downfield to retrieve the ball, Bobby about twenty-five yards from him and I about fifty. It took two of our kicks to get the ball back to Hooks. We were proud of ourselves and have always remembered this incident because he came to be the team captain, and a good one. Perhaps those days out in the field taught me to be a fair punter and dropkicker, although I never was a varsity football player. Nowadays, with specialists in kicking, I might have been an asset.

I can truthfully say I played on the worst football team that Noble ever had. We lost to Middlesex, 58 to 0, to Groton, 59 to 0, and to St. Mark's, 60 to 0, all in the same year. But baseball was different. I played on three Noble and Greenough baseball teams and was captain of two — the last of which was very successful, for seven out of the nine players batted over .300 and, I think, we were undefeated. We practiced and played on the old field at Dexter's on St. Paul's Street in Brookline.

When I entered Harvard we were told that the best way to make new friends was to go out for freshman football. I did so. I went out for the early practice and played through the autumn, as a substitute guard or tackle, weighing 155 pounds at 6 feet. (Think of what a guard must weigh now!) Our captain was Tudor Gardiner, a good friend of mine. Besides playing tackle, I also continued punting and drop-kicking, although the only time I was actually called on to kick was in the Yale game and then from behind the goal line, so it was a kind of nerve-wracking experience. But I managed to get away with it and received my numerals. That game, which we won, was marred by a very serious injury to our best running back, Bill Chatfield, who came from St. Mark's with a fine record. He was about to catch a punt when he was tackled by the Yale ends. One threw him back and the other pinned his legs so he almost broke his neck. He was carried off in an automobile to a hospital; he recovered but never played another game of football.

In my sophomore year I played on the second team, and again I did the punting, the placekicking, and the dropkicks. It was fun until I was clipped from behind and sprained my right ankle. Fortunately, as it proved, this accident forced me out of football and into a rowing career that lasted happily through the rest of college.

I loved all sports, and since I was a plugger, I tried them all. In 1914, in my senior year, I made the varsity hockey squad but only as the last substitute on the forward line. In the longest college game on record, against Hobey Baker's Princeton team (two overtimes and a sudden death of more than thirty-two minutes), I was the last forward to be sent on the ice, and, probably because I was so fresh, was lucky enough to sneak in the winning goal. After that game, Bill Claflin, our star on defense, said to me as we had a beer together, "Lev, if you're wise, you'll hang up your skates and put away your stick tonight." I didn't take the advice, and he was right.

Sophomore year I rowed in our class crew, and in my junior year I made the varsity squad and became a member of the four-oar that beat Yale at New London. My last year — a year that I shall always remember — I rowed on the varsity crew that lost to Navy at Annapolis. But the second crew won, and after that race I was put at the bow of the second crew and designated its captain. We went on to win all our remaining races and beat Yale quite easily before going to England after graduation to try for the Grand Challenge Cup at Henley.

That has proved to be one of the great events of my life. We surprised the English by taking our own water supply in five-gallon demijohns because we had been told that the change of water in the few days before the races would upset our stomachs. We stayed healthy. We lived in a house up the hill above the town, and next door was the German crew, so we hobnobbed a bit with them. Think of it: World War I broke out the first of August, less than a month after we were together at Henley. I have always wondered how many of that German crew survived.

In our first heat we beat Leander in a tough race. Then we took on a Canadian crew and won fairly easily. In the finals, on the Fourth of July, we were pitted against the Union Boat Club crew of Boston, who were all Harvard graduates. The day before they had had a very close race with the Germans and were more worn out than we were — and older. So our youth and freshness enabled us to beat them by over a length, and we became the first Harvard crew to win the Grand Challenge Cup. (Now, when I am introduced at political meetings, that ancient victory seems to assume greater and greater importance. I don't dispute the moderator, but just smile happily.)

One amusing recollection I have is of the sight of our coach, Robert F. Herrick of the Harvard Class of 1890, who accompanied us in practice mounted on a little white pony. He wore his city clothes with a stiff collar and could only barely get his short legs across the top of the pony as he trotted along the towpath. He had tough work to stay on and coach at the same time.

The excitement of being at Henley sparked several memorable incidents. One occurred after the race, when we winners were expected to entertain the various English crews who had won their events. They were a thirsty lot, as I well remember for I had to collect the money from the members of our crew to pay for the sixty-eight quarts of champagne, much of which was poured into — and out of — the Grand Challenge Cup. (In 1914 it didn't leak; in 1939, when Harvard again won, it did.) We gathered for dinner that evening in the garden behind our house. Above us flew the flag of the United States and the Union Jack. Our landlord, as the owner of the house of the winning crew, had also been celebrating. He and our manager, Bobby Cobb, were having a drink together, and our landlord lifted his glass. "Here's to the Stars and Stripes!" So they drank solemnly to that toast. Then the Englishman proposed: "Here's to the Union Jack!" To which Cobb replied:

"Here's to you, Jack! How are you?"

That disrespect resulted in a bit of discussion which I finally settled by proposing a toast to our landlord.

Eventually we ended our victory celebrations at Henley and the next day went to London, where the English Speaking Union, hosted by a distinguished lord, gave us a dinner. I remember it well for as we entered, we were met by a gentleman in a red coat. I supposed, of course, that he was our host and went up to shake hands with him, but instead found he was the factotum who presented me to the distinguished president! It was a mighty pleasant affair, but you can imagine my nervousness when, after the brandy had been passed, the same factotum in the red coat banged the gavel and proclaimed: "My lords and gentlemen, pray silence for Captain Saltonstall of Harvard!" That introduction knocked about every thought out of my head, but I did succeed in thanking them and telling them what a good time we had had.

After Henley, four of us went over to Germany and at Mainz hired bicycles to ride through the Black Forest. It seemed to me a mighty little forest, but gave us pleasant riding. The one bit of German I could say was "Ein Flask Mineralwasser," our only recourse when we grew thirsty since we did not dare drink the water out of the faucets. We rode through the Black Forest, down through Zurich and Lucerne, and up over the Uberal and Julian passes to San Moritz. After that wonderful ride we took the train down to Milan and Venice, and then back to Paris.

At Venice we had begun to read war news of Germany and France. England had not yet come into the picture. Paris was up in arms, and we were told to get home or we might be stranded. We were lucky to get passage on a German ship, the *Cincinnati.* When we were in the middle of the ocean, England declared war on Germany and our ship opened its secret instructions and headed for the Azores until the captain received a radiogram to continue to Boston. To avoid English destroyers the ship traveled in complete darkness at night. This upset some of the first-class passengers to such a degree that they sent a committee to the captain to tell him that it was extremely dangerous to travel without lights. Naturally he paid no attention.

* * *

I had entered Harvard with a good memory, little imagination and no ingenuity, but the expectation that I would practice law. I have always remembered the remark that Walter S. Gifford made when he was chosen to head American Telephone and Telegraph Company: "Success in life is relative. In my judgment, success means making the most of such ability, personality, and physique as you have. Don't measure your success against others but against your own potentialities. Never fret because somebody else has done better. . . . "

I had no trouble with my courses in college. Freshman year was easy because of the work I had anticipated; as an upper classman, I satisfied the requirements by taking George Lyman Kittredge's famous course on Shakespeare and courses on astronomy and philosophy. But the courses that meant the most to me and for which I worked the hardest were those in government and economics under Professors William B. Munro, Edward Channing, and Frank William Tassig.

My faculty adviser was Theodore Lyman. He was a friend of my father and we got along on easy terms. By senior year I needed only three courses for my degree, although according to regulations I was obliged to take four. When I called on him for permission to take less than the usual requirement, he asked why, and in all innocence I said, "Well, Professor, I am the class secretary; I am rowing; and next year I am going to law school. I want to rest my brain." He sprang up and exploded: "Lev, if I ever again hear you say you want to rest your brain, I'll not sign another paper for you!" That brought me to my senses.

When I graduated I had some B's, more C's, but only one D, in a half course on psychology that came at 2:30 in the afternoon, when it was hard to stay awake.

* * *

Going back for a moment, in the summer of 1911, I went north with two friends, Harry Parkman and Dunbar Lockwood, to work as a volunteer for the Grenfell Mission in Labrador. It was a five-day trip by steamer from St. John to St. Anthony Harbor, some twenty miles from the Straits of Belle Isle. Among the passengers was Captain MacMillan, later to be an admiral, who shared a cabin with the three of us. One day we were in the midst of a Chinese wrestling match, gripping a broomstick in an effort to throw the other fellow off balance. I'd beaten them all when MacMillan said, "Let me try," and with his powerful arms he somersaulted me right over his head. But on the second try I jumped him, and only slid over his shoulder. He was a tough customer.

Dr. Wilfred Grenfell and his young American wife lived on a hill above the hospital, and we saw him only occasionally since he and his medical staff, including Dr. David Little of Boston, were busy in the hospital or coasting along Newfoundland visiting the sick, many of them ill with tb., in the tiny, hermetically sealed settlements along the coast. I went on one voyage in the schooner presented to Grenfell by Princeton University; I stood watch from midnight to 4 a.m., on the outlook for icebergs, trembling with the cold. The Grenfell boats were known, and in every little harbor, as soon as we anchored, dories would put out from shore bringing the sick for the doctor's attention. Mostly we did the heavy work — unloading provisions from the schooner, digging peat for winter fuel, or chopping ice off bergs with hands so cold that our iron tools would stick to the flesh. One morning when Parkman and I were unloading the schooner, a Chicago gentleman who had chartered the ship for a cruise looked down on us and asked Dr. Grenfell, "Are those two typical natives?"

* * *

Law school was more demanding than college, and I made the common mistake of taking so many notes during the lectures that I was always racing to keep up with the discussion of a case and if suddenly called on I seldom had an answer ready. I studied criminal law under Felix Frankfurter the first year he ever gave that course, and I received one of the highest marks. My second year I attended his lectures on public utilities. He asked me a question on the very first day, I flubbed it, and he never called on me again. At the time I felt hurt but relieved.

But for me law school was not only books. The first two autumns I spent my afternoon coaching freshman football, and there were some fine athletes on the squad. Eddy Casey, Babe Felton, Hank Flower, and Gus Thorndike were among those whom I admired and who became my friends. It was good to be back on the field again, and I could count on Jimmy Lowell as our most loyal rooter.

Then at the end of my second year, on June 27, 1916, Alice and I were married at her summer home in Jaffrey, N.H. Alice had four bridesmaids; my brother Dick was my best man, and there were a dozen ushers — fellow members of the Porcellian Club, Lawrence Hemenway, and George Aspinwall. (Jimmy Lowell, who should have been one of them, was in Texas with the National Guard.)

We had asked the manager of the Ark, the summer hotel, for comfortable accommodations for the ushers, but what he gave them was an old cottage with a shower of sorts in the cellar and a thirsty hired man who soon discovered the carefully hidden bottle of whiskey. The wedding party the night before was held in Dublin, four-and-a-half miles away on a rainy, muddy road. On the way my father, who was driving an elderly lady, one of the out-of-town guests, skidded off the road and got stuck in a ditch. It was some time before he could be pulled out.

But the day of the wedding was clear and sunny and sometime before the ceremony, brother Dick and I went down the aisle looking for a place at the side of the chancel where we could be inconspicuous while waiting for the ceremony to begin. There was no side entrance or vestry room from which we could enter, but behind an evergreen decoration was a chair where we hoped we could wait concealed. Unhappily, the old minister from Chestnut Hill who was to take part in the service had the same idea, so I gave him the chair and Dick and I crouched down behind the green and stayed there like baseball catchers, listening to the rustle of the guests and waiting for the wedding march. When at last it began, my knees were so wobbly that I could hardly stand erect. Alice found that she had to hold me up — and has done so ever since!

The Porcellian Club song is always sung at a member's wedding, secretly in a room as the bridegroom is changing his

Leverett Saltonstall, at two years, with his mother Eleanor and his sister Nora, 7 months.

Saltonstall at about six years.

Saltonstall's father, Richard M. Saltonstall, about 1910.

At left, Saltonstall's mother, Mrs. Richard Middlecut Saltonstall. Below, right, great-grandfather, Leverett Saltonstall, left, grandfather, Leverett Saltonstall.

In 1917 before going abroad in World War I.

Saltonstall and his bride, Alice Wesselhoeft, on their wedding day, June 27, 1916, in Jaffrey, New Hampshire.

Alice Saltonstall in 1916.

In Mesa, Arizona in 1909.

The Saltonstalls with first child, Leverett Jr., in 1917.

The Harvard second crew in 1914, which won the Grand Challenge cup at Henley. Back row, left to right: Henry Meyer, Tick Morgan, Jim Talcott, Louis Curtis and Charlie Lund; Front row: Bill Mittendorf, Saltonstall, Henry Mittendorf, and sitting, Heinie Kreger.

clothes. But not this time. The members repaired to the cottage close by the tent where the guests were enjoying their champagne and proceeded to sing at the tops of their lungs.

As a married couple we had our first disappointment immediately. We started off in the family Cadillac, but as we got in George Aspinwall slammed the door on my hand, hurting it quite badly. John Gannon, who was driving us, had difficulty finding where our honeymoon car was hidden and we were still surrounded by the wedding guests when we reached the village. I managed to drive off with my hand bandaged in my handkerchief, but it throbbed so painfully that night we drove back to Jaffrey the next day to ask my father-in-law, Dr. William F. Wesselhoeft, to see what damage had been done. Luckily, no bones were broken. Then off we went to Chestnut Hill and to the dock where the old *S.S. Belfast* was waiting to take us to Rockland to start our ten-day cruise on the *Dragon*. Alice knew nothing about sailing, so I took over single-handedly — the other in bandage — and at the outset even had to scramble the eggs for breakfast.

I had forgotten all about my hand by the time we came ashore. Father had given us a wedding trip to California; we stopped at the Grand Canyon on the way out, and in San Diego we purchased a second-hand Model T Ford and started up the coast. After about thiry miles, the bottom of the engine dropped out and we were hung up for two days waiting for repairs. When at last we reached Los Angeles, I traded it in, plus $390, for a new Model T, and with our suitcases strapped on the running board, we took to the high road, burning out two sets of brake bands before we reached Portland, Oregon. There I sold the Ford for only a little less than I had paid for it and we boarded the crack train for Victoria, Vancouver, and, later, Glacier Park.

* * *

That autumn we went to live in Westwood, which in those days was quite a long commute from Cambridge. Matrimony was more of a distraction than I had allowed for, and when my marks dropped from B to a D+, I was so shocked that I called on Dean Roscoe Pound and told him that I had worked *almost* as hard in my third year as before and could not understand why I had dropped so low. He picked up that word *almost*, showed me the reports that had come in from Edward H. Warren, who was the sternest member of the law faculty, and from Austin W. Scott, whom we all loved, and I had nothing more to say.

But the real distraction was the war, which was coming closer to us in the early spring of 1917. Many of my class had gone off to Plattsburgh and were awarded their law degrees without having to take final examinations. It was a tough decision, but I stayed behind and took my finals for the private reason that our first baby was due in July and I wanted to be with Alice at that time. I also took and passed my exams for the Massachusetts Bar, which meant that I could begin to practice immediately when the war was over. As soon as our son Leverett was born, I applied for the Second Plattsburgh Camp and emerged with the rank of first lieutenant.

At Camp Devens I was assigned to a battery of horse-drawn artillery, the 301st Field Artillery in the 76th Division. We trained the horses and learned to fire the three-inch guns. It was one of the coldest winters on record — snow, snow, snow, from December to March — so we rode our horses on blankets, which was much warmer than being in a saddle, and safer, too, for if the unshod horse fell on the ice, one could slip off more easily.

To be close to me, Alice and the baby had moved into the station agent's little house in Shirley, and we parked our Hupmobile in a barn four of five houses away. In those days there was no antifreeze, so in the early morning I would go down the street carrying a kettle of hot water, pour most of it into the radiator, pour a little on the carburetor, and then crank and crank — there was no self-starter — and pray. The Hup was good to us, she always started except when Alice poured the water on the magneto, which cooled things off effectively for that day. Also, the roads were not plowed out; we drove in deep ruts and it was almost impossible to pass another car.

My military career was like thousands of others. Our training at Devens ended in the late spring of 1918, when with fellow officers I was sent to France to learn all about the famous French 75s. We went over on the brand new Holland-American liner, the *Justicia*. Boat drill was held twice daily and I was present when one of the more enthusiastic drillers showed his gang how to release a lifeboat from the davits. "You pull this crank," he said, which he did, and the lifeboat tumbled down three decks and hit the ocean upside down. The two men in her were thrown clear and were picked up by a ship following us in the convoy. The *Justicia* was a beautiful ship, but her life was a short one, for after she landed us at Liverpool she was torpedoed north of Ireland as she was returning to the United States.

We passed through Paris on Bastille Day at the time when General Ludendorff was making his final drive to break through the Allies' lines and to reach the seaports. At Camp DeSouge, a huge artillery cantonment south of Bordeaux, we learned how to plot a map, aim our guns, set the elevation for range and the angles for direction, and how to allow for the wind.

Then about the middle of August we rejoined the 301st Artillery at Besancon, where among our instructors were Rex Hitchcock from Hawaii, a Harvard classmate, and Harry Cabot, a lifelong friend from Brookline. Any evening that Harry and I could get off, we would stroll down the hill to a little French estaminet, where we would sit out back at a table under the trees — but within close range of the manure pile — and be served sweet but good champagne at ten francs a bottle. The taste made us forget the smell and we began to reminisce after the first glass.

In camp we were issued harnesses but we never saw a horse. First we were to be horsedrawn, then motorized, as reserve artillery for General Pershing's disposition. It all seems rather funny at this distance. For instance, we were given gas masks and were supposed to march and live in them, but they were suffocating, and as one who always breathed through the mouth, I never learned how to breathe in that mask. One sunny summer day we stopped to watch a dog fight between two German reconnaissance planes and a couple of French ones that went up to meet them and drove them away. That was the only time I came within sight of a German.

There at camp I played my last football, in a game between the First and Second battalions. I played end and did the kicking, and Lord, how stiff I was the next day! My former Harvard roommate, Griscom Bettle, was of all things the referee and subsequently the guest of the evening. Gris had celebrated a bit when the game was over and so slept peacefully through the band concert that our colonel had put on for his benefit.

I was walking to a lecture one morning, taking salutes, when an enlisted man ran squarely into me. I was surprised and was about to blast him out when I recognized Jimmy Lowell, now with corporal's stripes. Jim had become an instructor of field telephones and lived with the French company in their barracks. They were off limits for us because the French had a way of stacking the cards, even a new pack, and would clean our boys out on payday, so to see me Jimmy had had to pass through our sentries. He was halted with the usual

"Who goes there?" Jimmy replied that he had been ordered to shine Lt. Saltonstall's shoes. "Go ask the sergeant if I'm not right," Jimmy added, and when the sentry left his post to inquire, Jim walked in and we spent the first of many pleasant evenings together.

At the end of our training at Besancon we were okayed for duty and sent to Chalvraines, a village close to the front, to wait for orders that never came because the armistice came first. On Nov. 12, Capt. Ray Wilkins, our adjutant (whom I was later to appoint to the Massachusetts Supreme Judicial Court), got ten days' leave for us both. He wangled a staff car to drive us to Verdun (where we spent the night in a Red Cross hut), and the next morning we walked over that appalling battleground with its wrecked guns and haunted trenches where there were still bones, helmets, and the discards of war to be seen. We visited Fort Doumont, one of two vital forts the Germans had never captured, and were warmly greeted by the French officers. They showed us over the fort, described the battles, and set us up for a good lunch. Afterwards, we boarded the train for Paris; we bribed the conductor twenty-five francs to give us a compartment to ourselves, but when we woke up from our naps people were crowded in the aisle, even sitting in the baggage rack overhead. Paris three days after the armistice was still a madhouse and full of excitement for men as green as Ray and me. Of course, we overstayed our leave and were reprimanded when we returned, but not disciplined by our colonel, who rather liked Paris himself.

Soon after Christmas we were shipped home through Brest and deloused for the last time at Camp Devens, and I received my discharge in early February. I could not get back to Boston fast enough to be with Alice and our second baby, Rosalie, who had just arrived.

Perhaps the most valuable aftermath to my Army life occurred in April, 1919, when, at the suggestion of my friend George Cutler, I became one of the founders of the American Legion Post No. 48 in Newton. I was pretty regular in attendance for the next ten years, little realizing what a help the Legion would be in the days to come.

II. Scandals, law and legislation

My father felt it would be best for me to begin law in the office of his younger brother, my uncle, Endicott Peabody Saltonstall. There I would gain some knowledge of the justices and the officers of the court and take part in the cross-examination of witnesses; then, after being broken in, I might be ready to enter my father's firm, Gaston, Snow, Saltonstall and Hunt, a much larger office in which, incidentally, the senior partners took a dim view of enlisting young sons without experience.

Uncle Cotty, as we all called him, was really more of a friend than an uncle. He and his wife, Bessie, lived in the old family house in which he was born, the house my grandfather Leverett built when he moved from Salem to Chestnut Hill, only a short distance up the hill from where Alice and I lived on Chestnut Hill Road. Uncle Cotty was a big, heavy man — over 6 feet and over 210 pounds — slow, no athlete except for an erratic game of tennis. He was blond, whereas my father was dark; he was always courteous, very patient with us younger folk, and full of play. I can see him now riding on a Flexible Flyer behind our Shetland pony with his youngest daughter perched behind him screaming with laughter, or coasting down the hill on his belly on a toboggan.

On his way to the 8:32 express he often dropped in on us while we were eating breakfast. He liked to leave the train at the Huntington Avenue station and walk the rest of the way to his office at 60 State Street, usually with his lawyer friend William Thompson (one of the defenders of Sacco and Vanzetti), arguing over some point of the law every step of the way.

In court he was scrupulously honest — his word was his bond. He seldom lost his temper but would persuade a jury, often with humor, rarely sarcastically. Lawyers for the plaintiff respected and liked him. At home he was of necessity economical: he used to carry in his vest pocket a little leather book in which he jotted down all personal expenditures, even to his car fare.

In the late spring of 1919, I went to work for him at Saltonstall and Blood at a salary of $50 a month, high pay in those years for a starting lawyer. My desk was in a corner of his office, and my job more like that of an aide than a junior lawyer. He would occasionally call over to me to ask my interpretation of a witness's testimony while preparing his argument to the jury. When he went to court I went with him and generally carried his books and papers.

Few will remember the explosion of the molasses storage tank on Atlantic Avenue in Boston in the summer of 1919. It hurled tons of molasses over the freight cars on the siding; the molasses forced its way into buildings on the waterfront, injured pedestrians, and finally drained off and flooded Boston Harbor. Uncle Cotty was asked to defend the old Bay State Railroad Company, forerunner of the Eastern Massachusetts Railroad, and there were literally hundreds of claims for damage to the freight and for personal injury. It was my job to gather evidence of the value of the property losses and of the personal hardship, and in so doing I got my first insight into the exaggeration of claimants. I kept a list for my uncle of the stated claims and of the values that I believed were reasonable, and we watched to see how these might be modified in the final settlement. Several years later, after numerous suits, some of them involving millions of dollars, the claims were adjusted and paid, and the accident forgotten. In that case I learned how much molasses could be put in a tank without danger of its exploding — and how tempting it was to try to soak a corporation in trouble.

Uncle Cot was senior counsel for the Boston Elevated Railroad and repeatedly defended it against accident claims. Some of the cases were amusing: for instance, how long can a banana peel lie on a platform and not be considered a hazard? Is the El as responsible for a banana peel freshly dropped as it is for an old dirty one on which a passenger slipped? Uncle Cot made a distinction that set a precedent: if the banana was old, it should have been cleaned up, and the El was at fault; if freshly fallen, the El was not to blame.

There were other complaints, some of them mere pretext. If the trolley car comes to a sudden stop, may it cause a miscarriage? Who really had the right of way when an auto and a streetcar collided? How truthful are witnesses, and how easily can jurors be prejudiced in favor of the plaintiff? These are some of the questions I used to shop out with Uncle Cotty; my years with him broadened my understanding of human nature.

At the time I began practicing, Boston was shortly to be convulsed by the Boston police strike, by the scandals and corruption of the offices of the district attorneys of Suffolk and Middlesex Counties, and by the Sacco-Vanzetti murder case, which attracted interest far beyond the limits of the commonwealth. I was involved in two of these affairs and was intensely interested in the third.

In 1919 the mayor of Boston was Andrew J. Peters, a Democrat and a former congressman. The commissioner of police, Edwin U. Curtis, appointed by Gov. Calvin Coolidge, was a man of great firmness. He was well aware that the Boston police were unhappy about their pay, about the high cost of their uniforms, which they had to pay for themselves, and about peripheral matters. The mayor, who was finishing his vacation in North Haven, Maine, was in a conciliatory mood and would have compromised, certainly to the extent of paying for the uniforms, but before an agreement could be reached, several thousand patrolmen went out on strike, leaving the sergeants and captains and a handful of loyal policemen to protect the city. Commissioner Curtis was furious and told Governor Coolidge in no uncertain terms that he would resign if the governor yielded to the police.

Meantime, in the open city, stores were looted, crap games took place on Boston Common and the sidewalks at South Station, there were holdups at night, and one man was killed. Ex-veterans, I among them, volunteered for police duty, serving without arms under the police sergeants who had remained and patrolling the streets in pairs — no guns, no sticks — just ourselves. I recall Robert Choate of the *Boston Herald* directing traffic on horseback at the corner of Tremont and Boylston streets and my friend Bayard Tuckerman, patrolling in South Boston after dark, having to duck into a subway entrance to save himself from the vandals. Commissioner Curtis fired the strikers, the National Guard was called in to relieve the volunteers, and Governor Coolidge telegraphed to Samuel Gompers,

"There is no right to strike against the public safety by anybody, anywhere, any time."

But the problem remained of what action to take with the patrolmen who had been dismissed. The old officers were without work, without pay, and embittered. They organized and became a legislative problem for ten years or more. I recall having discussions with them when I was Speaker of the House in 1929. While I never advocated assistance through public funds, I did try to find them jobs in business concerns, and they were always grateful.

The Boston police strike was, I think, the first walkout of its kind by public servants, and received national publicity. Governor Coolidge's statement of "no right to strike" made him famous; he was nominated and elected Vice President in 1920.

* * *

It was while the police strike was in progress that I was given an unexpected opening. One evening as we were walking home together after our return on the 5:18, Uncle Cotty asked, "Lev, how would you like to run for alderman in Newton?"

"How much time is it going to take?" I asked.

"Oh, about one night every other week."

"Will there be any opposition?"

"No," said Uncle Cotty quietly.

"Judge Lowell and I will attend to that."

It was our precinct's turn to present a candidate since Mr. Bemis, our former alderman, was retiring. I was nominated in his stead; I did no campaigning and was unopposed. You might say that I made my start as a "machine politician," except that the alderman of that day received no emolument — not even money for expenses — and the amount of work involved was a good deal more than Uncle Cotty had allowed for, requiring at least one night a week and, when I was appointed to the subcommittee on zoning, a good deal more than that.

Zoning was a new issue in those days, and we divided the whole of Newton (which is actually nine separate communities) into several zones. We proposed a residential zone with setbacks and everything else that go with it, a second residential zone for smaller holdings and apartment houses, a commercial zone, for stores and business, and a small manufacturing area close to Watertown. There were compromises galore, and our first ordinance was actually vetoed by the mayor and not overridden. But the revised ordinance that later emerged is still enforced, with some modification.

The subcommittee's work on zoning was a long-range project and of course there were things that I wanted to have done closer to home. I drew up a petition to have cement sidewalks replace the old wooden boardwalks with their protruding nails that had run from Beacon Street to the railroad station, and for this I had to secure the signatures of all the property owners and their consent to bear half the cost; it took time, but was finally put through with only one objector.

I was not so successful with my plans for Commonwealth Avenue: in view of the increasing automobile traffic, I wanted to make Commonwealth Avenue — which in 1920 was divided in the center by the trolley track and had two-way traffic on both sides — one-way traffic on either side, but the residents who lived on the northwest side resisted and gave me my first political setback.

During my two years as an alderman I was often opposed by the most powerful member of our board, Tom White, who fought against both the zoning and the Commonwealth Avenue proposal. He later took a more kindly view of me, first when he was commissioner of Administration and Finance when I was serving in the legislature, and, more intimately, in 1938, when he became my campaign manager for the governorship.

As an alderman I marched in the long parade on Memorial Day. Traditionally we were at the head of the parade, in cutaways and high silk hats, followed by troops from Camp Devens, the National Guard, and several high school bands. We would foregather on Washington Street in Newtonville at ten in the morning, and when the music struck up, we climbed the hill, moving towards Commonwealth Avenue, where we paused to sing "The Star-Spangled Banner" before the war monument. Thence we moved to the cemetery, where there was a second ceremony before the Civil War monument, and then back to City Hall, where we were reviewed by the mayor and the final speeches were made. Not a long march but one is on one's feet from ten in the morning until one, and for most of the fifty-three years that I attended I was expected to speak. Then, still wearing that high hat, I would take part in the Dedham Horse Show in the afternoon, a strenuous day but one I would never miss 'till I became governor.

* * *

I moved over to Gaston, Snow, Saltonstall and Hunt in

1920, after about a year and a half at my uncle's office. I became once more an apprentice: I had no desk or room of my own, just a seat in the library. What papers I had were kept in a drawer of the library table. That was all. In time the partners gave me small matters to carry out. William Gaston asked me to conduct the proxy fight for control of the crematories in the Forest Hills Cemetery, which we won for our client after several months' struggle. Afterward, he asked me to sell a mausoleum in the Forest Hills Cemetery that had two bodies in it. I thought I did pretty well to get $2,000 for it — but only after I had moved the two caskets and buried them elsewhere with stone markers.

Mr. Hunt gave me a small accident case that I settled quite amicably, but he criticized me for not charging enough in doing so. My father told me to settle the estate of Harvey James, the butcher in Chestnut Hill who came around three times a week in a horse-drawn cart. He would inquire what my mother wanted; then proceed to cut and weigh the meat in the back of his cart. He was a fine old American who owned two delivery carts and lived in a small house with about seventeen acres not far from our home in Chestnut Hill. He left no will, and his only heir was a niece to whom I turned over the proceeds of the sale of his land, his only asset. Today, that area is fully settled with valuable homes, and I cannot go through it without feeling that I sold Harvey James's estate off too cheaply.

During this period of time, every edition of the Boston papers published accounts of the alleged corruption and misconduct of the district attorneys in Suffolk and Middlesex counties. Joseph Pelletier, the DA in Boston, and Nathan Tufts, the DA in Cambridge, were accused of accepting large sums to nol-pros disreputable cases in their courts. In the disbarment proceedings that were to follow, Dan Coakley testified that a member of the Hunnewell family paid $50,000 to have a case involving one of the family removed from the court with no publicity. But it was the famous Mishawum Manor Case in Middlesex County that blew the whole thing open. A group of movie magnates from New York went on a wild spree in Woburn in a house of ill fame; they were blackmailed and subsequently paid $100,000 to keep the case out of the press and courts. But one of the men present had the courage to file an affidavit revealing the facts and this affidavit led first to the prosecution of Tufts and later to the disbarment of Coakley.

I have always thought that the commonwealth owed much

to J. Weston Allen, who was then the attorney general. He had quite a fight to win that office and he now took a courageous part in presenting the petition to the Massachusetts Supreme Judicial Court to have both DAs removed from office. Dan Coakley was the brains of the conspiracy; it was said that his share of the movie hush money was substantial, and estimates of what he received from other cases ranged well over the $100,000 mark. The Supreme Court under Chief Justice Arthur Rugg sat in on the two DAs; Tufts resigned and Pelletier was removed from office, which in turn led to their disbarment by the Massachusetts Bar Association.

Dan Coakley's case took longer, and in that fight the Watch and Ward Society, which was largely financed by Godfrey Lowell Cabot, took a vigorous part. Cabot pitted himself against Coakley, and each man hired his own sleuths. Cabot bribed a man employed by Coakley to turn over papers and information in Coakley's office, and Coakley allegedly employed a man who was in Cabot's confidence. As things turned out, Cabot was indicted for the theft of the papers, was found guilty, and paid a fine. Then it was Coakley's turn, and on his own naive testimony he was disbarred.

Channing Cox had followed Calvin Coolidge as governor and now that the dirty business was in the open and Nathan Tufts had been forced out, it was necessary to find someone of unimpeachable character to clean the stable. The governor asked Uncle Cotty to fill out Tufts's unexpired term as district attorney of Middlesex County. Uncle Cotty was reluctant to do it; he felt he couldn't afford to, but the governor kept putting pressure on him and my father urged him to do so and offered to help financially, and I was eager for him to take the job and said I would go with him if he did. So one spring morning at 7:30 a.m., while Alice and I were having breakfast, he burst in to tell us that he would go to Cambridge, taking with him his law partner, Charles Blood, as his first assistant, and me. Later that day, the mayor, James Michael Curley, always curious, asked one of his aides if the governor had made the appointment yet. "Yes," was the reply, "Endicott Peabody Saltonstall." "What!" said Curley. "All three of them!"

With some trepidation I asked Mr. Gaston, the senior partner, to give me a leave of absence in order to fulfill my agreement. He looked at me with a smile and said, "Lev, since you have already agreed to go, what is there for me to say except, good luck and do a good job!" So I became a second assistant district attorney of Middlesex County with an office in the courthouse in East Cambridge. Uncle Cotty wanted to round out the staff with a good trial lawyer from the other end of the county, in Lowell. James C. Reilly was highly recommended and agreed to come along. The other second assistant was Raoul Boudreau of Marlboro, the only attorney carried over from the Tufts regime. I was actually the junior second assistant.

The court, which had its dramatic moments, was presided over by superior court judges serving in rotation. To the left of the judge sat the jury, and to their left on a dais sat Deputy Sheriff Walker, a big man and corpulent, who would call the court to order and a few minutes later would be slumbering peacefully with snores that could be heard by all.

The court interpreter, an Italian, was likewise a big man, weighing well over two-hundred pounds, who tried to clarify the testimony of witnesses with little or no English. I remember in one instance the interpreter intervened with, "Well, what do you *want* him to say?"

The liquor cases were of course the most numerous and not without their light side. We once tried a man who had been arrested on the charge of selling liquor at noontime. He had no attorney, and in such cases it was our practice for the government to put in its case and hear the defendant but to make no argument to the jury. "I know I couldn't have been selling it at twelve o'clock," stated the defendant, "because that was the time I was making it." Everybody laughed and the jury found him not guilty.

Because of the shady business that had occurred in that court so recently, there was now a tendency to take Uncle Cotty's word, or Mr. Reilly's findings, or even mine, on faith and without question. In my work I never forgot what Arthur D. Hill, who once served a term as DA in Suffolk County, told me: "In a prosecutor's office," he said, "you have a tough time to stay normal and balanced; the temptation is to become either too easy or too hard." Uncle Cotty was critical of me for becoming too sympathetic. But it was difficult for me to recommend a tough sentence when I looked at a tearful wife and her appealing kids and listened to an emotional plea put forward so eloquently by her lawyer of Irish descent. Yet I will say that the court did take my recommendations in every instance but one.

Uncle Cotty had been in office only a few days when he was involved in a gruesome murder in Littleton. It occurred on a Friday, the paymaster of a road construction company was shot and the bag of currency he had been carrying, stolen. The body was found in a field up a little side road, and some days later a man was apprehended on the way to Holyoke with the moneybag. He of course protested his innocence and said he had had nothing to do with the shooting; the case turned on the time of how long the paymaster had been dead.

Uncle Cotty, with Sy Smith, the state detective, and several others of us had lunch together in Concord on our way to visit the scene of the shooting , and my uncle asked Sy, "How do you know how long a man has been dead?"

"Oh," said Sy, "when the flies settle on his nose he has been dead for at least twenty-four hours."

When we got to the spot where the body lay, Sy squirmed under the barbed wire. "Look, here, Mr. Saltonstall, there are the flies, as I told you.

"But my uncle with his ham and eggs churning in his stomach said, "Sy, I believe you." The accused finally pleaded guilty to second-degree murder and was sentenced to fifteen to twenty years in jail. Many years later with my acquiesence he was released and deported.

Other cases that I helped with were that of Clarence W. Loud, who was accused of murdering a police officer, but was found not guilty, and the murder of the station agent in Winchester, where we believed that a Marine who was AWOL committed the crime. But the grand jury refused to indict him.

* * *

One can never foresee the future. Early that spring — the spring of 1922 — my father had told me while out walking one Sunday that he was to have a difficult operation. Dr. Chute, his surgeon, considered him well on the road to recovery when a blood clot from the operation stopped his heart, and he died very unexpectedly on April 17, 1922. His partners, especially Mr. Gaston, were mighty good to me. Take over your father's office, clean up his affairs, and carry on, they said. So I continued my work as an assistant district attorney and stayed late enough in town each day to take care of family affairs.

But in December of 1922, Uncle Cotty who had really been overworked, had to give up and rest in bed to get rid of boils. Again, all was going well when a blood clot, as with my father, stopped his heart and he died suddenly. So I found myself in charge of all the family affairs in Chestnut Hill, an adviser to my mother and to my Aunt Bessie. My mother finished the alterations to her home that my father had planned but never saw. Alice and I lived in the house my father had given me, and my aunt lived just across the road. Almost every evening I paid her a call while she began her new life, and every morning I stopped on my way to the train to see my mother.

We all know that life must go on. We finished our term in Cambridge. Governor Cox had appointed Raoul Beaudreau to take my uncle's place until the newly elected district attorney took over in January of 1923. But I soon discovered that my office work had changed. I took over my father's position on various family trusts. My maternal grandfather, who had died in 1920, left a will with estate-tax problems on which decisions had to be made — no easy job, as the income-and estate-tax laws were still virtually new and unsettled. Investments had to be considered and real-estate questions studied and decided.

The loss of those two men whom I loved and on whose advice I so often depended compelled me to take stock of myself. I had no very high regard for my prospects as a lawyer, but I knew from my experience in the DA's office that I enjoyed working with people, even those who were in trouble.

Earlier in 1922, when Uncle Cotty and I used to commute to Cambridge together, it cheered him when I first mentioned the possibility of running for a seat in the Massachusetts Legislature. Newton was entitled to three seats, and I knew that one of them would be vacated that autumn because the incumbent had decided not to run again. I asked Alice if she approved, as I had when Uncle Cotty suggested my becoming an alderman, and her reply was, "Go ahead." So I became a candidate. Newton at that time was heavily in the Republican column, and I felt that if I could survive the primary in September I might have a fair chance.

That summer before Uncle Cotty's death, I went on a cruise Down East with my friends Jimmy Lowell, George Aspinwall, and Lawrence Hemenway. You wear old clothes when you are cruising, and when we came ashore at St. Andrews in New Brunswick, we dressed Jimmy in the best we had, which consisted of my black Harvard sweater and a pair of clean trousers, and sent him ahead of us to the hotel to make arrangements to eat. When we reached the hotel we found Jimmy at the bar having a drink with the son of the president of the Canadian Pacific Railroad; he had broken the ice, and the management agreed to feed us out of sight at the bar.

Jimmy, who knew everyone, introduced us to Jack Maloney, the hotel barber, who came from Belmont, and he told Jack that when he got home he must be sure to pass the word in Newton that I was running for election. By coincidence, the head waiter, as Jimmy discovered, came from Newton, and Jimmy told him the same story. I took all this more or less as a joke, but when I got home in August, I found that the word had indeed been passed down from St. Andrews. I put on a door-to-door, store-to-store campaign telling the people my name and shaking hands. I was shy at this at first, but people were responsive and I warmed up to it. On the night of the primary I went down to City Hall, where there were always a couple of men who could judge from the first returns how the election would go. They said it looked good for me, and they were right. When I went home I stopped and told Uncle Cotty that I had won a place on the ballot. It might even be the first place. He grinned and told me to "Keep a-rollin.' "

Uncle Cotty said that now it was time for me to get my name in the newspapers, so he called George S. Mandell, the publisher of the *Boston Evening Transcript,* a conservative Republican organ. I went in for my appointment and Mr. Mandell, who had a high, squeaky voice said, "I think you ought to talk to Henry Cabot Lodge." My heart jumped because I thought for a moment that he meant the elder Senator Lodge; actually he meant the senator's grandson, who was then a cub reporter. I introduced myself and Cabot asked if I planned to speak. No, I said, I wasn't going to make any speeches. He next asked me if I planned to set up any general meetings. "No," I said. "We don't have meetings in Newton."

"Well," he burst out, "how do you expect me to give you any publicity in the paper if you're not going to attend any meetings or make any speeches?" So much for my effort to get publicity.

What I actually did was to use up shoe leather, going around to the drugstores, the groceries, the soda fountains, the American Legion Post, everywhere, and shaking hands. I sent out a number of postcards as Election Day approached, and Uncle Cotty made some telephone calls for me and spoke to his friends on the street and in the train. He was genuinely elated when he knew that I had been elected, but he never lived to see me take office. The cost of the campaign had come to about $17.

III. Eight years as House Speaker

On the first Wednesday after the first Tuesday of January, 1923, I was sworn in by Gov. Channing Cox as a representative of the Massachusetts General Court.

The Massachusetts Constitution of 1779, the oldest written constitution in the world, gave the assembly that title, designating it as the court to which any citizen could appeal when he believed that his rights were in jeopardy, as they certainly had been under the British monarch. The idea that it is essentially a court of appeal persists, and a citizen of the commonwealth still has the right to file a petition of grievance through his representative. This tradition, in part, accounts for the extraordinary number of bills that come before the legislature every year. When I first took my seat, we had two to three thousand bills to dispose of annually; today the number has risen to over eight thousand. It seemed to me that there were far more bills presented than need be, and I resolved to file as few as possible.

In the preceding December, Loring Young, the Speaker of the House, had conferred with each new member, assigning us, as far as possible, to the committees of our preference. I had known Loring at Harvard and was pleased when he selected me for the Judiciary Committee, which together with the Ways and Means Committee were the two most important committees of the House. All bills dealing with problems of a legal nature came up before the Judiciary, and this entailed an enormous amount of paper work. In addition, Loring suggested to the committee chairman, John C. Hull of Leominster, that I be chosen clerk of the Judiciary Committee. As clerk, I sat at a desk directly in front of the chairman; it was my duty to record the various bills and, after the vote on a measure had been taken, to make sure that the member in charge of that bill was ready to state the position of the committee to the full House should there be a debate.

At a public hearing, the proponents and opponents of a bill stood, according to tradition, in front of my desk — and so I had my first exposure to lobbyists, generally lawyers, representing the utilities, the real-estate and insurance interests, the Boston and Maine Railroad, and the foundations. Some of the lobbyists were able debaters, some were not, but I remember especially Edward C. Stone, who represented the Employers Liability Insurance Company. He was masterful in his handling of the various measures having to do with automobiles or with accidents on the highway. The proponents would often base their case on an emotional appeal. When the turn came for the opposition, Stone would rise and make an apparent concession: "Of course, if your committee wants to report this bill favorably, it is entirely within the jurisdiction of the committee to do so, *but* if this measure should become law, it will undoubtedly increase the cost of liability insurance and may well force a car owner to install new, expensive equipment." In this calm, firm manner Stone would "throw the case out the window," to use the legislative expression. After listening to Stone's presentation, the Judiciary Committee time and again gave the proponent of the bill "leave to withdraw," which was the formal method of killing it. Whenever on later occasions I appeared before a committee in the State House or in Washington, I tried to adopt Stone's quiet, pragmatic way of stating the facts in such a way that they would help to clinch my argument.

It was my luck in 1923 to draw a seat in the second row, only one seat away from the chairman of the Ways and Means Committee, my older friend Henry L. Shattuck. Shattuck was 6 foot 1, a strongly built man, a bachelor, and a dedicated public servant, respected on both sides of the House for his decency and financial responsibility. He was a loyal alumnus of Harvard and eventually served as treasurer of the university. He loved the Irish and had a romantic feeling for Ireland, which he was fond of visiting. On Sundays he would entertain groups of boys from South Boston at his private club in Dover, and no one will ever know how many students he helped through college.

In the House he spoke in a heavy, forceful voice that could be clearly heard, and as the chairman of the Ways and Means Committee he was cautious, careful, and thorough, making it a point to give the report himself on the more difficult cases that came up before his committee. At almost every session he would bring in a briefcase full of papers, and put on the desk in front of him the particular memorandum that applied to the debates that afternoon. As I say, he was cautious, and at first when I leaned over to speak to him or ask him some question, he would cover his folder. I could not help noticing this, but gradually I was pleased to see that he was gaining enough confidence in me to leave his folder open. It would be impossible to say how much a young legislator like myself learned from Henry Shattuck; certainly I was not the only Republican to profit from his example.

I also got aid from another quarter when my friend Sinclair Weeks, serving his first term as an alderman in Newton, gave me a copy of a letter he had received from his father, John W. Weeks, who was then secretary of war. It is so full of salty advice that I have kept a copy, and because of its suggestions I rarely spoke on the floor of the House during my first two years, and never unless I knew the facts. The secretary had served three terms in Congress before being appointed to the cabinet, and he wrote to his son from experience:

> "There are two or three things I want to impress upon you as it is your first experience in a legislative body. Success in such a place, more than in almost any other, depends on knowledge. A man is a leader, legislatively, when he knows more than those who are serving with him. He does not have to be an orator, have wealth or any other qualification than to have the facts, and therefore you ought to take some part of the work, perhaps all of it if you have time, and know all about what is going on. Study the rules which are used, so that you will be entirely familiar with them. Attend committee meetings, so that you will be entirely familiar with the work of the committee, and above all things do not attempt to speak unless you know exactly what you are talking about.
>
> There is no place in the world where you get sized up quicker than you do in a legislative body. If you are on your feet every few minutes talking about something which all the others know as much about as you do, you do not acquire but lose influence. If you get the reputation of knowing what you are talking about, then every one will listen and will be likely to accept your views. I have seen

> hundreds of cases which confirm this statement. The greatest orator who has been in Congress since I have been in Washington is ________________.
> Members and others listen to his speeches because he is a great orator, but he has no more influence, and never has had, than the most inconspicuous member, because he has the reputation of not having carefully and fundamentally studied his subjects, but depends on verbiage rather than information.
>
> "Do not get into the habit of quarreling with a man who does not agree with you. He is entitled to his opinion as much as you are to yours. The thing to do is to convince him that he is wrong — not to suppress his speech, but to argue him out of his position. If you cannot argue him out of it, he may be right and you wrong."

There were two members of the Judiciary Committee whom I came to know well and to whom I listened. The first was Chairman Hull, formerly a high school teacher, who had been in the House for a number of years and who was to succeed Loring Young as Speaker in 1925. The other was Martin Hays, a Republican from Brighton, an able speaker whose language could get very salty, and one whom a new member like myself would think twice before challenging.

I remember one bill having to do with the quality of bread, a bill that Loring Young favored. Hays, who opposed the Speaker, ended the debate with laughter when he stated that Loring really didn't know what he was talking about "because he'd been brought up on cake." There had long been an undercurrent of rivalry between those who had a Harvard background and were supposedly indentified with banks and investments and those who did not. I came to realize that Hays shared some of this suspicion towards me.

During Hull's chairmanship, he occasionally called on me on the floor to support a committee report when the discussion seemed to be going against us. Hays and Hull were not close to each other, and Hays would not help. Victor Jewett, the floor leader, never took much part in floor debates, so Hull turned to me. At first it certainly made me nervous when the page came down with the message that the Speaker was about to recognize me to speak in behalf of the committee's report. I had to learn to think fast and do my best. I was not too convincing, I am sure.

Then as now the Massachusetts Legislature was the only one in the Union to have sessions continue until all of the business was completed and the governor had signed or vetoed every bill we had put up to him and until we in the legislature had withdrawn or let die in committee those that we believed were unnecessary.

We were a body of 240 members, next to New Hampshire the largest state legislature in the nation, and during my service our shortest session began in January and ended May 29; normally, we did not adjourn until the summer or early autumn. We assembled Monday to Thursday at 2 p.m. and Friday mornings at 11, when traditionally the uncontested bills were presented. Our annual stipend was $1,500, which meant of course that every member had to have some other means of supporting himself; the great majority were lawyers, quite a number were in insurance, and some were farmers from Bristol County and the Berkshires.

In Washington, President Harding's death in 1923, followed by the Teapot Dome scandal, opened the door for the safe and clean successor, Calvin Coolidge. The Naval Disarmament Treaty signed by Great Britain, Japan, and the United States gave us a false assurance of security. Prohibition was openly violated but the Drys were still influential. When Loring Young encouraged a referendum on the 18th Amendment," establishing prohibition, the bill passed both the House and the Senate but was vetoed by Governor Cox.

Times were also changing in Boston. The city had always had a low skyline; except for the Custom House Tower, which had been built before the regulation, there was a limit of ninety feet for any building in the city. In the boom, this restriction held back new building in downtown Boston, and the maintenance of this limit became an active issue in the 1920s, when Statler proposed to build a modern hotel in uptown Boston on the condition that the limit be raised to 125 feet. The labor unions were naturally in favor of raising the limit. Henry Shattuck led the opposition, but the House was ready for a change, and once the height of business buildings started to go up it never stopped.

Another innovation, which was passed against a solid Democratic opposition, was the two-cent tax on gasoline. That, too, was in the early 1920s; think how it has gone up since then!

The most controversial bill I filed had to do with the automobile. By the end of World War I the Model-T Ford was selling well. The Hupmobile and the Dodge, the Stutz, the Packard, the Pierce-Arrow, and the Cadillac, to name but a few, were also in increasing demand, and the speed limit was going up. (Think of my father-in-law, Dr. Wesselhoeft, being stopped by police in Concord when he was going 12 miles an hour and the speed limit was 8!)

But as the automobile traffic increased, so did the accidents. People were now buying automobiles on credit, and the impecunious owner became more prevalent. Pedestrians were run over and permanently injured, but the shoestring owner, if he were caught, had little or nothing to pay for his negligence. Increasingly and indignantly, the question was raised, "Why sue a dangerous driver and pay the cost of a high-priced lawyer only to get a verdict that the driver could not pay?"

Various bills for protecting the innocent from injury were submitted to the legislature. Some had merit, but were difficult to work out practically. Others with less merit continued the controversy. Lawyers wanted the business. The insurance companies needed to make certain that their policies provided adequate coverage. The worker or salesman who used a car in his business was opposed to regulations or higher taxes. And so it went with no satisfactory solution to the problem for some years. Finally, in 1924, the first compulsory automobile insurance bill for personal injuries was offered. But as I remember, the insurance companies and individual citizens opposed it, and it was killed.

A year later I took the bill that had been turned down, smoothed it out in several particulars, and reintroduced it. The joint Judiciary Committee reported the bill to the Senate, where it was debated, amended, and finally referred back to the House Ways and Means Committee. The chairman of that committee, Henry Shattuck, moved that it be referred to the next annual session, intending to kill it. It was not often that Shattuck and I found ourselves on the opposite sides in debating a bill, but in this instance Shattuck was defeated. The House passed the bill, and the Senate finally passed it, and it was enacted on May 1, 1925.

Massachusetts thus became the first state in the Union to have a compulsory-automobile-insurance law.

Many years later, insurance litigation jammed up the courts, and legislation to relieve the situation — the no-fault insurance bill — was introduced in the legislature. This time, in 1970, my son William, a senator from Manchester, led the support.

* * *

When we lived in Chestnut Hill in the early 1920s, Alice and I used to ride horseback on Hammond Street and through the bridle paths around the Brookline Country Club. The roads were not tarred in those days and there was still a good deal of woods and pleasant country. I was never as good a horseman as my father and sister, Nora, but now at the age of twenty-eight, I began to ride and jump and loved it.

We had in mother's stable one well-bred jumper, "Bully Boy," and it was not long before I began to take part in the drag hunts of the Norfolk Hunt Club, whose devoted master, Henry Vaughan, was a man of great charm and generosity. After the first year, Alice joined me; she had always ridden cross saddle but now she hunted on a sidesaddle. She had plenty of courage and really handled herself well, and how we came to enjoy those rides, especially when our children — Lev Jr., Emmy, and Pete — were old enough to join us! Mr. Vaughan never made the hunts too stiff for family riding, and with his tact he won the cooperation of the neighbors who owned the land through which we hunted. I remember our consternation at a check one Saturday when Lev, who was on a little pony, failed to appear. Finally he came cantering in, perfectly happy. He knew where he was all the time, but his pony was so small and he had to go around so many jumps that he could not keep up.

On Tuesdays and Thursdays on frosty mornings Alice and I would rise at 6:30 a.m. and motor out to the Norfolk Hunt Club in Dover, where our horses were stabled. There we would mount and follow the drag for perhaps forty minutes then back to the club, drive home, take a shower, and after breakfast I went to town. On Saturday mornings we would ride with the hunt for two hours or more. There were beautiful trails through the woods and open fields along the Charles River, and I remember that on one Saturday I must have covered well over thirty miles.

We both came to love the Norfolk country and in 1928 we bought and settled into Lone Oak Farm in Dover, within sight of the Charles River. Now we could keep our horses in our own barn, closer to the scene of action, and spend the night before the hunt in our farmhouse, which we were enlarging. (In 1945, when we went to Washington, it became our only home in

Massachusetts.) A barn as big as ours was intended for more than horses, and we soon had goats, sheep, and, at one time, sixteen dogs, counting puppies. Lev Jr. was fond of foxhounds and when he was older, he and a friend, Louis Neilson, would hunt the fox on foot by night. The neighbors were not wholly pleased about this. One rather annoyed lady, Mrs. Gelston King, was the owner of a swimming pool, and the vixen who lived in her woods and who had cubs to protect would run round and round the pool leading on the hounds, who were baying lustily. She finally protested that if this almost nightly bedlam didn't stop she would have a nervous breakdown.

Alice and I both took part in the Dedham Horse Show, which is held on Memorial Day, and when the children were old enough to ride with us, we won a blue ribbon in the family class with Lev Jr. and Emmy on their ponies, and Alice and I all dressed up in our best hunting coats and hats. We were very proud of our performance.

In 1929 we spent ten glorious days in Mallow, County Cork, County Limerick, and County Meath, riding horses that were loaned to us by Dick Sheehan, a horse dealer. We purchased our favorites from the Irish horses that he brought to Dover each year. I remember one occasion in County Meath when I had my first experience with those enormous Irish ditches with a bank in the middle. A well-trained horse would jump the ditch, scramble to the top of the bank, change his feet, and then slide down and hop over the other ditch, provided he had a good rider aboard and was going slowly. No Irishman would consider trying to jump over the whole bank.

Everyone who rides occasionally comes a cropper. I had a horse that did not like sheep hurdles, so-called. One day in Dover I drove him at one. He swerved suddenly and hit poor Mr. Dutton, who was following me and had just taken off. He was knocked off his horse but fortunately was not hurt. However, he never hunted again and I felt badly.

Then my turn came on a June morning when I had ridden over to school a mare at my brother Dick's jumps. There a large telephone pole had been laid on a stone wall. My mare came to a sudden stop in front of the jump and then rolled into it; I was thrown over her head and landed heavily on the back of my neck. I picked myself up, and since things seemed all right, rode home. That was on a Sunday and when I told Mike, our stable man, who disapproved of my riding on the Sabbath, he said I got what I deserved. On Monday I had a prepared speech to deliver on the Boston Common in honor of a visiting Polish general, in which I naturally paid tribute to Casimir Pulaski, the Polish officer who had served us so well in the Revolution.

So Monday morning early, in cutaway and high hat, I was driven intown for the ceremony, and I well remember it was quite an event. But something seemed uncomfortably wrong with my back, and on the third day I went to see my doctor, who, after taking X-rays, told me that I had broken a vertebra in my neck. All through that hot summer I had to wear a leather rig over my head and chest, and it was a great relief when I could finally discard it.

Then in 1934 at the start of a hunt I saw Alice's horse get kicked on his hind muscle. It has always bothered me that I did not stop her, for the leg had no strength. The horse fell over the first jump and rolled on Alice. We decided that we should take things more cautiously after that, though I continued to hunt for another two years — with rather less enthusiasm — and finally gave it up when I became a candidate for governor.

* * *

Loring Young, the Speaker of the House, was very popular with both the Democrats and the Republicans. When Sen. Henry Cabot Lodge Sr. died in office in 1924, David I. Walsh, who had been the first Irish governor of Massachusetts, announced that he would run for the Senate seat. He was so strong that no Republican was willing to take him on; but Loring finally decided that the election would not go by default and that he himself would run. He lost, and in the upshot John Hull, the chairman of the Judiciary Committee under whom I had served as clerk, succeeded him as Speaker in 1925. When in my second term I met with Mr. Hull to discuss my committee appointments, he told me that he had no choice but to make Martin Hays, whose seniority outranked mine, the new chairman of Judiciary. So Hull asked if I would accept the chairmanship of the State Administration Committee and also serve on his Rules Committee.

As chairman of the State Administration Committee, I had as my opposite in the Senate Charles Hartshorn from the town of Gardner, famous for its manufacture of chairs. Charlie was a gruff elder who terrified witnesses, particularly women, but who was really a very softhearted man when you came to know him. We spent four years together working on problems of state administration with very few differences. In fact, Charlie did not show up too much and left the hearings to me.

One year when the State Administration Committee had finished its work, I invited the members to a supper party at my house in Chestnut Hill. This was during Prohibition, but I did have some gin and whiskey that was pre-Prohibition, so I felt free to offer it. "Doc" Finkelstein, a Democrat from the North End who sat beside me and finished the cocktails of those who didn't want them, said to me during supper, "Leverett, most of the bootleggers are in my district. If you ever run out of liquor, just let me know and I'll get you anything you want." Later, even more confidentially, he said, "Lev, a good many of the automobile thieves live in my district. If you ever have a car stolen, give me a ring; I think I can get it back for you." That was Dr. Finkelstein, a dentist by profession, and very popular in whatever district he served.

* * *

All through this period, the trial and conviction of Sacco and Vanzetti for first-degree murder was publicized not only in Massachusetts but throughout the world. At the time they were finally put to death in 1927, our embassy in the Argentine was bombed, Gov. Alvan T. Fuller had left the state for security reasons, his family was in the top floor of the Phillips House at Massachusetts General Hospital, and Lt. Gov. Frank Allen was out of the city.

While I personally had no connection with the case, I did believe that the men were guilty — for two reasons. In 1922, when I was an assistant district attorney, I studied intently the report of Captain Van Amberg, the state police officer in charge of ballistics, when he pointed out to Uncle Cotty and me the markings on three slugs that were found in the body of a victim in Middlesex County. Every revolver or rifle has its own markings, similar to our fingerprints, and these markings showed distinctly that the three slugs had come out of the same barrel. In the Sacco-Vanzetti trial, Van Amberg testified that the slugs fired from a pistol found on Sacco when he was arrested in a streetcar were similar to the slugs that were found in the dead paymaster and that therefore could have come from Sacco's gun.

Secondly, after an appeal to the Massachusetts Supreme Court had been dismissed, Governor Fuller, because of the enormous interest in the case and the great publicity given to it, requested President A. Lawrence Lowell of Harvard, President Samuel W. Stratton of M.I.T., and Judge Robert Grant of the Suffolk Probate Court to examine the record and advise him on whether Sacco and Vanzetti were guilty. They did so, and unanimously agreed with the verdict of the jury. Incidentally, President Lowell felt so strongly about the case that one evening when I sat beside him at dinner (and I was always nervous in his presence) I brought up the subject. From that moment, through a long dinner, he never stopped talking about the case. He cited many facts that convinced him of their guilt. I never said another word and he never turned to the person on the other side of him, he was so engrossed in the subject. Regardless of much other testimony, some of it circumstantial, I felt that the verdict seemed to be correct.

I might add that one afternoon when I was in the office of Arthur D. Hill, a former district attorney of Suffolk County, he asked me whether he should take on the defense of Sacco and Vanzetti. (As it happened, William Thompson, my uncle's great friend, had defended these men and had become so nervous in doing so that he resigned from the case and asked Mr. Hill to take it over.) The case had been through all of the Massachusetts courts, and I believe the United States Supreme Court had declined to review it. I advised Hill against taking it on, and he replied, "That is the same opinion my partners have given me." Then I returned to my office and found a call from Mr. Hill. He said, "Please don't say anything about what I spoke to you because I have not made up my mind."

Next morning I read in the newspapers that he had gone to Rockland, Maine, hired a fisherman's launch, and motored across Penobscot Bay in a thick fog to Isle au Haut, where U.S. Supreme Court Justice Harlan F. Stone was spending the summer, in a last-minute effort to have Stone grant a habeas corpus. Stone refused, and the men were eventually executed. But the interest continued with such intensity that on the first anniversary of their death, the State House was guarded by a National Guard truck with machine guns in it to prevent a disturbance.

* * *

Somewhere in this period, I was reminded that my great-grandfather had been president of the Senate in 1830, and I decided it would make me mighty proud if I could be Speaker of the House a hundred years later. So when in 1927 John Hull decided to run for lieutenant governor in the upcoming election in 1928 and the speakership would thus become vacant, I thought, after canvassing some Republicans, that I might have a chance to take his place.

In 1928, I began to work in a quiet way to see if I could get a majority of Republicans to support me for the job. Naturally, I first approached members whom I knew to be friendly and was pleased when others they had spoken to indicated that they hoped I would be a candidate and that they would vote for me. In that year there were 153 Republicans and 87 Democrats in the House (think how that number has changed today!), and it was up to me to get as many written pledges as I should need for my election. This took much time and considerable traveling around the state, although of course while we were in session I buttonholed as many as I could at the State House. My goal was 90 pledges; my opponents were Martin Hays and Victor Jewett, both of whom had stated their desire to succeed Hull. Jewett never made much of a campaign, but Hays was another matter. He had been in the House for a long time and knew a good many members quite well and had done many favors.

Fortified with the pledges that I had picked up at the State House, I began to track down other representatives in their home towns, at their offices, or even in the fields. Two instances stand out in my mind. Al Bullock of Waltham had a small cottage at Ipswich, and there I found him on a ladder painting the second story of the cottage. He stayed on the ladder while I looked up at him and pleaded my case. After some talk in which he considered my opponents, he climbed down and signed my pledge card, we shook hands, and up he went to continue his painting.

The other episode was slightly embarrassing and had to do with an old gentleman, Henry Estabrook of Fitchburg, who had his little place of business on the main street. His business consisted of making tight corsets for women, things I don't think they wear today. The store had a small office space with one chair in it and a cubicle where his customers changed their clothes. The walls to the cubicle did not reach the ceiling, so while I waited for Henry to appear, his squeaky voice was quite audible as he fitted a corset to what sounded like a rather stout woman. Of course, I heard the whole conversation, so when the lady came out I did not dare to look at her but glanced the other way. Then out came Henry, who apologized for keeping me waiting and with no argument signed my card.

In only one instance was I rebuffed. Izzy Fox of Hyde Park wanted to be on the Judiciary Committee and wanted me to promise that I would put him there, before he gave me his pledge. I told him time and again, as we talked, that I was making no commitments; if I made a promise to one member, the word would get around and then no one would sign my pledge unless I agreed to give him the committee of his choice. So I received no pledge from Izzy; that is, until he knew for certain that I had the majority of the Republicans signed up and and then over he came with his pledge to tell me once more that he hoped he would get on the Judiciary Committee. (I finally did give him the appointment, but only after Martin Hays, whom I had defeated for the speakership, asserted loudly in his speech against me that he would not accept any committee appointment from me. This gave me a break, for I had planned to place him on the Judiciary, where he had sat for years; I scratched him off the assignment and gave it to Izzy.)

I can assure you that the last ten or fifteen signatures came hard, but when the word got around that I finally had a majority, the others began to roll in. Martin Hays all this time was talking big. He kept asserting to anyone who would listen that he had a majority of signatures in his pocket. I knew that he didn't, but I couldn't say so. I finally got every vote pledged to me except one. One representative stayed home sick from the caucus, and I always suspected he had signed cards for both candidates.

* * *

On the morning of Jan. 2, 1929, both parties met to caucus at the State House. In the Republican caucus, Martin Hays and I were nominated for Speaker, a roll call was taken, and, as I expected, I won by a comfortable margin. Hays was not happy about this; he had an antipathy for Harvard graduates and had a chip on his shoulder when we were summoned into our respective chambers by the governor. According to tradition the oldest member of the House presides until the Speaker has been elected. The governor was informed that we were in session. After he had sworn us in, we proceeded to the election. I was nominated by the Republicans, and Leo Birmingham by the Democrats, but before a vote could be taken, Hays insisted on being heard; he had prepared a long brief that he asked the sergeant-at-arms to distribute to each member. I did not object.

In his indictment, which he read aloud, he questioned my affiliation with Gaston, Snow and the work I had done for the Boston Elevated, the Massachusetts Gas Companies, and the telephone company; in short, he argued that because of my "connections" in such legal work as I had done, mainly with

Uncle Cotty and my father, I was not a proper person for the office. His suspicion was typical of the animosity which then existed and which still occasionally comes to the surface in political rivalry. I asked permission to reply, and this is what I said from the notes I had jotted down while he was reading:

> Mr. Speaker, for a good many years my family has lived in this state. During that time, its members have held many public offices and positions of trust. One member has been president of our honorable Senate, member of Congress and the mayor of Salem; another member has held the office of the collector of the Port of Boston, and a third has been the district attorney of Middlesex County. There has been no word of the betrayal of public trust by them. They have also held prominent business positions. Now, I have sought for the past six months the votes of the Republican members of this House for the high office of Speaker. I have asked the men to whom I have spoken to investigate and find out all they desired to know about me; during that time, Mr. Speaker, I have made no promises of any kind to anyone.
>
> Now, Sir, to you and to the other members of this House, with whom I have been associated for six years, I can say nothing. You know me, and you have to judge me by what you know. To those members of the House, particularly the Republican members who are new today, I cite the past, not on which to ask them to vote, but as a precedent on which they may base their vote.
>
> I have been in public office ten years. I have been a member of the board of aldermen of the city of Newton; I have been assistant district attorney of Middlesex County; I have, during the past six years, served as a member of this House. I have also held positions of private trust, and do so now, but I will never let those positions of private trust interfere in any way with my public duties. Those that I considered might conflict I no longer hold. I no longer hold the position of trustee of the Massachusetts Gas Companies. I am no longer a member of the firm of Gaston, Snow, Saltonstall and Hunt. Those positions I now hold of a private trust I will relinquish, and gladly, if they ever interfere with any public trust or public duty.
>
> Now, Mr. Speaker, I ask your support for the office of Speaker. I know of nothing in God's world why I should not hold that office and serve while I hold it the best interests of all the people of this great commonwealth.

Then Martin Hayes spoke:

Mr. Speaker, of course, with my colleagues, I take this gentleman from Newton at his word, that he has severed his connection with the firm of Gaston, Snow, Saltonstall and Hunt. A recent severance! Of course, I take his word that he has given up, no matter how recently — and it must have been recently, Sir — his connection with the Massachusetts Gas Companies, but, Sir, the associations are there, the financial interests are there, the connections are there. They cannot be severed by a temporary elimination for the purpose of grasping high office. Of course, Sir, his family has held high office. Of course, we had a Saltonstall mayor of Beverly, and we had one — and an efficient one — appointed as district attorney of the Middlesex district. And, of course, a Saltonstall presided in the Senate. It has always been the prerogative of wealth and social position, whatever that may mean, to get everything there was, at interest and at no low rate.

Sir, he made an appeal that he would not betray the public trust. Sir, I believe he means it. I believe he is absolutely sincere. He cannot help it. He was not born, Mr. Speaker, the way you and I were born. He didn't have to go through the hardship of life and know the punishment of life. He only knows one side of life, the coupon-clipping side. Subconsciously — unconsciously, if you will — he will play into the hands of those who first stuck the diamond-studded spoon in his mouth when he was an infant. . . .

He got out of Gaston, Snow and Saltonstall, but he is only a few doors removed, and I daresay he still knows their telephone number, and they his, and they can run across the corridor and possibly may at some time consult him. Did you ever know a multimillionaire to give up anything?

Of course, his family has always grasped for power. My position and point is, Sir, that we should put a stop to it. They have had enough. They have had enough.

Oh, Sir, recent trustee of the Massachusetts Gas Companies, Speaker of the House of Representatives! Former associate counsel of the Boston Elevated Railway, Speaker of the House of Representatives! Sir, I never believed the day could come when such a person, with such affiliations, could be seriously considered. Have we not in our midst, a score of eminently fitted men to fill that great position of honor and of power? Are we going to say to the people of

Massachusetts, "There is only one man, the man who by his own act has run away from and discredited and severed temporarily his connections. That is the only man to be Speaker of the Massachusetts House of Representatives?" Oh, Sir, I know the votes are pledged to him. I know, Sir, that the caucus, short and, for him, sweet as it was, is unanimously in his favor. I yield to no man in my allegiance to and work for the Republican party, but, Sir, if he should be Speaker, I would not stultify myself to hold a committee appointment under him.

Sir, the time has not come, I believe, when we with full warning, with the complete knowledge of the facts, would not at least pause at the information that I have given this House today, that we will not at least pause and think. Shall we go through with this blue blood? Shall we, notwithstanding everything that is hostile to the interests of the decent, hardworking people of this commonwealth, elevate to that exalted office a man who is more contaminated with corporation control than any member I have ever known of in the years I have been permitted to be a member here?

Then Henry Shattuck rose:

I abhor demagoguery. I love honor and high standards. I have no fear that we shall not today uphold the high standards of the commonwealth and the high standard of the office we are about to fill.

Something was said regarding the caucus. The caucus was held in the usual way, the way it always has been held. All members of each party were invited to his or her caucus. All could come who desired. If any were absent, it was through their own choice.

I have the utmost confidence in the nominee of the Republican caucus. I have known him for many years, and particularly for the last six years, during which time we have served together on the floor of this House. He is independent, courageous, and true. He is not the servant of any man or set of men. He stands on his own feet, and he does his own thinking. I think, Sir, that the attack which has been made upon him is a despicable attack, and I hope it will receive the reception which it deserves.

It touched me that Henry Shattuck should speak out so strongly in my behalf; and his statement swept away any misgivings in the House. I was elected and escorted up to the dais

Riding Kilbrach at Millwood Hunt show in 1934.

Saltonstall being escorted into the Massachusetts legislative chambers for inauguration as governor on Jan. 7, 1941.

Saltonstall's family in 1938: Front row, from left, William, the Saltonstalls and Susan. Back row, Leverett Jr., Peter and Emily.

A familiar pose in parade in Charlestown, Mass. in 1941.

With his great uncle, Bishop William Lawrence, left, and Frank Stearns, Boston store owner, while Saltonstall was in the House of Representatives.

With Boston Mayor Maurice Tobin, left, and Secretary of State Fred Cooke at annual field day of Ancient and Honorable Artillery.

by two friends of my party and by the leading Democrat. I spoke briefly, accepting my new responsibility, and privately I was pleased to assume my office just short of a century after my great-grandfather, an earlier Leverett, had been elected president of the Massachusetts Senate.

* * *

The Speaker's first and immediate duty is to read off the committee appointments, and this I did with one instant change, scratching out Martin Hays's name and putting in Izzy Fox on the Judiciary Committee. This sticky business of the appointments I had worked out in the preceding December in the Speaker's office loaned to me by Mr. Hull; there every afternoon for hours on end I interviewed each one of the 239 members, asking their preferences and seeking to place them to the best of my judgment. This is a delicate adjustment and one, incidentally, that wouldn't be allowed in Washington, where the caucus of each party determines the appointments of its members.

It was inevitable that some would be glad and some would be mad. In my second term, for instance, I put Henry Cabot Lodge Jr. on Labor and Industries, warning him that it was a tough committee; he did so well on it that he had the support of labor thereafter. Where I went wrong was with Eliot Wadsworth, who came into the House as a former vice president of Stone and Webster and an expert on utilities. In my innocence I made him chairman of Power and Light, and I couldn't have made a worse decision, since the older members of the committee resented his being given seniority; if I had simply put him on that committee at the bottom as a new member they would have listened to him and supported his opinion.

After the appointments are made, there are always a few who ask to swap and a few sensitive spirits who feel hurt, and when possible I made a readjustment. The Rules Committee is the Speaker's committee, and to it he appoints members from both parties who he believes will advise and support him in the year ahead. It was my practice to have the 15 members of Rules lunch with me in the Speaker's room each Tuesday on chicken sandwiches and apple pie sent up from Thompson's Spa; there we would calmly discuss some of the more controversial matters, and from members like Joe Roach of North Adams I could get the sense of how the Democrats would react.

A presiding officer, new to the job, must seek the advice of an expert parliamentarian, and in Frank Bridgman, the clerk of the House, who sat directly beside me, I was fortunate in having an expert who was long familiar with the rules. Whenever a question arose that required a ruling by me, I could lean over for Frank's advice; if I was still in doubt, I would hold over my decision until I had more opportunity to examine the precedents and then give my ruling at the next session. Only three times in my eight years on the rostrum was there an appeal of my ruling. When there is an appeal, the Speaker must take the floor and clarify the basis on which he made his decision; in each instance, I was upheld and the House refused to grant the appeal.

The calendar is freshly prepared for each day, and at the outset the noncontroversial bills or those for which there is little support are quickly disposed of. For instance, an ancient statute of colonial days permits a he-goat to run at large in the morning but not in the afternoon; this law came up for repeal, but the members horsed around with it and were so amused that the repeal was laughed off. They refused to repeal the statute and it is still on the books.

On another occasion, a serious-minded Republican member from Taunton, deeply troubled about the state's responsibility for the children of the mentally deficient, filed a bill, 900 copies of which were printed, to the effect that those who were hopelessly insane should be castrated. I wanted to avoid a debate, but Paul Dever, who was later to become governor, signaled that he wished to amend the bill and ignored my efforts to kill it quietly. Up to the Speaker came his amendment, scribbled in longhand, stating approval of the bill — provided "that members of the present House and General Hooker's horse should be exempt." (The statue of the general on his proud stallion stands on the State House lawn.) I shook my head at him, refused to put in the amendment, the House roared with laughter, and the bill was given leave to withdraw.

I served my first two terms as Speaker with enthusiasm and keenly enjoyed my contacts with the members of both sides of the House. Our Rules Committee, as I have said, met each Tuesday at lunch, and through my friends who were on it I kept in pretty close touch with what was going on in the House. In the daily House sessions when I was fresh, I could call every member by his name, but if the session lasted into the evening and I became tired, my memory would slip and I had to rely on my page, Joe Humphrey, to call the names for me when a member I knew only slightly rose to speak.

During my first two years as Speaker, Harry Shattuck was chairman of the powerful Ways and Means Committee. He seldom asked for or needed help on the floor. He managed the work of the committee, set the time and extent of the hearings, wrote the committee's report, and was so much respected that his committee was seldom divided. Shattuck gave the appearance of being stiff, firm, and unyielding, but he was, in truth, none of these things. He was willing to compromise if he felt it was the only way to accomplish his objective. His reports on the floor were always factual, with carefully prepared reasons for either passing or killing a bill. His strength came from his knowledge rather than from his oratory, which could be quite cumbersome; but, win or lose, he was the most respected member of the House.

A Speaker must have allies on whom he can depend. Naturally, I was relieved when Martin Hays buried the hatchet. We went back on a friendly footing; he resumed his place on the Judiciary Committee, became its spokesman, and continued to be one of the most forceful voices in the Legislature.

Albert Bigelow, who succeeded Shattuck as chairman of Ways and Means when the latter withdrew to become treasurer of Harvard University, proved to be a hard worker whose reports on the floor were clear and well reasoned. He was conservative by nature and became stubborn when he disagreed,and found it hard to accept a compromise. In his unwillingness to do so, he sometimes lost all when he could have gained most of what he sought.

A third member who was increasingly helpful to me during my speakership was Horace Cahill of Braintree. He too was a competent chairman of the Judiciary Committee, and later was to serve me loyally as lieutenant governor throughout my three terms as governor.

* * *

Shortly after my election as Speaker, I was invited to lunch at the Parker House by James Michael Curley, who was then the mayor of Boston. When I arrived, I found the table set for two in a private room, but no one appeared. Finally, I called the mayor's office and was told that he was on his way but had been delayed. Curley at last arrived, gave me a substantial luncheon, reminisced in his usual charming manner, and when we had finished our coffee, he paid the bill with no mention of legislative matters. I thanked him and as we walked out he said to me in those grave tones he affected, "I'm sure, Mr. Speaker, that you will find many bills of great interest to the city before the House this year." I got the point; it was his way of telling me why he had given me a lunch, and of soliciting my interest in the affairs of Boston.

Inadvertently, the mayor made trouble for me later. The Arnold Arboretum, headed by Prof. Charles Sargent, wanted some new roads from the city, and the professor, a careful gentleman of the old school, was told that the best way to get Boston to build the roads was to invite the mayor to a white-tie dinner with the trustees at home. The professor did so. Curley entertained them all through the dinner. When cigars were lighted up, the mayor turned to the professor and said, "Now, professor, what is it you want of me?" The professor told him, and Boston built the roads.

I had been Speaker only a short while when a friend of my father's and a distinguished lawyer, Bentley Warren, invited me to lunch at the Union Club. We had a pleasant conversation. I knew he followed the activities of the Legislature closely, so at the end of dessert, remembering Curley and the Arnold Arboretum, I said, "Now, Mr. Warren, what is it you want of me?" His answer was an abrupt, "Nothing!" Next day, William Snow of my father's firm wished to see me. He asked me what I had said to Mr. Warren and I told him the story I had remembered about Curley and said that if Curley could say it, why couldn't I? He laughed heartily, but suggested that I had better write Mr. Warren an apology. I did.

* * *

The governor who was in office when I became Speaker was Frank Allen, a veteran Republican, who had made his mark as president of the Senate and subsequently as lieutenant governor under Fuller. He was not what I would call a forceful speaker, partly because he relied on notes prepared by an assistant who was a master of cut-and-dried statements. All of us were groping in those dark days of the Depression, and from hearing Governor Allen's speeches, I learned how important it was to have a touch of humor ready in advance of a meeting where I might have to speak.

In private life Governor Allen was a manufacturer of gloves, and when he was affably inclined, he would reach into a desk drawer, bring out a new pair of kid gloves, and present them to you. One way or another, I went home with more gloves than I could possibly wear, and I still have one pair in tissue paper today.

During the first year of the Depression, Governor Allen bore the onus of having to put through the public ownership of the Boston Elevated. The El had long been operating on a subsidy, yet by law it was obliged to pay a six percent dividend to the stockholders as if it were still running in the black. During the Depression, the payment of these dividends out of a state subsidy naturally became increasingly unpopular, and although Governor Allen, like mose conservatives, was opposed to public ownership, it gradually became clear that there was no other alternative. Henry Shattuck was convinced that public ownership was inevitable, and so was I, and so was Jim Twohig, a legislator from South Boston who harped on the subject. So, as it became clear that the bill for public ownership must pass, the *Boston Herald* on its front page published this squib:

"Twohig, Shattuck & Saltonstall
All for one, and one for all."

* * *

Governor Allen ran for a second term in 1930 and was defeated by the Democratic candidate, Joseph B. Ely, an able lawyer from Westfield and a conservative. Ely and I got along well together, and it came to be my practice that when the legislature passed a bill that I thought to be a poor law, I got in touch with his secretary, Robert Bradford, and told him why I disapproved. In every case but one, Governor Ely vetoed the objectionable bill. The exception was the case of building a state pier at the Buzzards Bay entrance to the Cape Cod Canal. When I told the governor that I doubted if we needed the pier, he replied, "Well, if you were in my position, would you have signed the bill?" I grinned at him and assented.

Any bill originating in the Massachusetts House or Senate comes up for three readings. Before it reaches the floor for the second reading it will have been reviewed by committees; it will be debated, and, when necessary, amended, and in those days would have been reviewed by the House counsel. A hot one would be debated even on the third reading. I made it my first order of business, early each morning, to examine the bills that were coming up for a third reading, to make sure I was informed of their content. I had Harry Wiggin, the House counsel, at my elbow, and if I were in any doubt, I'd ask, "Harry, what does this mean?" For after a third reading, a bill is engrossed and, with the signatures of the House Speaker and Senate president, goes up to the governor. When a bill has been engrossed, it cannot be altered.

During one of the closing sessions toward the end of my speakership in 1935, at about two in the morning, I discovered that an insertion had been made in an engrossed bill granting salary raises to certain of Governor Curley's aides. No one knew how this had happened, but I knew that those raises were not in the bill we had passed. I was so angry that with a slam of the gavel I called for an adjournment, reached down to the drawer in which I kept an extra gavel, and with them in hand strode out of the room. (I was later accused by the Democrats of not putting the negative vote on the adjournment.) The commonwealth eventually had to pay for that secretive insertion.

* * *

In one of the early years of my speakership, 1930, the convention of the American Legion was to be held in Boston, and I was asked to be the aide to ex-President Coolidge. President Hoover was to be the main speaker, and it was thought appropriate to arrange a meeting between the President and his predecessor. So up I went to Northampton to present the invitation in person. I found Mr. Coolidge in his office, and after we were seated he turned back in his swivel chair and pulled out of his desk drawer a small box of cigars — none of them, I noticed, of the same brand — and offered me one. I thanked him and accepted a cigarette. I suspect that those cigars had been given him at various banquets, and judging from the dryness of the cigarette I was smoking, I am sure I was right. Frugality was something he never lost.

Coolidge said he would be happy to come and would stay with his friend Frank Stearns. On the day of the convention in early July, I called for him at the Stearns's home on Fairfield Street. I had never served as an aide, and I wanted to do it right. I was spruced up in my American Legion uniform and I carried a large bouquet of flowers that Alice had suggested I present to Mrs. Coolidge. Then I drove them over to the Copley Plaza. In the lobby I paused to telephone to the President's suite to say we had arrived. "That isn't necessary," said Mr. Coolidge, "I can get you in." The sixth floor, as we stepped out of the elevator, was in turmoil, but as soon as the Coolidges were spotted, they were shown into the reception room as a path was cleared for them. I stayed outside and talked with Hoover's secretary. Shortly, the door opened and Mr. Coolidge called to me. "Mr. Speaker, he said, "come in here." I found the conversation most formal, for even when Hoover was serving in Coolidge's cabinet, the two men were never very compatible.

Later, still acting as the ex-President's aide, I waited in the lobby of the Copley Plaza while he attended a formal luncheon. A lady whom I did not know passed by and asked, "Where is Mr. Coolidge?" I told her that he was attending the luncheon, and my friend Alvin Sortwell, who was standing beside be, added, "And there is his hat." She went over, touched the hat , and that was that. It showed the affection that was felt for him by many in the commonwealth.

From that time on he and Mrs. Coolidge were unfailingly kind to us, and when Alice and I were invited up to spend the night with them in Plymouth, Vt., we accepted with pleasure. I went, hoping to get his support for holding a pre-primary convention in Massachusetts.

It was Mrs. Coolidge who carried on the conversation through supper, and when she put a question to the President, I noticed that she always called him "Pa." It was the middle of October and cold. Toward the end of the evening she said, "Pa, I think the Saltonstalls would like a fire in their bedroom." Without a word, Mr. Coolidge left the room and went to a closet door. I couldn't sit there with the two ladies just doing nothing while the ex-President was building a fire for us, so like a little dog I followed him. Outside I found Coolidge picking up stray pieces of wood left from the enlargement of the porch, one by one, until the basket was full. Then upstairs he went, laid the fire and lit it, with never a word, as I tagged along after him.

Next morning we were having breakfast with the Coolidges, and Mrs. Coolidge remarked, "We have been invited to New York in connection with the campaign." (This was the campaign in 1932, when Hoover was running for a second term and Coolidge was expected to speak in his behalf.) She continued, "Pa has been building up his voice by reading poetry to me aloud." It interested me that he was training his voice in that way. Actually he did not have a strong voice — nor do I — but what he said in his dry, quizzical style came over. I made a point to listen when Coolidge made that radio address for President Hoover, and I remember his opening in that nasal voice, "When I was in Washington ... " and how the crowd roared with laughter.

President Coolidge gave me only one bit of political advice, but it was good. I had been asked to take an interest in the *Boston Transcript,* but I did not want to do so for two reasons. I thought it was a bum investment and I considered that it would be poor judgment for one in politics. I asked Coolidge what he thought. In his nasal voice he said, "When you are in politics, don't have an interest in a newspaper, but when you are in town, drop in on the local editor. They like it." I always have.

* * *

I was to complete my third term as Speaker in 1934, and well before the election that autumn, Alice and I had quietly decided that after twelve years in the House, six of them as Speaker, the time had come to withdraw. But unknown to me, my friend Christian Herter had circulated a petition among the members of my party insisting that I stand for a fourth term as Speaker, and when he had the necessary signatures to insure my election, he added his personal persuasion.

I am indebted to him, for I did run again and in the ensuing years made the decision to try for a still higher office, which I probably would not have done otherwise. The matter of timing is all-important in a politician's career, and I have always credited Chris Herter for having kept me on the ladder.

In 1934, James Michael Curley defeated my friend, Gasper Bacon, for the governorship. So in 1935, during my last year as Speaker, the conviction grew on me that since Gasper had retired from politics, it might be my turn to try for the governorship in 1936 if I could get the necessary support.

I began kiting around the commonwealth, speaking wherever I had the chance, nosing out how the land lay. In the months preceding the pre-primary convention in June, I had found out two things. First, there was only a limited number of people who had any idea who I was or what a Speaker did; and, second, that my leading Republican opponent would be John Haigis, a banker from Greenfield, who could pull rank on me since he had been president of the Senate and for two terms had been state treasurer. I knew that he would have strong support in the western part of the state and that if the convention were held in Springfield, he would be on his home ground. If it were held in Boston, I would have the advantage.

When the Republican executive committee chose Springfield by a 5 to 4 vote, the odds were against me, and I suspected that some of the party regulars were too. The competition between Haigis and myself proved to be a hot one, as close as that between Sinclair Weeks and Henry Cabot Lodge Jr., who were competing for the nomination for the US Senate seat vacated by Marcus Coolidge. In the end, the Republican slate of Weeks or Lodge and Saltonstall was thought to be too highbrow. The vote for the governor came first (I deliberately stayed away from the convention floor, which was perhaps a mistake), and it was so close that instead of a recount, it was decided to proceed to a fresh ballot after lunch. Haigis was eventually declared the winner by a margin of three — 648 to 645.

I had supposed that the party machine would count me out as a candidate for lieutenant governor, but I calculated without my friends. When the supporters of Joe Warner, the attorney general, who seemed to have the edge on the nomination, went down into the basement to decide how to handle the situation, their return by the only staircase was blocked off by two good friends of mine, Dan Lynch and Abe Casson, who were wedged on the top step and did not move. So the Warner boys were too late to interrupt a voice vote for me that became unanimous.

I draw three conclusions about the campaign of 1936: First, that no Republican in the United States could have beaten Franklin D. Roosevelt for the presidency; second, that no Republican in Massachusetts could have beaten Gov. Charles Hurley, the Democratic candidate, who rode in on the landslide when, as James A. Farley quipped, "As goes Maine, so goes Vermont"; and, third, that it was a very lucky thing for me that I lost my bid for the lieutenant governorship. Haigis lost to Hurley by a plurality of more than 100,000, and I to Frank E. Kelly by 7200. Sinclair Weeks, chairman of the Republican Finance Committee, insisted on a recount since a close defeat would not disqualify me from considering a try for the governorship in 1938.

* * *

Looking back on the eight years I was Speaker, if I were asked to single out the type of legislation most carefully considered during that period, I would answer: laws protecting the individual. Workmen's compensation laws were broadened and tightened; I particularly have in mind the efforts to protect the worker in the granite quarries and in the other more dangerous trades. An old-age pension law was passed, and was of course amended several times as experience taught us how to make it more effective and easier to administer. Amendments were made to the regulatory laws affecting railroads and public utilities. And there were, of course, emergency measures arising out of the worst of the Depression. I remember that on one Saturday morning in 1933 I was called at 5 a.m. and asked if there could be a meeting of the legislature that day to close the banks of the commonwealth so as to prevent runs on the deposits. I agreed to send messages to the members for an immediate meeting — only to learn that the President himself had closed the banks throughout the nation that morning.

IV. The sweet and sour of being governor

After my fourteen years in the House, I returned to my personal office in the National Shawmut Bank Building feeling as if I were temporarily out of a job. The consolation was in having time with the family in Chestnut Hill, and when on weekends we went out to our farm in Dover, I found plenty of work to do, things that no one else had time to do, the kind of exercise I still enjoy.

Back in 1933, when I was serving in my first six-year term as a Harvard overseer, our most important duty was to confirm the nomination of James B. Conant as successor to President A. Lawrence Lowell. Jim Conant was a classmate of mine, and the president of the overseers. George Agassiz asked me to sound out Jim's roommates and other friends to see how they felt about the nomination. They were strong for him, as indeed were the overseers when the time came for a vote.

On Sept. 18, 1936, President Conant presided at the Harvard tercentenary exercises, which were held in Cambridge. Distinguished scholars from all over the world were invited to participate, and sixty-two of them were to be awarded honorary degrees. When the day dawned, the weather was blustery, the skies dark and forbidding with rain forecast. But Harvard has always had such good luck with weather at the June commencement that at the last minute it was decided to hold the morning exercises in the open as planned.

The procession formed in Widener Library with the scholars in their academic robes and hoods — all the colors of the rainbow — and other dignitaries in cutaways and silk hats, and then precisely as President Conant led the way down the steps of the library, rain began to fall. And it never stopped. Apparently, I was the only overseer who had brought along a raincoat, so I put it on with my top hat, took my place in line, and marched along. As I passed Charles Francis Adams, who was one of the marshals, he said to me in his Yankee way, "Lev, aren't you puttin' on your slicker kind of early?" But I was glad I had it. The tarpaulin that was supposed to cover the large platform at the side of Memorial Chapel was blown about and was quite inadequate to shield the guests, and I wondered how many head colds were in store for all this eminence. John Masefield, poet laureate of England, sat directly in front of me in his brilliant scarlet and black Oxford gown, and I noticed that when it rained the hardest, he took off his floppy cap as if to protect the velvet, while the water ran down his neck.

President Lowell, who had been in charge of arranging the celebration, had written a rather abrupt letter to President Roosevelt, Class of 1904, inviting him to attend and deliver a short address. It is not customary to tell the President of the United States what he is to say or how long he is to say it, a point which Lowell in his brusqueness overlooked. Prof. Felix Frankfurter intervened as the peacemaker. He suggested a dignified reply to the undiplomatic invitation, and FDR did attend, but with a grim expression on his face. There he sat unsmiling, in the rain with no umbrella or raincoat. (Bishop William Lawrence, my great-uncle, told me afterwards that at the luncheon, when sherry and spirits had helped to restore the dampened guests, the President did warm up and took a lively part in the conversation.) Because the rain did not abate, the afternoon meeting was held in Sanders Theater, where President James Roland Angell of Yale opened with the witticism: "This is the way in which Harvard soaks its alumni. . . . "

When President Roosevelt was introduced, everyone rose. In his smiling, confident manner, he began by saying that at the 200th anniversary of Harvard, Andrew Jackson was President, "and all Harvard alumni were worried"; at the 250th anniversary, Grover Cleveland was President, "and all Harvard men were worried;" "and at the tercentenary," I am President. . . . " And he paused. There was a roar of laughter and applause, and he continued in his best vein.

* * *

I knew I was in for trouble on a day in early December, 1937, when Charles Francis Adams, a former Secretary of the Navy, and two colleagues of his appeared in my office. Mr. Adams had been a great friend of my father; I sometimes turned to him for advice, and I knew that when he asked one to do something, it was almost a command performance. What he had on his mind now was that I should accept the chairmanship of the Community Fund campaign for the upcoming year.

The Community Fund was a new experiment in those days, and there was some opposition: the Red Cross did not wish to join, the Salvation Army and the Christian Scientists kept outside the fold, and the leaders of the Jewish community felt that they would be just as well served by the United Jewish Appeal. The chairman of the first Community Fund drive was my old friend James W. ("Mike") Farley, and he met his quota of $4 million, which was to be divided up among the agencies and hospitals that served Greater Boston. The chairman of the second drive, Robert Cutler, filled his quota of $4,250,000. If these figures look small in comparison with the $16 million collected today, it must be remembered that we were working in the Depression and with a much smaller area than that of the United Fund today.

I thanked Mr. Adams and was more easily persuaded when he said that he would be glad to help. I suspected that I was taking on a full-time job for the next ten months; but what I did not appreciate in advance was the opportunity it would give me to work with and get to know citizens of Greater Boston with whom I would otherwise have never come in contact.

I have not found it easy to ask for contributions, whether for charity or for political campaigns, and there were many businesses in 1938 that felt that it was illegal to contribute company funds for charitable purposes. But Mr. Adams lived up to his promise, and in his direct, courteous way he was very persuasive. When I lined up a good prospect who might be tough, I would call up Mr. Adams's secretary and ask what his appointments were for the afternoon. She would say that he had one at 2, another at 3:30.

"Well," I'd say, "Put me down for 2:45." Then I would call up our intended victim and ask if I could see him for not more than ten minutes. When the time was set, I would pick up Mr. Adams in a taxi, tell him whom we were going to see and what resistance I thought we might encounter. After our prospect got over his surprise at seeing Mr. Adams with me, I would take the lead and Mr. Adams would follow along, answer the questions, and point up the need. Few could resist him.

Cardinal O'Connell's nephew, a vice president of the National Shawmut Bank, told me that the Cardinal wished to see me at his home in Brighton. I had heard that he had tentatively agreed to give $5,000 as a contribution from the Catholic

Church but that he wanted to see me personally. We had a pleasant talk in which I explained the nature of our organization and who its officers were, and in the end I came away with a check for $5,000. The same experience was repeated with the leaders of the Christian Science Church. The leaders of the Jewish appeal agreed to give a very substantial figure with the understanding that it could be counted in our general drive but would be distributed to those agencies in which the people of Jewish faith were most interested. This helped to swell our total as we came down the homestretch.

I gave many talks, all short, using some of the amusing episodes that occurred in the fund drive. I shall always remember one luncheon at which my mother and some of her friends were sitting directly under the speaker's rostrum. After a good deal of persuasion, I had secured Bill Cunningham, the well-known columnist for the *Boston Post* as the speaker for that meeting, though I knew he was given at times to some pretty questionable language. Bill began by telling how once while in New York, a terrible toothache had forced him to go to a strange dentist. The nurse, seeing he was in pain, assured him that the doctor would take care of him as soon as he finished with his present patient. Well, from the office Bill could hear a voice exclaiming in stentorian tones, "Jesus Christ! Jesus Christ!" (I wondered how this was sounding to my mother and her elderly friends in the front row.) Finally, Bill could stand it no longer and he asked the nurse, "What is the doctor doing to that man in there?"

"Don't worry," said the nurse, "our patient is a minister who speaks over the radio. He's testing his voice with a new set of false teeth."

To this day, I am uncertain what that story had to do with the Community Fund. But it certainly stirred up the crowd — and did not shock mother or her friends.

Our goal was $4,300,000, and to my disappointment we fell short by about $140,000, But my campaign that year had a cheerful result, for the Red Cross and some of the other hesitant agencies agreed to join the fund in the future.

The Community Fund drive also proved to be one of the most edifying jobs I had ever undertaken; the campaign exposed me to Bostonians in parts of the city I had scarcely known before, and the few professionals and hundreds of volunteers gave me an enthusiastic backing that I treasured as much as the cigarette case with the names of the various chairmen inscribed on it that was presented to me at our final dinner.

The fund also brought me a full-time lieutenant who was to help me for the rest of my political career. Dan Lynch was a young, red-headed Irishman of twenty-six, even-tempered, and full of savvy in his knowledge of South Boston and Dorchester, a man whose advice and friendly encouragement I came to depend on. Dan, who had been working for *The Boston Globe* and studying law at night, had been recommended to me as a part-time aide when I became Speaker; in the fund drive, I paid him out of my pocket to work for me full-time. His loyalty has never wavered to this day.

* * *

When the drive was over, and my successor, Francis C. Gray, had been chosen, I was ready for a holiday. Alice and I cruised to Jamaica on a United Fruit boat, and while at sea I mulled over the question of whether I should try for the governorship again. I knew that John Haigis, despite his defeat, had been talking about making a second bid. I suspected that Joseph W. Martin, a rising power in the US House of Representatives, would be against me. I remembered him sitting on the platform at the convention in Springfield in 1936 growing more and more nervous when he thought I was going to beat Haigis for the nomination. On the other hand, I had heard that Charlie Hurley, the Democrat who had defeated Haigis, had not been conspicuously successful in the State House, and that there was a likelihood of his being challenged for renomination by Mayor Curley, who was eager to have another term in the governorship. If the Democrats were split, a Republican would have a better chance. Alice and I talked this over during the cruise, and my mind was made up by the time we had returned.

I wrote out my statement of intent on the morning of April 19, Patriots Day in Massachusetts, and took it to Sinclair Weeks, the chairman of the Republican State Finance Committee, whose backing I would need. "Sinny," I said, "I'm ready to release this to the newspapers if you'll say that you will be responsible for raising the money for the campaign." Sinclair deliberated, asked a few questions, and then said he would. So that afternoon I released my copy to the press and then on my return uptown paused at the Harvard Club, where, from the roof in company with a tipsy alumnus and the prettiest of the waitresses, I watched the finish of the Boston Marathon.

As I had anticipated, there was some uneasiness in the Republican ranks. When John Haigis and I met in Worcester a few weeks after my press release, he said to me hesitatingly,

"Leverett, I thought we were going to talk things over before we came to any final decision."

"Well, John," I said, "I've made up my mind to try for it. If you want to come in, God bless you, and we'll have a good primary fight. But I'm in it to the end."

John procrastinated for a time, but that talk really ended the matter, and he did not run. Then came Joe Martin, who was not yet the minority leader in the US House, but was already formidable. He was pushing for the nomination of George Bates, his fellow congressman, formerly the mayor of Salem, and he brought with him another representative, my old friend Richard Wigglesworth, evidently hoping that Dick would help persuade me to step aside for Bates. But I said again that my mind was made up and I was in it all the way. These two skirmishes discouraged some of the opposition, but not all. A group of State Street bankers and industrialists, apprehensive perhaps that I was too liberal and Ivy League, put their money and support on a more conservative candidate, Charles Whitcomb. To be honest, he did not scare me too much.

We began putting together a campaign team. I wanted my brother, Dick, who was a partner in one of Boston's most successful investment trusts, to handle the money. I tried to stay out of the finances. "I'm just the front man," I'd say when people spoke to me about contributions, "You talk to Dick." I knew he would be a cool treasurer; he never splurged and when, at the close, people got excited and wanted to throw in more cash, Dick said firmly, "No." I learned that it was of first importance to have by your side a strong "No!" man who will object when it is all too easy to say "Yes." Dick did the collecting, tapping all members of the family, and the contributions from all sources totaled less than $100,000.

Now that I was planning to speak all over the commonwealth, I needed someone to drive me, and my nephew, Renouf Russell, who had recently graduated from Harvard, volunteered. Ren did not content himself merely with driving. As we were returning from one trip, shortly before the primary, I noticed that we must have something extraordinarily heavy in the trunk that was weighing down the rear end. When I asked what was in there, Ren chuckled and said nothing. Finally he admitted that he had stuffed it full of leaflets attacking me that he had purchased from a discouraged Whitcomb supporter for $15 and that he was taking them home to burn.

Another who was to be at my right hand through the governorship and during my early years in the US Senate was Henry W. Minot. Henry had formerly been the head of the Boston office of Dillon, Reed and Company. Illness had forced him to withdraw from business in 1936, but on his recovery I learned through a mutual friend that he might be glad to help with my campaign. In his tactful, decisive way he proved to be invaluable — he was my safety valve, and I could blow off steam to him as to no one else. He was a quiet worker, intent on making independent surveys in the course of which he might appear and disappear, but when an important decision was to be made, he was always there and his advice was sound. At the outset my other leaders, Horace Cahill, Carroll Meins and Lynch, who didn't know him, used to say, "Who is that fellow Minot?" — and only a month later, "Let's see what Henry thinks about it."

Henry and my brother, Dick, were usually on the same wavelength, and it was they who now authorized the first political poll ever taken in New England. They used the American Institute of Public Opinion in Princeton, N.J., then in its infancy, and were secretive about the initial poll showing that I would receive 80 percent of the votes in the primary. This proved to be just about the margin with which I defeated Whitcomb.

Meins, who had represented West Roxbury in the legislature and whom I had come to know well, threw himself full time into the campaign and was to stay on as my top secretary. Carroll was a good talker and a good listener, and he proved to be indispensable in settling intraparty and personal disputes. Often I would say to him, "Carroll, I wish you would get Jim Brown and Martie O'Toole together and shake out their differences." He really liked doing it. They would have supper together, talk for two or three hours, and early the next morning he would come to me and say, "It's all settled."

Abraham B. Casson, also of West Roxbury, was another of my close personal advisers. Abe was Jewish; ethnic distinctions were touchy, but he was one of the most objective men I have ever known, and was always considerate in handling sensitive problems affecting the Jewish people.

Such was my team. After the primary, when I had been nominated for the top spot and Cahill for the lieutenant governorship, we worked out our strategy, planning to cover the state without appearing on the same program and thus get the maximum mileage. To run the campaign, we chose Tom White, with whom I had served as alderman in Newton. In 1936 he had managed Henry Cabot Lodge Jr.'s successful campaign against Curley for the Senate. Now it was my turn against Curley, who I knew would be tough. People loved to hear him talk, for he was witty and eloquent and always attracted good crowds. But Tom White was astute, he knew the commonwealth, he had beaten Curley once, and we felt he could do it again. One piece of his early advice I have continued to observe. He said to me, "When a quick line of repartee or humor occurs to you, don't say it. Try it on me the next morning. If it comes back to you that evening, try it on me a second time, and if it still seems pretty good, we'll let it go."

I learned this lesson quite forcibly one rainy Saturday afternoon in Melrose, where I was dedicating the wing of a hospital. Mrs. Saltonstall had come with me. I said in my opening that I was so glad to be there with them, that I seldom had the opportunity of enjoying the smell of a hospital except when Mrs. Saltonstall was having a new baby. That went over all right with the crowd, but not with Alice. As we drove home, she said emphatically, "Never try that one again!" And I never have.

The day after the primary I went back to my office with a stern injunction from Alice to take things easy. That was Sept. 21, the day that the hurricane of 1938 hit us full force. It was the first of three devastating blows that were to ravage New England within a decade, and we didn't believe what was happening. The drenching rains that preceded the wind had left the largest and oldest trees vulnerable, and they pulled out of the soil like mushrooms; the wires came down, the roads were blocked. Dan and I were the last to leave headquarters on Beacon Street, and the streets were already full of broken glass from the windows above. Heads down, we forced our way against the wind, passing Curley's campaign headquarters on Tremont Street across from the Parker House. Inside a band was playing and there was the sound of cheering. Dan says that I turned to him and remarked, "It will be different in November!" And I am glad to say it was.

The trolley car to Chestnut Hill could get only as far as the reservoir in Brookline, where the lack of electric current and fallen trees made further progress impossible. I started home on foot and was almost immediately picked up by Alice, very angry that I had not returned sooner. Parts of Chestnut Hill Road were blocked, so we drove up over the fields toward my uncle's house, and then down across his lawn. The damage to the trees and the flooding was appalling.

This great storm was to contribute unexpectedly to my campaign. There was an immense amount of repair work to be done throughout the state and on the highways, especially in the central part of the state, which was hard hit. In the emergency, quick contracts were let, often without open bidding, and the friends of Mayor Curley and of William J. Callahan, the commissioner of Public Works, had much to be thankful for.

In my speeches throughout the campaign I aimed my criticism against Curley's regime of 1935-1936. Time and again I repeated the fact that during his administration the state paid $25 for scrapbaskets used in government offices and $75 for highway sandboxes that at the most were worth no more than $25. We stressed the need for economy in the state at large, and in Boston and the suburbs we hit at the way Curley had administered the city.

During his campaign Curley gave me a break by constantly referring to me as "a man with a South Boston face and a Back Bay name."

Actually that description had originated some years earlier in Bob Washburn's column in the *Boston Evening Transcript*, and I really think that Curley's revival of it helped me perhaps as much as anything I could have said, the more so when Jake Spiegel (now a retired Supreme Judicial Court judge), who coached me, especially for the radio, prompted me to retort, "I'll have the same face *after* election that I have before election"— meaning that I would live up to my promises and not make statements that I had no intention of following up. I used this constantly and it went over well.

Members of the family were always there to do their part. My oldest son, Leverett, then about twenty, and Pete, his younger brother, piled signs into an old Dodge pickup truck that my brother loaned us and drove all over the state placing them in opportune spots. Some, of course, were torn down, but most were guarded by the owners of the premises and stayed up until we won. A picture of Alice with our five boys and girls on a platform in Newton while I was speaking made a strong appeal when it was published.

In those days FDR reached the people on radio in his fireside talks, but radio was little employed in state electioneering, and there was no television. One reached the voters in mass meetings, and we had big ones in Worcester, Springfield, Lawrence, Haverhill, and Lowell.

I also made up my mind that we would put on a rally at the Boston Garden on the Sunday night before the election. I figured that I might as well know on Sunday rather than Wednesday morning whether I was a winner or a loser, so through the assistance of my brother-in-law Bill Barron, I secretly engaged the Boston Garden at North Station for a meeting that Sunday. We engaged a band and all the fixings, and we organized a gigantic parade through downtown Boston to the Garden. I still get excited when I think about it. The floor was crowded, the gallery was crowded, and the balcony was full — I think there were over 20,000 people present. With Henry Cabot Lodge and Horace Cahill, I came down to the basement of the auditorium from the little club where we had been hiding, and we made our entrance up a narrow passageway between crowds of cheering people to the platform at the far side of the Garden. The three of us spoke, with Cabot building up the enthusiasm. I have no idea what I said that evening, but the crowd yelled encouragement. After the meeting was over, it was a struggle to get out. I came away with confidence that victory would be ours on Tuesday, and so it was, by a majority of 140,581 votes.

In this first campaign for the governorship and in the two that followed, we estimated that if I could get 40 percent of the vote in Boston, break even in the other thirty-eight cities, and receive 60 percent of the votes in the towns, I should be pretty sure of election. A second public-opinion poll gave me 52 percent of the vote and indicated that I even might beat Curley in Boston. My brother Dick kept these figures secret; he never let the papers know. He and Meins believed them to be accurate, but I was skeptical. Actually the final count ran quite close to those estimates, and I must have gained a sizable number of anti-Curley votes from the Democrats.

I shall never forget that Election Night of 1938. I had anticipated a quiet evening at home, and being confident that we would win, had invited Alice's father, Dr. Wesselhoeft, for supper and to listen to the returns. It never occurred to me that newspaper reporters would want to keep in touch with us, but half a dozen of them came to the house while we were having dessert and when we went into the living room, there they were, drinking coffee and eager to ask questions.

Our family gathering grew larger and noisier as the evening progressed, and it was Dr. Wesselhoeft who first noticed that something unusual was going on outside. About nine o'clock, an automobile had suddenly driven up to our front door; the men in it had sprung out and placed a live flare on the wooden porch and then sped away. Luckily, Dr. Wesselhoeft was quick-minded. He ran out on the porch, grabbed the flare, and hurled it on the grass before any serious damage could be done. It had already burned a hole through the floor and might well have set the whole house on fire had he not been so alert. We never knew who did it.

Later in the evening, when the election was assured, Mrs. Saltonstall and I drove into Boston and made the customary tour of the offices of the *Boston Herald,* the *Boston Globe,* and the *Boston Post,* and then on to the triumphal meeting in the ballroom of the Parker House, where our supporters had been enjoying the returns and were awaiting our appearance.

When I had gone to console my supporters after my defeat in 1936, an aide said to me, "Tell them something bright and amusing. Don't be serious." The only thing that came to my mind then was the old song I used to sing at club dinners, "School Days." So I sang it lustily but off-key, and they all joined in. You might say it became my theme song; the big crowd in 1938 sang it again now that I had won, and hereafter when as governor I made my appearance at receptions or dances where music was being played, the orchestra leader— Ruby Newman or Herby Sulkin, for example— would switch to "School Days" the moment I appeared.

* * *

According to tradition, the old governor swears in the legislature on the appointed day in mid-January, and on the day following the newly elected governor is sworn in by the president of the Senate. A committee of the members from the House and Senate came to escort me to the dais of the House, and with the sergeant-at-arms in his silk hat and armed with his staff leading the way, I took my oath of office.

My first responsibility and one that had worried me was my inaugural address. I wanted to speak about what most needed to be done in the commonwealth and to make those needs sound as convincing as if I were speaking man to man. But I knew that the peace in Europe was trembling in the balance and in the preamble, which Jake Spiegel helped me to write, are phrases more familiar to Tom Paine than what I customarily used. I said:

"These are tragic times. Times which truly try men's souls. The world has gone mad with tyranny and persecution. There is but one hope left. Democracy must not fail. It is the one thing to which helpless minorities cling. . . . " The words sound thumbworn now, but in those days when democracies were giving ground before the threats of Hitler and Mussolini, they had the true ring.

After that, I launched out on my specific recommendations for Massachusetts, as the state emerged from the Depression, and what I asked for was not greatly different from the recommendations made by Gov. Francis Sargent in 1972. The unemployed needed jobs, and to find jobs meant attracting new industries. We needed stronger laws for the protection of the workers; we needed unemployment insurance and old-age assistance. As I re-read that speech, it seems to be relevant; the same needs exist today, though on a larger scale. For scale, I compare my first state budget in 1939, which was balanced in the amount of approximately $65 million, with the 1976 state budget of $3.4 billion.

Alice, my mother, and other members of the family were in the Speaker's gallery for the address. The chamber of the Representatives was filled with members of the Senate who were sitting in the front rows, and the gallery had standing room only. A speaker can tell when the audience is friendly, and this one was.After the ceremony, Lieutenant Governor and Mrs. Cahill and Alice and I shook hands with those who had come to greet us in the Hall of Flags in the State House. That evening, in full dress, we all attended a ball in our honor in the Armory of the First Corps Cadets, where my mother was one of the guests of honor. I cannot remember how long we danced, but home certainly looked good when we got back after that full and exciting day.

Under the state constitution, the governor was obliged to submit his budget within the first ten days of his term. But the budget is drawn up during the previous term, so I had to assume responsibility for a budget that had been planned by my predecessor, a Democrat, with little time to alter it. This seemed to me decidedly unfair, and in my budget message I said so, adding that when I had a chance to study it I hoped to send the legislature a request for certain reductions. It riled me when Reginald Bird, who was head of the Massachusetts Tax Foundation, and Norman MacDonald, its executive director and workhorse, called a mass meeting in Mechanics Hall at which MacDonald, Bird, and others disregarded my statement and were extremely critical of the figures I had submitted. This taught me my first lesson as a governor: never give critics an opening by saying what you intend to do. Either do it, or keep silent.

This was the first of several headaches. The second, which occurred only a few days after I had taken office, was a strike of truck drivers which brought to a complete stop the transportation of food, fuel, and other necessities within the state. I remember the shock with which I listened to the telephone warning by Russell Fessenden, president of the Massachusetts Eye and Ear Infirmary: "Mr. Governor, we have coal for only two days. We can't let our patients freeze and get pneumonia. What are you going to do about it?" I could not give him a satisfactory answer, not even when he pressed me to call out the National Guard. When I asked the adjutant general how many members of the National Guard were capable of operating big trucks, his reply was that there were probably fifteen men at the most; he also asked what might be the liabilities of the state if we did put guardsmen in charge of trucks owned by private companies.

My most helpful advice came from Jim Moriarty, the chairman of the Labor and Industry Committee; he was an experienced member of the AFL and just as anxious as I to put the trucks back on the roads. We were not having much success when there was an announcement in the afternoon papers that strikers had stopped a truck on the highway and a man had been killed. This brought matters to a head. We learned afterwards that there had actually been no violence. As the truck slowed down, the driver had been seized by a heart attack and had fallen out of his seat to his death. The accident turned the tide. That evening, on Moriarty's advice, I attended a meeting of the truck owners where to my surprise I was greeted with cheers and applause. Many of them, I found, were small operators, owners of only a couple of trucks, eager to get back in operation. The following morning, in Moriarty's company, I went to a meeting of the truck drivers that was being held in the South End, unaware that the state police were worried about what might happen to me. My coming was something of a surprise, since an election was in progress there, but when I mounted the platform I was received with applause, except from one leader, Nick Morrissey, who felt that my appearance might have hurt his chances for election. Those two meetings ended the strike; the hospitals received their coal, and my first crisis as a governor was over.

Since I was the first Republican governor after eight years

of Democratic administration, I knew that I would have some tough problems in the appointments I made — or declined to renew. The first and most thorny problem concerned William J. Callahan, commissioner of Public Works. Callahan was a competent road builder, no one could deny that, but mile for mile, the highways of Massachusetts were said to be the most expensive in the nation. Callahan, Dan Coakley, who was then a member of the Governor's Council, and Mayor Curley seemed to share a common interest in the construction of highways; and in the contracts which were let after the hurricane, Callahan was responsible, as I brought out in my campaign, for charges far in excess of what was justified. The $75 sandboxes were only one example. I asked Callahan for his resignation. He was furious and refused to give it.

Paul Dever, a Democrat who had been elected attorney general, had assured me of his support, but he added that he did not want to have anything to do with removing men from office. Accordingly, I appointed a special commission composed of Henry Shattuck, Charles P. Howard, and John L. Hurley to investigate and report to me on the alleged excessive expenditures after the 1938 hurricane. Their report narrowed the charges to two based on "the squandering of public funds," and with it in hand I called for an open hearing. Raymond Wilkins represented me at the hearing before the Governor's Council to seek the removal of Callahan as commissioner of Public Works. The commission was represented by Charles Rugg, one of the senior partners of Ropes and Gray, who volunteered his services and acted without fee; and Callahan, who did not appear, was represented by his lawyer, Atty. Murphy. The hearings before me dragged on for nine days, and at one time Henry Shattuck feared that I was vacillating. In due course, Rugg brought out that the widening of the Mohawk Trail in the Berkshire Hills had run 27 percent above the estimate, and that the work on the Jacob's Ladder section was 44 percent in excess. The defense called no witnesses. Rugg's summing up was devastating, and the Callahan supporters left the last hearing muttering, "He has demolished our man."

Following the hearings, with the support of the council, I dismissed Callahan and appointed a new commissioner, John W. Beal; the appointment was ratified by the Governor's Council by a vote of 6 to 3, with Dan Coakley in the minority.

None of my other appointments was so troublesome. In Tax Commissioner Henry F. Long, we had one of the ablest men in the State House in my time. Long was a Republican and, because of his competence and honesty, was untouchable.

Short, dark-haired, not easy to change when his mind was made up, he repeatedly saved the commonwealth large sums through his extraordinary knowledge of detail. For instance, monies from the estate of Hetty Green, which he proved should come to Massachusetts, helped balance one of my budgets to the tune of $2 million when we were hard pressed. Long, I knew, had been a roadblock to Curley and others, and I was relieved to have him in my administration.

* * *

I entered the governor's office with a solid Republican majority in both the House and the Senate. Maurice Tobin was to be the mayor of Boston, and throughout my three terms, we worked together with a friendly understanding that would never have existed had Curley been in his place. We had, as I remember, only one difference of opinion involving the state and city — that was over the MBTA toll rates.

Our concern for domestic legislation was overshadowed by the threatening events in Europe. President Roosevelt's proposal for a world conference to reduce armaments, promote economic security, and cool down the threat of war, which he made to the British government on Jan. 11, 1938, was rejected and in any case would have been nullified by Hitler's timetable. The surrender of Sudetenland, Germany's stiff demands on Warsaw regarding Danzig and the Polish Corridor, and the signing of the Russo-German Pact at Moscow on Aug. 23 were sobering evidence that Hitler was not preparing for peace.

Here at home the country was deeply divided between the interventionists and the isolationists, a breach that was not completely healed even after Pearl Harbor. We on the Atlantic Coast were more worried than those in the Midwest, and although it was good politics to say that we would render every aid short of war, if war came, it was my personal belief that we would undoubtedly get involved. We could not stand by and see Britain invaded. She was too close to the shores of New England, and if she went under, we would lose one of our ramparts against the dictators. I spoke to this effect at a dinner given for me by the Republican State Committee early in 1939, and when echoes of what I had said reached Washington, I heard that Joe Martin and others of the conservative wing had not been pleased. But I felt I was on the right course. I also heard that President Roosevelt was pleased by my remarks and I had word of commendation from U.S. Secretary of State Hull.

* * *

In a state as old as Massachusetts there are a number of occasions when the governor must put on his cutaway and high hat and smile. The first on my calendar for 1939 was the celebration of Washington's Birthday, which holds a special significance for Bostonians, who can point to the day when General Washington took command of the Revolutionary Army under the Great Elm in Cambridge. For the governor, the lieutenant-governor, and their wives, the day began with a reception in the Hall of Flags in the State House at ten o'clock in the morning. Representatives from all the old colonial organizations, the Sons of the American Revolution, Colonial Dames, and the Society of the Cincinnati, lined up with many friends and the other citizens intent on shaking hands with the heads of the state and their wives. While the music played, Cahill and I literally shook over 2000 hands. Several times the medical officer took me into an anteroom and rinsed off my right hand with alcohol and soap — as far as I could see this simply stung my hand — but I must say I enjoyed it all and inwardly was grateful to General Washington.

When the last guest had been greeted, I had two luncheons to attend. The first was the luncheon of the Society of the Cincinnati, the organization of the descendants of the officers in the Colonial Army. They made me an honorary member, which I was proud to be, and I enjoyed the rather formal function, attended by the Army and Navy commanders stationed in Boston and members of the society. From there I went to Faneuil Hall, the headquarters of the Ancient and Honorable Artillery. This affair, traditionally, is in honor of the chief executive, and they always sent one of their distinguished representatives to escort me to the hall. The Ancients gave me a pair of dueling pistols — but with proper caution not to use them on any political rivals — and at a later meeting, a 38-caliber pistol.

Equally demanding, but much more political, is the great celebration in South Boston and Dorchester marking the anniversary of the British evacuation of Boston on March 17, 1776. Of course, this is also the feast day of St. Patrick, the patron saint of the Irish, and the fusion of the two anniversaries generates an emotional and spirited warmth in the historic part of Boston.

The governor is first expected to salute the monument on Dorchester Heights, where the guns captured at Ticonderoga forced the British fleet to retire. Then on to a luncheon in Dorgan's Restaurant, where after generous helpings of corned beef and cabbage, toasts were drunk and speeches made. I was the first governor to walk the four miles of the parade that followed; I did it in 1939 to set an example because of the wartime scarcity of gasoline, and for the next five years I walked the full route before deciding that it was time to ride in an open automobile. As we tramped along there would be many pleasant greetings, some boos, and an occasional baby held up to salute. The parade ended opposite a large church, where I was greeted by the pastor and offered a most welcome libation.

April 19, 1775: "Hardly a man is now alive who remembers that famous day and year," it is said, but Lexington and Concord will never forget how the British confronted the minutemen on Lexington Green and then marched on toward Concord to fire the "shot heard 'round the world." The governor is expected to share that day with the citizens of both those towns and to congratulate them on the courage of their ancestors.

To jump ahead for a moment. In the spring of 1950, Concord celebrated the 175th anniversary of the Battle of Concord; Gen. Omar Bradley and representatives of the British armed services stationed in Washington were invited, and I accompanied them as the senior senator from Massachusetts. I introduced General Bradley and in my prepared remarks I had a scathing comment on the actions of the British Navy during the Revolution. But as I looked down from the rostrum and saw Admiral Dalrymple-Hamilton, who was representing the British Navy and was also a good friend of mine, I toned down my rather strong remarks about the navy and its conduct in Boston Harbor. General Bradley flew us all back to Washington in his plane, and that gave me the chance to show the admiral the remarks I had deleted. "Why didn't you use them?" he asked. "They were really most appropriate for the occasion."

Next on the calendar comes the Harvard commencement, to which the governor has always been escorted by the Massachusetts Lancers. I was about to shelve this old custom during the war, but President Conant asked me as a favor not to give it up, for he was afraid that if we did it would never be resumed. So in the state car S-1, in low gear, we followed the Lancers to Harvard Yard, where I was received by the proper authorities and conducted to the platform. For six years I sat out in the broiling sun through the morning ceremonies, which lasted several hours. At length several of us suggested that Harvard could assist its dignitaries by erecting a canopy over the speaker's platform and it was finally covered — though too late for me as governor to get the full benefit. After a luncheon for the recipients of honorary degrees in the Fogg Art Museum, it was the governor's responsibility to open the alumni proceedings in the afternoon with a speech limited to three minutes — a limit not always respected.

Massachusetts used to be the only state in the union to commemorate Columbus Day Oct. 12. This is a relatively new holiday but very meaningful to the leaders of the various Italian organizations and citizens of the North End who join forces in a magnificent parade and the evening receptions which follow. I attended and was impressed by the heartfelt unity of this ethnic group who love to keep fresh the traditions of their old country.

Apart from these occasions, Boston also attracts a good many conventions and historic meetings. I soon learned that those in charge of the programs wished the governor to appear, speak briefly, and then clear out. I liked to enter with the head table guests, welcome the guests of honor, then depart via the serving rooms — with which, in the Statler, I am very familiar. If I were scheduled to appear at three dinners, as sometimes occurred, I found that I would probably get a cup of soup at the first, miss the main course at the second, and get a melting dessert at the third, with the result that I would go home hungry and have a beer and a hot bath to put me to sleep. Eventually, I learned to space my evening parties so that once or twice a week I could relax at home without any nervous strain.

At a dinner when Dr. Hans Zinsser, the distinguished pathologist, was seated between me and my brother-in-law, Dr. George Bigelow, he learned over and remarked, "I don't see how you boys go out so often."

"Why, Doctor," I said, "I always have a good time, as I am with you tonight, though it is often difficult to get to sleep after I get home."

"Why don't you take a drink then?" he asked.

I replied, "I'm out so many nights I'd run it up."

"You're dead right," he agreed. "I got it up to about a half of a bottle — and then quit altogether."

I found it did help to get my exercise on my way to the office. With other commuters I took the Boston and Albany train from the Chestnut Hill station, usually in the company of my friend Jimmy Lowell. We would get off at the Huntington Avenue station, walk from there to the State House at a good clip, and I usually reached the office at about 9:15 a.m.

Our walks took us through the Boston Common, and I noticed that the trees on the Common were always trimmed in the spring but never fertilized, so rather persistently I urged Mayor Tobin to use a fertilizer to stimulate the growth of the elms. He finally said, "All right, I'll put in the budget whatever you suggest."

I replied, "$2000."

Several months later when Jim and I were on our way through the Common I noticed that little heaps of manure had been placed along the paths, presumably by the Park Department, so I picked up some of it, which was very dry, and remarked to Jimmy, "This is secondhand manure."

Jimmy agreed, and immediately I called up Tobin and told him he had been soaked. He sounded very stern and asked me how. I explained, and he laughed and said he would call the park commissioner. The commissioner was on the line within a few minutes: "What do you mean by telling my boss that I bought secondhand manure? It is firsthand."

I asked, "Where did you get it?"

"From Orchidvale, the Burrage's greenhouse," he answered.

"Yes," I said, "I knew it was secondhand manure."

Jimmy always supplied the light touch. He sometimes accompanied me when I had to make a speech, and on one occasion, noticing that I was getting nervous, he said, "Now, don't worry, Lev. I'll make your speech for you if you want."

"On what subject?" I asked.

"The love life of the whale," he said with a grin.

But I never was so nervous that he had to deliver it.

* * *

In the spring of 1940 there were three serious contenders for the Republican nomination for the presidency: Sen. Robert A. Taft of Ohio, conservative and the voice of the Midwest; a younger man, Thomas E. Dewey, the district attorney of New York County who had made his reputation as the special prosecutor in the investigation of organized crime; and a dark horse, a native of Indiana, Wendell Willkie, a public-utility administrator, the president of Commonwealth and Southern. Willkie was a magnetic, broad-shouldered man with a shock of dark hair that fell over his forehead. A convincing speaker, he had caught the ear of the nation with his sensible approach to our domestic problems.

During the campaign, Wendell Willkie spent a night at my house, and in the morning I gave him a breakfast with some of the leading Massachusetts Republicans. He arose early and while waiting for breakfast was reading close to our front door when there was a crash in the hall. My daughter Susan, in her usual manner, had dropped her school books from the second floor to the bench, and it scared the presidential candidate so that he jumped up to greet her and later wrote Mrs. Saltonstall this letter:

> Dear Mrs. Saltonstall:
>
> Many thanks for the gracious hospitality of your home. Also, congratulate your daughter for me on the best method I have seen of conveying school books to their proper level.
>
> I really enjoyed the breakfast and all very much and I am in your debt. My regards to the governor, with many thanks,
>
> Cordially,
> Wendell L. Willkie

The convention that year was to be held in Philadelphia, and well ahead of time Dewey came up to Boston to look for convention votes. The meeting I had with him at the Hotel Statler was difficult because even then I felt drawn to Willkie and was unwilling to commit myself. What was said in those 15 minutes I cannot recall; we parted with a pleasant handshake, and I came away relieved but still so nervous that I forgot my briefcase and had to go back for it. Dewey was very polite and passed it off with some humorous remark, but I was sure I had not misled him. He was followed by Taft and Willkie, and I arranged for each of them a luncheon at which they met the Massachusetts delegates. As the host, I tried to make my introductions impartial, but I could see that Willkie made the strongest impression, and I knew that I would be for him.

The national convention that year was the most exciting one in my experience. Willkie started out with only 75 votes compared to Taft's 189 and Dewey's 360. But there was no clear majority, and as the voting continued, Dewey's strength shrank as Willkie's grew. The galleries took up the chant, "We want Willkie! We want Willkie!"

On the fifth ballot, Willkie had 429 votes, and when Pennsylvania switched to him, he had the nomination won.

The Massachusetts delegation had made me their chairman, and it was my responsibility to announce over the loudspeaker the vote of Massachusetts. Underneath the mouthpiece was a little sign saying "When the name of your state is called, put your face close to the mouthpiece and speak slowly and distinctively."

I was nervous when the first time came because the delegation was divided, so I did just what the instructions called for and proclaimed: "Massachusetts paasses." The southern delegations burst into laughter, and I was mystified until I realized that no one with the exception of the governor of Vermont spoke as I did, with a broad *"A."* It was either "pas" or "pauss" but not "paass," which was the only way I knew to say it.

The instant Willkie's name was put in nomination, some of his strongest supporters reached out for the Massachusetts placard on its two-by-four, intending to join in the parade marching around the hall. The placard was right in front of me; I stood up on my seat and held fast to it, as I was determined that we would not join Willkie's bandwagon until there was a clear majority among our delegates. Bob Bradford, later to be our governor, became so excited that he threatened me with "political extinction," and Fred Steele of New Bedford shook his fist at me and promised to knock me off my perch. But I hung on until we had polled the delegation, and when we had a majority for Willkie, out we went to join the parade for him. (Back home when the emotions had subsided I received letters of apology from the two who had wanted to knock me out.)

As I have said, Willkie won on the fifth ballot, and I was glad. I had been asked to make a seconding speech and had prepared what I though might be helpful. But I never made it since our senator, Henry Cabot Lodge, had requested the opportunity and two seconders from Massachusetts would have been too much.

I intended to help Wendell Willkie in every way I could although by this time I was in the thick of my own campaign for re-election against a strong opponent, Paul Dever, the attorney general. In late September Willkie came north to Massachusetts and Rhode Island. A special train brought him to North Attleboro, where he spoke in the square. Then, with Joe Martin and Mike Farley, we drove to Attleboro and Taunton, where Willkie spoke again, but during this time I found there was sharp rivalry between the two Massachusetts factions supporting Willkie — the one headed by Joe Martin and the other headed by Mike Farley, the state chairman for Willkie. They bickered about who should ride in the limousine with Willkie and me the next day, and since I had no wish to arbitrate, I walked over to the two state police to thank them for the efficient way they were handling the cavalcade.

Meanwhile, Willkie had motored back to Providence; Mike Farley continued to fume, and he finally determined to go down to Providence to see who was really to be the boss in Massachusetts. He found the Willkie train in the Providence railway yard, and except for the porter there was only one gentleman aboard, a classmate of mine at Harvard Law School named Pierce, the son of a justice of the Supreme Court, who was putting the finishing touches to Willkie's speech for the evening. He was a brilliant fellow, with a great sense of humor. Mike looked into the compartment and said to him, "Can you tell me who's in charge of this train?" And he said it in that polite, soft tone that Mike always used when he was very angry.

Pierce looked up from his writing and replied, "Mr. Farley, this place is like a house of easy virtue on a Saturday afternoon when the madam has gone out to buy the Sunday provisions."

This answer so tickled Farley that whenever he came to me with some trouble all I had to do was to ask him if he knew who was in charge on Saturdays. He would laugh and that ended it.

The day after his Rhode Island speech, I met Willkie early in the morning in New Bedford to drive him through the various towns to Milton and thence into Mattapan and on to the Hotel Somerset in Boston, where he was to rest before visiting Essex County in the afternoon. There was no bickering about seats. We left New Bedford with Mrs. Willkie in front and Congressman Wigglesworth and me in the back seat, with Willkie between us. As we approached the crowds, Willkie would stand up to wave and respond to the cheers as we went slowly along. We finally came into Mattapan, and as we went towards Boston on Blue Hill Avenue, a ripe tomato was thrown at Willkie. It was in the Jewish section, where he was not popular. He used some very strong language, wiped the tomato off his shirt and vest, quickly put on the best smile, and regained his com-

Associated Press

Saltonstall gets ready to throw out the first ball as the Red Sox opened their 1939 season in Boston. From left, Connie Mack, manager of the Philadelphia A's; Tom Yawkey, Red Sox owner and Joe Cronin, Red Sox manager.

In 1939, on the 25th reunion of Harvard's second crew, Saltonstall was back in the boat's bow.

Pruning a tree at his Dover farm in 1952.

Leaving the State House in Boston in 1945 at end of last term as governor.

Talking with Queen Wilhelmina of the Netherlands at Boston's Museum of Fine Arts, 1943-44. Alice is at right.

Alice Saltonstall, left. Below, son Peter in World War II uniform.

posure. A little later he turned to me and said, "Governor, how much longer is it before we reach our destination?" He did not know where we were going. I looked around and said, "Oh, about fifteen minutes, Mr. Willkie."

Then he resumed his waving to the crowds. We went about another ten minutes, not in the direction of the Hotel Somerset but towards City Hall, and Willkie again asked the question. Again, I replied, "about fifteen or twenty minutes, Mr. Willkie."

A third time Willkie turned and I gave the same answer. Finally, Willkie turned to Congressman Wigglesworth and said, "Congressman, I think that governor of yours is just a plain goddamn liar."

I laughed, Wigglesworth laughed, and no more was said.

After his rest, our tour resumed to Essex County, and for the first few minutes all he did was to apologize for his remarks about my being a liar. I think Mrs. Willkie, during their lunch hour, must have told him that it didn't sound very good to call the governor of the state in which he was seeking votes a liar. But I laughed it off.

That evening Willkie made a speech at the old Braves Field, which he did not do well. I was very disappointed. It was a chilly evening, and his talk was delivered in a stereotyped manner, not in the spirit with which Willkie usually spoke. The truth was, he had practically lost his voice. In small groups he could be very persuasive; on the stand, before large crowds, he was not so effective.

* * *

Once we had finished paying for the havoc wrought by the hurricane of 1938, I tried to administer the state finances carefully. There could be no large, new capital outlays with the country on the verge of war, and it was easy and good politics to tighten the belt. The fighting in Europe came even closer to us in the spring of 1940, when Hitler's blitzkrieg smashed through the defenses of Belgium and Holland and forced France to capitulate in a campaign that lasted only three weeks. The evacuation of Dunkirk was followed by a bombing of the British cities, and we who admired England held our breath.

On Sept. 20, 1940, when the Blitz of London was at its height, I made a broadcast in honor of the Massachusetts National Guard. We had always been proud of our National Guard, which had served with such distinction in World War I under General Edwards. Once again the 26th (or Yankee Division) was to be called into federal training and since there were a number of vacancies, I made an appeal for volunteers. I said, "Massachusetts had her pilgrims and her minutemen. Today she has just as brave and loyal citizens in the membership of the Guard. . . . "

"'Don't fire until you see the white of their eyes' was a stirring command at Bunker Hill, yet it will not do today. 'Don't let them get within a thousand miles of us' is the present secret of security."

Following that address, with the approval of the legislature and the Governor's Council, I organized two units to be responsible for our statewide security. The first was a semiuniformed outfit called the State Guard, under the command of Captain Foley, chief of police of Worcester and himself a retired national guardsman. We had no trouble with enlistments, for many citizens who were too old for the draft but physically fit were eager to serve. The State Guard soon grew to be 2000 strong.

The second unit, called the Committee on Civil Defense, was organized by Mike Farley with the women in it under the direction of Miss Natalie Hammond. And in addition, for special emergencies, we had the Massachusetts unit of the American Red Cross under the leadership of Joseph R. Hamlen. One of their first missions after Pearl Harbor was to help the merchant seamen whose ships had been sunk by the German U-boats and who had been brought safely to our harbors.

* * *

In my 1940 campaign against Paul Dever I asked the voters repeatedly: "Do you want to go back to the old Curley days?" And then I went on to emphasize the economies that we had put through during my first term. I stated that we were on the threshhold of war and that we must assist in every way possible the preparations for national defense and for the safety of the Atlantic seaboard.

As we came into the last weeks I was campaigning with confidence because of a private poll which reported that I was running three to four percentage points ahead of my opponent. But I was in for a shock, for as the pollsters told me afterwards, they had underestimated the pulling power that President Roosevelt, running for his third term, contributed to all on the Democratic ticket.

The truth came out on election night, with Dever showing unexpected strength in the industrial towns of Fall River, New

Bedford, and Lowell. Alice and I were following the returns on the radio at home. Willkie, in whom I had set such high hopes, was being snowed under. At midnight Tom White, who had been managing my campaign, telephoned and urged me to come into Boston to show myself "as the electors' choice." But I was too uncertain of the outcome and so, Dan Lynch, who urged me just as earnestly not to appear. I agreed with Dan. This brought about an angry dispute between my top advisers, and so to get away from the argument and uncertainty, Alice and I took a ride out through Cambridge and the suburbs. When we came to the State House to talk to Dan, the prospects seemed so unpromising that we went home to bed.

At breakfast the next morning the headlines reported my defeat, and on my way in town I stopped at my mother's and told her that I was out. It was not a happy morning in the governor's office. But in the mid-afternoon Fred Cook, the secretary of state and a good friend of mine, who had been overwhelmingly re-elected, came to my office to report that there were two wards in Springfield, both fundamentally Democratic, and two in Quincy, both Republican, whose returns were not yet in. There was still hope that the vote in Quincy would swing the majority my way, and so it did. When the last vote had been counted, I was elected by a majority of less than one-fourth of one percent.

Naturally Paul Dever asked for a recount. Now, a recount of 351 communities is a tremendous job. It was Abe Casson who protected my interests and who made certain that we had vigilant watchers wherever a recount was taken. The Governor's Council would have to announce the final tabulation, and I was certain that there was at least one member of the council, Dan Coakley, who would be happy to see me defeated. But Coakley made no interference. The recount was finally determined in my favor early in December, and at the Clover Club dinner the evening of Dec. 8, I smiled with relief from my spot at the head table when I saw Dever rise and courteously concede the election — and heard the cheers that followed.

I had many friends among the members of the Clover Club and I rarely missed their annual banquet, which is held on the Saturday evening preceding Evacuation Day; I enjoyed their Irish humor and the banter that was sometimes directed at me. How many times have I joined in singing "The Wearing of the Green" or listened to the Hon. John F. Fitzgerald as his high tenor reached the rafters in "Sweet Adeline?"

When they honored me with full membership after I retired, I was happy to accept, adding jokingly that from now on I would have to pay for my dinners. The Charitable Irish Society also used to invite me to their banquets, and on one occasion I bragged that seven generations back a relative of mine was married to a Mary Sullivan, born in Limerick in 1690. That remark brought down the house and in the next morning's mail I received an invitation to join the Charitable Irish, paid my dues, and have been a full-fledged member ever since.

In my 1941 inaugural address I took a certain pride in reporting the turnaround that had taken place in our state finances. At the end of my first term we had a surplus in free cash of over $3.3 million in the general fund and a surplus of $2.6 million in our highway fund. The state debt had been cut in half, and we had turned back to the cities and towns $10 million each year from highway revenues to assist them with local road building. As a result, 215 of our cities and towns had reduced their tax rates in 1940, the largest number to do so in thirty years. In fairness I must add that moving as we were toward a war economy, it would have been inappropriate to have spent money on new undertakings.

The federal government was re-arming the forts in Boston Harbor, and antiaircraft installations were being placed along the coast, and with these in mind I felt it was time to develop the airport in East Boston. Initially, this had been supported partly by the city and partly by American and Northeast Airlines, but, now on my recommendation, the legislature took the facility over from the city in 1941. I appointed a commission to determine the price that the state should pay the city for the control tower and the improvements that had been made to the runways, which then comprised 292 acres (just about a fifth of its present size). It was also my plan that the commonwealth should develop the facilities of the airport in Bedford, northwest of Boston, then used primarily for private planes and a few freight carriers, but after Pearl Harbor this responsibility was assumed by the federal government. The state leased Bedford to the government for $1 a year; the government took over its enlargement and has remained in charge ever since.

Our first priority in East Boston was to enlarge and increase the runways. We employed a professor from M.I.T. to determine the underpinning and the weight per square inch that the runways could support. We found that the soil under Boston Harbor provided excellent fill, but the problem was how to get hold of the big dredge we needed. At that time there were only two dredges capable of doing the work we wanted;

one of them was in the Panama Canal, and the other was somewhere in the Pacific. I think back with a smile to the skullduggery with which our contractor contrived to have the Pacific dredge diverted and towed up to Boston to make the new foundations we so urgently needed.

The Air National Guard and the Army Air Corps each owned a hangar at East Boston, and I was relieved when I learned that the latter had decided to build a very large airfield in New England — in Connecticut, Massachusetts, or New Hampshire. An Air Force general flew up to make a reconnaissance. He first examined the facilities at Hartford, where he was given a dinner by the governor, then went on to Manchester, N.H., and again was well fed. It was a very warm day when he landed in Boston, and I invited him to a light lunch at the City Club with blueberries, half-and-half, and apple pie for dessert. I had the president of the Boston and Maine Railroad, the chairman of the New England Electric Company, and the chairman of the State Public Utilities Commission meet with him. He questioned them on what services they could provide should the Air Force place the field in Chicopee, not far from Springfield, and their answers — and the cold lunch — seemed to satisfy him, for that is where the field was built.

* * *

As long as we live we will always remember what we were doing when we first heard the shocking news of Pearl Harbor as it came over the radio. I was in the woods at the Dover farm and getting ready to drive the family home; as soon as I reached Chestnut Hill, I asked the adjutant general to call out the State Guard to protect railroad crossings, utility installations, highway bridges, and other spots. Next morning I advised all of the public-service units to take the precaution of guarding their own facilities, and in two days' time they had agreed to do so, with the single exception of the Boston & Maine, whose president protested that they really had no funds with which to pay for a guard.

I had read somewhere a story about Huey Long when he was governor of Louisiana and how he persuaded the local railroad to provide a free train to the Tulane-LSU game. When the railroad at first said that they couldn't afford it, Huey had his utility commissioner inform the railroad president that a certain bridge seemed to be unsafe and might have to be condemned. The executive saw the point and decided that it would be cheaper to give the students a free ride. Acting on that example, I invited the admiral of the Boston Navy Yard, the commanding general of the First District, Lieutenant Governor Cahill, and other officials to my office together with the president of the B&M. There was some general discussion about security measures and their expense, at the end of which I turned to the president of the railroad and said, "All of your trains come into North Station over a causeway, which is dangerous if it is not protected. If you will not guard it, the only thing I can do is to close North Station." The president threw up his hands and said, with a broad smile, "You win."

Early in my governorship I said I would do everything I could to attract new business to Boston. My assistant, Jimmie Reynolds, thought we might get some out-of-state publicity by bringing to the State House the stars of some of the new plays that were opening in Boston, and thanks to his persuasion I met and was photographed with Dorothy Lamour, Fred Astaire, Jane Withers and others. On one night, five bright-eyed chorus girls from a popular musical comedy were lined up by the photographer along a wall with me in the center, and as they got set for the camera, he said to them, "Now, look at the governor."

One of the prettiest was standing next to me; she didn't quite come to my shoulder, and as she turned up her head, she remarked pertly, "That's a little hard to do, but I'll try."

I was to use that remark later to get smiles out of nervous visitors when we were photographed together.

I certainly proved to be a ham actor in the one and only performance in which I took part for the Stage Door Canteen. A radio writer had written a comedy in which he, Gertrude Lawrence, and I were to take part. I tried hard to get out of it, but he was so insistent, he said he had sat up all night writing it without a fee, that I felt I had to go along. The show was to go on the air for our boys in the service, and the Boston studio was packed with a radio audience, young and old, sitting on chairs and on the floor. In the skit I was to play the part of Captain John Smith, with Gertrude Lawrence as Priscilla.

It was a small stage, and not being sure of my lines I held my script handy. When Gertrude Lawrence came in with that famous line, "Why don't you speak for yourself, John?" I answered her with the words provided in my script but added something about getting the horse ready to race. I can't remember the exact words, but it brought down the house even if Gertrude didn't like it too well. When the show was over, I had to go down the fire escape to get out of the building, it was so crowded, and when I reached home, Alice said emphatically that she would never want to listen to another program like that one. But it couldn't have been too bad for my friend George Denny, serving as a doctor in a veterans' hospital in Texas, wrote me and said it gave him quite a feeling of homesickness to hear my Massachusetts voice.

In order to help the war, people were accepting all kinds of sacrifices. Meat and fuel were rationed, and so was gasoline — quite stringently. After long discussions I wanted as many of the state cars as possible put in mothballs for the duration. Over 400 such vehicles were stored in a public works shed in Framingham. The S-1 used so much gasoline that I picked up a state-owned Dodge and drove it home each night. In this way I saved my allotment of gas. During the early rubber shortage old tires were collected and piled up in pyramids in lots. They were never used. Then, during the drive for scrap iron, some public-spirited citizens suggested that the wrought-iron fence in front of the State House be given up. I agreed. It has never been put back, nor have the old gates around the Common, which Mayor Tobin ordered used for scrap.

* * *

When the national convention of the AFL was held in Boston, I knew that as the governor I must provide some form of entertainment, and when I looked at my very limited fund, the choice was either for me to hold an executives' breakfast at one of the in-town hotels, or for Alice and me to invite the convention wives to a tea party at our home in Chestnut Hill. The program chairman seemed delighted at the second suggestion, but we had not anticipated that there would be quite so many guests, nor that the pouring rain would eliminate any chance of our using the garden. The ladies arrived in sightseeing buses after a tour of Concord and Lexington; over 400 of them, wet, tired, and thirsty poured into our house. The walls bulged, people chatted in the bathrooms, sat in the boys' bedrooms on the third floor, and gathered together on the stairs and in the entry ways. The tea, cakes, and sandwiches were provided by the commonwealth, but, at my expense, I provided a small bar. Thank goodness it was so crowded that no one could really get to it. I asked Jim Reynolds how many drinks he served. He said with a smile: "My own, and one other" — to the head of the bartender's union.

Several years later, I was in Cincinnati at a United Fund gathering, and the head of the carpenter's union said to me that his wife was still talking about the fine time she had at our house in Chestnut Hill. I only wondered whether she had been sitting in the bathroom or on Alice's bed. But I am glad she had a good time.

* * *

In the Boston Navy Yard, which had never been busier, some 16,000 men were working around the clock, servicing the warships in battle gray or camouflage, and at the Fore River Shipyard in Quincy, aircraft carriers, destroyers, and LSTs were on the ways. I officiated at the launching and commissioning of many of these ships — the aircraft carriers *Lexington* and *Saratoga,* followed by the cruiser *Boston,* and finally by the magnificent battleship *Massachusetts.* Secretary of the Navy Frank Knox telephoned me from Washington to say that it was customary for the governor to designate the person who was to christen the ship named for his state. The rather formal way in which he said this made me hesitate to name my own good wife, though I wanted her to do it. Instead I suggested that Mrs. Charles Francis Adams, wife of the former secretary of the Navy, would be a happy choice, and Knox agreed. At the event Mrs. Adams did the christening in style; she broke the champagne bottle successfully and afterwards we all enjoyed a pleasant luncheon.

I know Alice would have liked to, but she felt as I did that the honor should go to Mrs. Adams, whose family had sent two presidents to Washington from Massachusetts.

To make amends I asked Mrs. Saltonstall to christen the first LST to be launched in Quincy and was proud of her. On the way to the scaffold I had asked the public relations officer what would happen if something went wrong with the bottle of champagne. "Why," he said casually, "we always have another on hand." As we were leaving he handed me a package: "Here is the bottle," he said. I thanked him and said that Mrs. Saltonstall and I would enjoy drinking it at supper that night. He looked a little strange, but said nothing. When we reached home and opened the package, we found that it was the remains of the bottle Alice had smashed on the bow, still in its network. That Alice had not been selected for the *Massachusetts* still hurts me though it does not bother her.

* * *

Meetings and conventions on the home front created many openings for me to speak. I remember one year when I had 600 invitations during one stretch of 180 days. As a rule I would scan the morning paper and try to tie in my remarks with something that happened that day. At one meeting at the Hotel Statler, where I was leading a rally for Victory Bonds, my garter slipped as I stood up to talk, and I could feel it sliding down my leg. So I began: "We are here to do honor to those boys who are fighting, and to our fellow citizens who are working around the clock in Washington, and the only thing I am suffering from at this moment is that my garter is worn out and is falling down."

The *Boston Herald* put that in a box on the front page the next morning, and within the week I received forty-eight pairs of garters. I also received forty-four requests for garters from people who evidently needed them as badly as I did. So I passed along those I had been given until I had only one new pair left. Evidently this made friends, for at a luncheon sometime later the lady beside whom I was seated remarked, "You know, we still have those garters you gave my husband. We framed them, and they are hanging on the bathroom wall!"

There are times when I have an innocent way of saying something with an unexpected effect, and this happened when I was asked to address the girls at Mount Holyoke College. I did not believe that many of them would come to hear me, but when I arrived, the auditorium was packed. The president gave me a flattering introduction, and in momentary embarrassment I cast about for a good opening and came out with an historical observation: "You know, in the early days our ancestors on the banks of the Charles had to compete with packs of howling wolves . . ."

The girls burst into laughter, and I had to start all over. On the drive back to town I asked Jimmie Reynolds why they laughed. He said, "Don't you know what 'wolves' are to college girls?"

But the most stirring engagements in those days were in the bestowing of the E Awards, for excellence in cooperation between management and labor in the preparation of military and naval equipment. I attended over eighty of these ceremonies, for Massachusetts received the second-largest number of such awards in the nation, topped only by Ohio. These meetings made me proud to be an American citizen. There was such intense good feeling on all sides: the workers were proud to be signalized as a vital part of the war effort, and management was just as proud to receive the award with the flag that spoke for their accomplishment.

These meetings, before as many as 16,000 at The Raytheon Company, or perhaps 75 at a small plant in Somerville, never ran longer than an hour, and it was remarkable how much emotion they generated in that time. Each speaker was allowed approximately three minutes, which was pleasing to me. At one of the first awards, there was an officious Army colonel who was in charge and who said, "I should like to see the speech you have prepared, Governor. I cannot let you speak without knowing what you are going to say."

Such absurd red tape made me angry. "I have no prepared speech," I said, "And I'll not speak at all if my remarks have to be vetoed beforehand."

I was never asked that question again.

Admiral Cloverius, who was then retired but very active, was usually the spokesman for the Navy, and he and I used to vie with each other to see which one of us could bring out the more timely incident in our brief remarks. I remember one case in which we were presenting an award to a company which had been working on bombsights. In my three minutes I alluded to the successful raid of B-29s that had been reported that morning in the newspapers and how their bombsights, built in Massachusetts, had helped locate their targets. The admiral laughingly conceded that I had won our contest that day.

* * *

When John Gunther was collecting material for his book *Inside America,* he came to Boston and visited me in the governor's office. That day I had a talk scheduled at a Rotary meeting in Needham, so I invited him to ride out with me and to visit with a typical Rotary group. Of course, we talked all the way and he asked me what I cared for most in life. I said my family and my desire to lead a happy life with them and, secondly, Harvard University. I added that I was the tenth generation of my family to graduate from Harvard and that I hoped there would be many more.

Early in 1942 I was surprised and pleased when I was informed that an honorary LL.D. degree would be conferred upon me that June; I was not to say anything about it. No governor of Massachusetts had been singled out for such an honor since 1882, when a degree was awarded to Gen. Benjamin Franklin Butler. Butler was not popular with Harvard men, partly because of his rough-shod behavior in New Orleans, where he was in command of the army of occupation at the end of the Civil War, and partly because of the uncomplimentary speeches that he made about Harvard during his term as governor. Thereafter, Harvard authorities felt that it was wiser not to award a degree to the governor and to discontinue the tradition. I was the first to be so honored after the hiatus of sixty years.

The awarding of the honorary degrees takes place at the end of the commencement exercises, after the graduates of Harvard College and of the many professional schools have had their hard-earned degrees conferred by the president. Then the university marshal announces the names of those who are to receive the honorary degrees. Each recipient as his name is called rises to receive the parchment in the traditional flat leather case from the chief marshal and stands while his citation is pronounced by the president. I was touched as I heard the words:

> "Governor of the commonwealth and former overseer of Harvard College; a multitude of devoted friends and proud fellow citizens applaud his high integrity and courageous public service."

Actually I served three terms as an overseer, eighteen years in all. Each overseer is the chairman of a visiting committee, and at various times I was chairman of the Committee on Public Health, of the School of Design, and of the Peabody Museum, where for the first time I learned about the Mayan culture, and I enjoyed the meetings at which I presided and the chance to pick up some adult education.

In 1943 I was elected president of the Harvard Board of Overseers, and I observed that when President Conant himself had reached a decision, he would argue, sometimes quietly, sometimes strenuously, to have the board follow his judgment. In ninety-nine case out of a hundred, the board was willing to do so. But there was one case where a fundamental difference of opinion developed, first in the corporation, and then among the overseers, as to whether William Marbury of Baltimore, a graduate of the Harvard Law School but not of the college, should be named a fellow of the corporation.

It was, I believe, the first time in history that the president had reached outside the alumni of the college for his choice, and the traditionalists, who had an alumnus in mind for the appointment, were in opposition. President Conant stated flatly that if the board did not care to follow his judgment in this case, he would feel compelled to resign. Personally, I have never liked that type of argument, and I was relieved when the board did not push Conant to his decision. Conant prevailed in a close vote, and over the years his judgment proved to be a sound one, for Bill Marbury was a conscientious, intelligent, and helpful member of the corporation.

I never willingly missed a Harvard commencement. The singing of the old college hymn by the Harvard choir, the graduates in their new robes who are summoned to the platform by the chief marshal, the women in their summer frocks, and the old graduates reaching far back in time touch my loyalty.

The speeches that follow in the afternoon are sometimes exceptional, sometimes not. I recall sitting beside Mr. Kettering, the vice president of General Motors and a great innovator of appliances for an automobile. He told me about the new spraying of paint on automobiles and how he had sold the idea to the president of General Motors by inviting him to lunch. They drove over in a black Cadillac, had a fairly long meal, and when they came out to return to the office, the Cadillac was painted gray. The president said: "This is not our car."

Kettering said, "Yes, it is, but I just had it painted while we were at lunch."

That day, too, I watched Kettering as he changed his notes after listening to the opening remarks by the president of the Harvard Alumni Association, a bank president from Indiana, who stated that the time had come for us to hold back and assimilate the many new inventions before trying any more new ones. When Kettering's turn to speak came, he began, "Ladies and Gentlemen, I have listened to your president say how we must catch up on the present inventions before we experiment further. I just want to tell you men of Harvard that General Motors will keep on making new automobiles, safer automobiles, faster automobiles, whether you men of Harvard buy them or not."

On Sept. 6, 1943, at the suggestion of President Roosevelt, Harvard conferred the degree of Doctor of Laws on Prime Minister Winston Churchill. I had been warned in advance by President Conant that he had no automobile and would be very grateful if I would drive him out in the governor's car to the Brighton yards to meet the special train bringing the Churchill party. I said of course I would be delighted and asked what we were to wear; he replied a cutaway but no silk hat.

Mr. Churchill's visit posed a political dilemma. An important conference of Republican Party leaders was to take place on the island of Mackinac in Michigan on the same date, and they offered to send a private plane to fetch me for the last session when they learned of the conflict. I had to decide whether to attend the party council or remain to welcome the Prime Minister to Massachusetts. As a Harvard man, I felt proud to have Churchill come to Cambridge and I felt honored that Conant wished me to present him to the alumni and undergraduates. Furthermore, I did not much like the idea of that long flight in a small plane, so I stayed put.

On the morning of the sixth, I put on my cutaway. Al Larivee, my driver, donned his uniform as a sergeant in the state police, and we picked up President Conant at his home in Cambridge and then followed the police escort to the Brighton yards. Shortly, Churchill emerged, wearing gray slacks, a dark coat and his famous blue and white spotted bow tie. Mrs. Churchill and their daughter, Mary, who was a subaltern in Women's Veterans Service, were with him, and he was attended by one bodyguard. On the ride back to Cambridge, Mr. Churchill was too conspicuous not to be recognized, and when people waved at him, he responded by holding up the first two fingers on his right hand in the famous V-for-Victory sign. At the President's house, the ladies were welcomed by Mrs. Conant; then President Conant in his academic robes, Churchill with his walking stick and black fedora, and I crossed the Yard and joined the academic procession which, as a bugle sounded, entered Sanders Theater.

It was a little before noon, and in that familiar old auditorium sat or stood more than 1200 people in what one man described as "the most exciting fever of a lifetime." The faculty, the governing boards, the officers of the Army and Navy units at the university and of the WAVES, and a semicircle of undergraduates all rose to their feet as we took our places on the stage.

Conant had requested that I, as governor, introduce the Prime Minister, and as we sat listening to the fanfare, the latter turned to me and asked, "What do I call you?"

I knew the customary language was "Your Excellency,"

but I could not bring myself to tell Churchill, probably the most prominent man in the free world, to give me that title, so I replied, "Just call me Governor," and he did so.

In my presentation, I concluded with these words:

> "He tells the truth in dark days as well as bright. That is why his people follow so confidently when he leads. That is why his Allies are his steadfast comrades in arms. That is why our country and his will work together for a greater security for each other and for those who love freedom throughout the world.
>
> "Mr. Churchill, you are an inspiring example of the biblical motto of our great President, Thomas Jefferson: 'Ye shall know the Truth, and the Truth shall make you free!' "

As I concluded, he laid his hand on my arm and said quietly, "Very good."

Then after the singing of the Psalm, President Conant conferred on him the honorary degree of Doctor of Laws with this citation:

> "An historian who has written a glorious page of British history; a statesman and warrior whose tenacity and courage turned back the tide of tyranny in freedom's darkest hour."

Churchill took his manuscript from his pocket, put on his glasses, and, with gestures emphasizing what he said, moved dramatically to the subject of Anglo-American relations. The audience gave him a standing ovation. I noticed that he left his notes, reminders on small white cards, on the rostrum as he resumed his seat beside me. So did Prof. Tom Barbour, the gigantic director of the Agassiz Museum, who sat directly behind us. Tom, 6 feet 5 and weighing something over 250 pounds, was determined to get those notes, and as he stood up and moved forward to do so, he told me afterwards, he felt a strong pair of hands on his shoulders and a voice which said, "Stay where you are until the Prime Minister leaves his seat!" That was Churchill's guard.

Tom stayed; Churchill picked up his notes as we filed off the platform, and the academic procession crossed Broadway and entered Harvard Yard, where the Prime Minister was taken by surprise. There awaiting him were the Naval units, student detachments of the Air Corps, quartermasters and

WAVES, more than 10,000 who broke into cheers at his appearance. I could see that he was affected. He mounted the steps of the chapel and, in the hush that followed, spoke these words:

> "Gentlemen of the armed forces of the United States: This is indeed an inspiring spectacle, and I am very glad that my hosts here today have not denied me the opportunity of meeting you here for a few moments, and of offering you a few words of salutation upon the work on which you are engaged.
>
> "We have reached a period in the war when many people are inclined to think the worst is over. In a certain sense, this may be true: that the issue—the final issue of the war—does not seem so much in doubt as it did some time ago.
>
> "I have no reason to suppose that the climax of the war has been reached. I have no reason to suppose that the heaviest sacrifices in blood and life do not lie before the armed forces of Britain and America.
>
> "I know of no reason for supposing that the climax of the war has been reached even in Europe, and certainly not in Asia.
>
> "The courses of instruction through which you are going are of the utmost value to those who will be charged with the responsibility of leading others in battle. If the troops have a good supply of thoroughly well-trained officers, then they get their tasks done with incomparably less loss of life. Therefore, the work you are doing here is of the highest possible consequence. I bid you all good fortune and success, and I earnestly trust that when you find yourselves alongside our soldiers and sailors, you will feel that we are your worthy brothers in arms.
>
> "And you shall know that we will never tire nor weaken. We shall march with you into every quarter of the globe to establish a reign of justice and law among men."

At the close, he lifted his right arm to give them his famous V salute and the audience on tiptoe gave it back to him. I know how the boys must have felt, for I had tears in my eyes.

A luncheon for about fifty members of the Harvard official family followed in the Fogg Art Museum, where I was seated between Mrs. Churchill and her daughter. There again, Churchill made a brief speech. Just what he said I cannot remember, but I do recall most clearly how carefully Mrs. Churchill watched him and followed his every word. I asked her afterward if she always watched him as carefully as that, and she replied: "I always do when he is speaking without notes."

* * *

Alice and I were very proud that four of our five children were in uniform during World War II. (Our second-oldest child, Rosalie, had died when she was just over a year old, and our fifth, Susan, was too young to take part.) Emily was the first enlisted WAVE in the United States. She was not eligible for a commission because she had had only one year of college, but at the end she was decorated for her long term of service, mostly in the communications center in Naval headquarters in Washington.

Leverett Jr. was twice inducted. He was discharged after his first induction because he needed an operation for a cyst on the bottom of his spine. The second time he was assigned to Devens and then to an officers' training camp in Virginia for airborne engineers. As a lieutenant, he saw service in the Far East and helped to build the road and the headquarters prepared for Gen. Douglas MacArthur in New Guinea.

After his first year at Harvard, Bill, our third son, enlisted in the Navy and served to the war's end as a quartermaster aboard a tug at one of our Naval stations in Newfoundland. His mother and I will always remember how he came home to see us in Washington on his first leave. He had our address, but no latchkey. We were sound asleep in our house on Woodland Drive when suddenly about midnight Alice woke up and said: "Somebody is coming in our window." She has the courage of the family, so I said sleepily, "Go and see who it is." She discovered that it was Bill, who had climbed the strong ivy to get in the window of the bedroom.

In 1942 I reviewed the Harvard undergraduate battalion of which our second son, Peter, then a sophomore, was a member. The captain of the battalion was Bayard Dillingham, who later became a flier and was shot down over the Pacific in the closing days of the war. One of the pictures that is very dear to me is of Peter shaking hands with Mrs. Dillingham on Soldiers' Field as I stood by. Peter's studies were not going too well, I think because he was so restless to get into service. That year he enlisted in the Marine Corps and was sent to Parris Island for his training. Another boy in boot training, presumably a Democrat, began making cracks about me in Pete's hearing. So Pete swung into action and his buddy never repeated himself.

But Pete came away with a very black eye, which he was reluctant to tell us about on his leave home. We learned later that his captain had called him on the mat for it; Pete related what had occurred, and the captain dismissed him with the remark, "You did right, but don't let it happen again!"

By the time he was shipped out to the South Pacific Pete had risen to be an instrument sergeant, which is the second highest rank in the Battery for an enlisted man.

He served at Guadalcanal and later became so sick that he was sent to an American hospital in Wellington, New Zealand. At Christmastime, 1942, my cousin, Dorothy West, entertained some boys from an English frigate being refitted in Quincy. One of them, Ian Lyons, came from New Zealand, so Dorothy wrote the mother and told her about her son. In the letter she said she lived next door to Governor Saltonstall. Somehow Mrs. Lyons learned that Peter was in Wellington. With difficulty she obtained a pass to visit Pete and invited him to stay with her when he was released from the hospital. He did so, and we had a happy letter in which he told us of his visit with the Lyonses in Hawkes Bay, New Zealand, before he had to return to the service.

I was working late in the governor's office on Aug. 13, 1944, when the Boston manager of Western Union called and said he had a message that he wished to deliver in person. I knew this must be ominous, and it was, for he handed me a cable from the commander of the Marines informing us that Peter had been killed, ambushed and shot by the Japanese on Guam while on a clean-up patrol. I thanked the manager for his consideration and shortly left to drive myself home in the Dodge, planning what to say to Alice, as we walked along our path to the river. It was a sad time for both of us.

Al Larivee had us very much on his mind and that evening drove out to Dover in the S-1 to ask if he could be of help. I gave him some of the eggs that I had been gathering, thanked him, and asked him to call for me the next morning.

I had to speak at a memorial service on Boston Common the next afternoon in honor of a young marine who was missing in combat and whose mother was to be presented with a medal honoring his bravery. I can only add that I had prepared my remarks before I had heard our news and simply added a personal note of sympathy without direct reference to my son.

* * *

My campaign for the governorship for a third term in 1942

was nothing like as strenuous as that against Paul Dever. My Democratic opponent was Roger Putnam, former mayor of Springfield and a nephew of former president Lowell of Harvard. He was not so well known in the metropolitan area, having long made his home in the western part of the state; I had the advantage of the incumbent and made the most of the argument that we had practically no state debt. Actually, the state debt at the close of my administration in 1945 was $3 million, with $6 million in the banks with which to pay it off (where permitted in the language of the bonds). In my earlier terms I had won the approval of many independents and not a few Democrats in Boston, and this time I did not need a poll to tell me that my hopes for re-election were good. But after my inauguration Alice and I agreed that when that term was over I would not seek another political office.

But politics is unpredictable. In February of 1944, when I was in Washington on business connected with the American Legion, Sen. Henry Cabot Lodge, who was laid up at home with a bad cold, telephoned to say that he wanted to have a talk with me. I knew that Cabot had been an active reserve officer since 1925 and that he had been sent out in command of the First American tank detatchment to serve with the British Eighth Army in Libya, with the understanding that on their return the troops who had been in combat would communicate the sense of the battlefield to the American armored divisions then in training. On Cabot's return in the early summer of 1942, he had received a letter of commendation from Secretary of War Henry Stimson urging him as a skilled observer to return to his seat in the Senate. So, heeding Mr. Stimson's advice, Lodge ran for re-election that autumn and was successful in defeating his opponent, Rep. Joseph Casey.

Cabot now told me he had finally decided that the only right thing for him to do was to go back into uniform. He wanted me to know in advance so that I could appoint someone to fill his seat until the election of 1944, and he asked me to keep the matter confidential until his letter of resignation was read in the Senate that coming Friday afternoon, by which time he would be airborne on his way to Prestwick, Scotland.

Back home in Chestnut Hill that Sunday, I met with Henry Minot, Dan Lynch, Charlie Rugg, and Carroll Meins to discuss the various prospects, and we were soon agreed that Sinclair Weeks was the best man available. When I telephoned him in Lancaster, N.H., Sinny sounded less than enthusiastic; he said he would have to talk it over with his business partners. I asked him to let me know his decision by Tuesday, and by then he had changed his mind. He said he would be happy to accept the interim appointment, but would not run for election in the autumn of 1944; in short he agreed to fill the seat for 10 months. This limited acceptance presented me with a personal problem: we were deep in the war, three of our children were in the service, and the fourth would soon be. Alice and I felt that if there was a job in Washington that I was qualified to do, I should try for it. I called a press conference in the governor's office the following Wednesday to announce the appointment of Sinclair Weeks and to say that I, myself, would stand for election to the Senate in the autumn of 1944. Horace Cahill at the same time announced his candidacy for the governorship.

Incidentally, what surprised me about all this was that Tom White, who had been my loyal campaign manager in 1938, was bitterly opposed to my appointment of Sinclair Weeks; evidently he had had a feud with Sinclair's father, John Weeks, when he was Secretary of War, and the fire had burned deep. Tom White never really spoke to me again.

* * *

In April of 1944, Wendell Willkie, on being asked by the press which Republican presidential candidate he favored that year, replied, "Governor Saltonstall of Massachusetts."

For me this was a bolt out of the blue; I was very surprised and of course pleased. *Time* Magazine sent a girl reporter to write me up, and although Mrs. Saltonstall never approved of her story, my picture for the first and only time went on the cover of that magazine. The reporter was followed by her boss, Henry Luce, whom I invited to have breakfast with me in Chestnut Hill. I don't think I made much of an impression on him, for I was shy and honestly could not take my candidacy seriously, but once the rumor was started, it continued to bring reporters on my trail for some time to come.

I had been chosen chairman by the governors for the national conference, which took place in Harrisburg, Pa., in late May of 1944. One highlight of our meeting was when Gen. George C. Marshall, the chief of staff of the Army, and Adm. Ernest King of the Navy, spoke to us in closed session about the progress of the war.

On Memorial Day there was a more emotional event: we were all driven over to Gettysburg, where the governor of North Carolina, J. M. Broughton, and I were to speak from the very spot where Lincoln stood when he delivered his famous address. I am sure that we were both aware that our words could not match the grandeur of Lincoln's, but this was the first occasion when governors from the North and the South had spoken together on the old battlefield, and it was this feeling of unity that I tried to stress at the close of my remarks:

> "The spirit of our soldier dead demands of each one of us for the other a feeling of friendliness, whatever may be our religion, or our color. Our boys fight side by side, whether they be Protestant, Catholic, or Jew, or whatever may be their racial descent. It demands that we by our actions at home show our men in active service that we understand the problems, the dangers, and the tragedies that they are daily facing in our behalf . . . Today, this invisible unity is our most pressing need."

Wendell Willkie's recommendation let me in for some friendly ribbing from the other governors. But we all realized that we had in our midst three more likely presidential candidates: Thomas Dewey of New York, Gov. John Bricker of Ohio, and Gov. Harold Stassen of Minnesota, and when they spoke we listened with that larger possibility in mind. I was a little nervous when I presided, since I wanted to show no partiality. On the last day, when we were voting on a final resolution, they each rose to speak with implications that went beyond the subject, and it was my impression at the time that Stassen's remarks were reasoned and well expressed.

There was a feeling of hope and buoyancy at the Republican National Convention in Chicago that June, which began a fortnight after General Eisenhower had made the successful landing at Omaha Beach. The majority of the Massachusetts delegation was in favor of Dewey, and I was among them. I felt that Dewey had made an admirable governor and that perhaps his only handicap was his youth. When I was invited to meet with Governor Bricker, I told him frankly where I stood and that our delegation was nearly unanimous for Governor Dewey. Bricker smiled at my directness and later, when we were both members of the Senate, he reminded me that I was one of the few who had spoken candidly to him, and that he appreciated it.

Dewey was eventually nominated, and when the fighting was over, he invited me to be one of those to help him select his running mate. There were perhaps a score of us in the room, the discussion was open, and as I remember we were unanimous in suggesting Bricker as the candidate for Vice President. This was the first of four conventions at which the nominee asked me to help him make his choice of running mate.

Dewey rightly decided to base his campaign primarily on domestic issues and to leave the war out of it. When General Marshall sent an officer-courier to Dewey with a confidential memorandum that would in effect have briefed Dewey on the immediate prospects, he returned it unopened, meaning that he would not make any issue of the conduct of the war. I admired him for this — I think it was an honorable thing to have done — but I also think that anything Dewey said or did not say would have failed to have carried the day against FDR. Sick as President Roosevelt was, failing in strength, he was a symbol to the country of confidence restored; the old axiom, "Don't change horses in mid-stream," plus his immense popularity resulted in his victory.

In New York City in the final weeks of the campaign, Herbert Brownell, who was managing Dewey's campaign, invited me to meet him at a morning press conference, as he liked to have interested outsiders join in the give and take. When a newspaper reporter asked me if I thought that Dewey would do better in Massachusetts than Willkie, who had been quite badly defeated in our state in 1940, I spoke impulsively, meaning to be helpful. "Of course he will; I hope that Dewey will carry Massachusetts this year."

This was quoted in the *New York Times* and was read by Willkie, who was then a very sick man in the hospital. Strong as he was, Willkie had followed his exhausting 1940 campaign with an even more exhausting tour of the world, and on his return had been operated on for cancer. Now he wrote me reproachfully asking how I could have made such a statement after the help he had given me in the press. In my answer I said I did not mean to hurt him; I wanted Dewey to win and only said what I hoped and believed. I never heard from him again, and shortly after that he died. I went to his funeral in New York City; the church was crowded with government officials and those interested in politics, and I came away with a feeling that many who were there had opposed him as a candidate.

As for my own campaign, I won my Senate seat by defeating my Democratic opponent, John Corcoran of Cambridge, with a record majority of more than half-a-million votes and looked forward to four full years in Washington before I would have to campaign again.

* * *

Massachusetts, I am quite certain, is the most cosmopolitan state in the union. California, New York, Ohio, and Illinois all have larger populations, and accordingly a larger number of citizens from different racial backgrounds, but none of them draw from as many bloodstreams in such a large proportion as we do here in the Bay State. This influx, which began with the Irish potato famine in the 1840s, has resulted in steadily increasing numbers from ethnic groups, from Irish, Italian, French, Canadian, Greek, Finnish, or Polish backgrounds; it is also responsible for the shift toward the Democratic Party that began midway in my political career and today makes Massachusetts virtually a one-party state. I had a warning that this change was coming half a century ago from a lawyer named Lawrence Ford, an Irishman, a loyal Catholic, and a partner of Gaston, Snow and Saltonstall. He said to me one day, "Lev, you Yankee Republicans had better look out. We Irish are breeding much faster than you are and one day we'll take over the state."

How right he was! Now when I am asked how many children we had, I answer, "Six. All we Yankees are trying to do is to keep up with the Irish."

During my three terms as governor I had, as I have said, some difficulty with my appointments—but no rejections. The three racing commissioners whom I "inherited" from former Governor Curley had none too savory reputations. But I had the goods on one of them, and without putting up a protest, he resigned; the other two, perhaps feeling a cool draft at the backs of their necks, did likewise. In their places, I appointed my friend Bayard Tuckerman, the former governor's councilor, who was honest and knew everything there was to know about a horse. He did not particularly want the job, but agreed to serve for the time being. For the chairman of the commission I reached out to the Country Club in Brookline for Harold Peirce, a famous golfer and a man of scrupulous integrity, who knew nothing about racing but could learn; and for the third, I appointed Robert Almy, a trustworthy horseman with experience in racing.

In Massachusetts the judges of the district courts, the municipal court of Boston, the Superior Court, and the Supreme Judicial Court are all appointed by the governor and confirmed by the Governor's Council. In my time, the appointment was for life, but with the referendum of 1972, judges must now retire on reaching the age of seventy. I learned from experience that it was helpful to make these judicial appointments as soon as possible after a vacancy occurred, and by doing so to avoid the political pressure for one candidate or another. In 1944, my last year in the State House, I had my first opportunity of appointment to the Massachusetts Supreme Court when two seats became available. Charles Rugg, my initial choice, was a man eminently qualified, a well-respected member of the bar and a strong supporter of mine, but he preferred to remain in private practice.

Accordingly, I turned to Raymond S. Wilkins, who had studied at Harvard Law School with me, was the adjutant of my regiment in World War I, and a longtime friend. He was a member of the Governor's Council when the vacancy occurred, and his appointment was confirmed unanimously. Later in the same year, I appointed John Spaulding to the second vacancy. Spaulding had an excellent reputation as a lawyer, and I had come to know him personally since he frequently took the long walk with me from the Huntington Avenue station up to Beacon Hill. Spaulding was a fast walker and so was I (it helped me swing by those who might have wanted to buttonhole me along the way). Both of these men served the court with distinction for many years and I was proud to have put them there.

At the end of any long assignment, one looks back and asks what one might have done differently had the chances occurred. While I was in office ten criminals were sent to the electric chair. I have no second thoughts about this, for I studied the facts and had the approval of the district attorney, the parole board and the attorney general. I believe I did my duty. I firmly believe that the death sentence should be enforced in some cases. The jury that tries the case should have the right to recommend it if in its judgment death is merited by the crime.

The changes I should like to see are long overdue; they would help our state's government, and they would definitely speed up the democratic process.

I should like to see the Governor's Council abolished. It is a hand-me-down from the days when a group of prominent, strong-minded citizens were chosen to aid, or more likely to remonstrate with, a governor appointed by the Crown. I am firmly of the belief that nothing will be lost if the council is abolished. Today the council seems to me an anachronism, a fifth wheel to the coach, and one which slows down the forward motion.

Although the size of the legislature is currently being reduced, those of us who feel that the legislative body is too cumbersome and spends more time than is necessary to conduct the business of the state must still exert our efforts.

A constitutional amendment was adopted in 1938, the year

I was elected governor, to have the legislature meet biennially instead of annually. In my humble judgment, this was of advantage to all of us because it gave the opportunity for the state government to carry out the laws without an annual effort on the part of the General Court to amend or change them. The executive had a better chance to become a true administrator of public affairs. But this amendment was killed by referendum in 1944, largely through the pressure of the unions and because our minds were on the war, and so again we have annual sessions of a very large General Court meeting for anywhere from six months to nine months every year.

* * *

Tradition and continuity mean much to me. There have been nearly seventy governors of Massachusetts, and when Loring Young was Speaker of the Massachusetts House, he collected the portraits of all but five of them to be hung in the State House. When I became Speaker, I continued the search and found three more: a portrait of one of the earliest governors I secured from the editor of *The Spectator* in London, another with the help of Henry Shattuck came from Philadelphia, and the third came from my friend Tudor Gardiner in Maine. We reluctantly concluded that the two governors who were missing had never been painted.

Now came the question of where to hang them. While I was governor, I wanted the portrait of Gov. John Endicott, who as a deputy royal governor preceded Gov. John Winthrop, to be hung over the mantel in my office. And there he hung during my three terms and through the term of Governor Tobin. When Bob Bradford took office, Governor Endicott was replaced by the portrait of an ancestor of Mrs. Bradford who had come over on the *Mayflower*. When Governor Dever came along, he hung the portrait of David I. Walsh, the first Irish governor of the Commonwealth. Then came Christian Herter's governorship, and he restored Governor Endicott. But there was a hell of a row from the Irish, and for self-preservation, he had to take it down. The place was left vacant until Gov. John Volpe came in and he felt that he owed so much to Chris that he had the portrait of Herter hung in the showplace. And after Chris died, Volpe replaced Chris with a portrait of me, and there, I believe, I hung through Governor Sargent's terms until he was replaced by Gov. Michael Dukakis. Now Sam Adams hangs over the fireplace.

V. Joining America's "most select club"

The press sometimes refers to the Senate as the most select club in America, although that seems to suggest more relaxation than I experienced. As I said, I won my US Senate seat in the election of 1944 and looked forward to four full years in Washington before I would have to campaign again. A letter of welcome came to me from Sen. Wallace White of Maine, the minority leader, and Mark Trice, the secretary of the minority, sent a questionnaire from the Republican Committee on Committees asking me to name the committees on which I would like to serve. With my knowledge of the Boston Navy Yard and the Fore River shipyards and my love of the sea, I put the Committee on Naval Affairs high in my preferences.

Meanwhile, we were looking for a house for ourselves and our daughter Susan, but houses were very difficult to find in wartime Washington. Eventually we leased for a year, sight unseen, a comfortably furnished dwelling on Kalorama Circle — at a rent that took practically the whole of my senatorial salary! (We moved to a less expensive house when the lease was up.) I arranged to take over Sinclair Weeks's secretarial staff and his assistant, Joe Larsen, agreed to familiarize me with how the Senate functioned from day to day. Sinclair had also given me his personal opinion of each senator and how he should be approached.

Finally, I had to make a tough decision. Newly elected senators are expected to attend the opening session of Congress, which was set for Jan. 3, 1945, and are ranked in seniority on that day, those who had been governors coming first in accordance with the age of their state. But as I had pledged that I would serve out my full third term as governor, I felt that I could not conscientiously leave the State House until my successor, Maurice Tobin, was sworn in on Jan. 4. This meant that I would not be present when the new senators were sworn in, and so instead of being first in freshmen seniority on the Republican side, I dropped down to sixth place in the ranking.

The guns were saluting the installation of Governor Tobin as I left the governor's office for the traditional walk down the long flight of steps leading to the State House (how often had I counted them!) and to our car, where Alice was waiting to drive me home. That weekend we took the Federal Express to Washington, and waiting to meet us next morning was our daughter Emily, looking very trim in her WAVE uniform. So, too, thanks to Wendell Willkie, were reporters from *Look* magazine; they came along with us to the house we had not yet seen, peppering me with questions — which was to be our bedroom, would we please stand there for a picture, and I don't remember what else.

Emily had laid in supplies and helped us get breakfast after the press had departed. Then she drove me down to the Capitol. Neither of us had any idea where the Senate Office Building was, and by mistake she eventually let me off at the House, a good half-mile from my destination. I walked across the Capitol grounds and asked the guard at the Senate Office Building the way to Senator Weeks's office, where Joe Larsen ushered me into my headquarters. On the vacant desk with its spotless blotter was a single postcard addressed to

THE HONORABLE LEVERETT SALTONSTALL
S.O.B.
Washington, D. C.

That was Henry Minot's sense of humor; he had come on ahead to set up the office.

I shall never be able to repay my debt of gratitude to Henry Minot, who was my executive assistant for the next eight years. As I have said earlier, he first became one of my aides in 1936. In his taciturn way, Henry was a unique figure in politics. He had a capacity for smelling out the pros and cons of any tough problem in which I was involved; his decisions were always realistic, and generally quite pessimistic, but his pessimism was invaluable as a counterbalance to the enthusiastic, sometimes overemotional views of others. During my governorship he never would have a desk at the State House — he simply came and went in his swift, quiet way. But when the heat was on, he was always there.

In Washington it was imperative for him to have an office next to mine, and, as in Boston, he soon won the confidence of not only my staff but of those who were serving the other senators and the clerks of committees with whom I had most to do. He would never accept a position in government service. Ostensibly, he was a dollar-a-year man (but he never got the dollar); his loyalty, his diligence, and his judgment never faltered.

With Henry came the second of my Boston team, James R. Reynolds, who like Minot, had given up his own business in the late 1930s and had accepted my invitation to help me in the governor's office. Now he moved down to share an office with Henry. Jim always had a smile, and while he could be firm with people who tried to take advantage of us, he had a charming, hospitable way of greeting all who came to my office. I could always tell when Jim was upset or angry because the top of his bald head turned a bright pink. He was very angry one morning when he came to me exclaiming, "I won't take any more of it! I won't be talked to that way!"

"Jimmy," I said, "what is the trouble?"

"Your friend Walter Cenerazzo has just called me 'a goddamn son of a bitch.' "

Walter Cenerazzo was no friend, but he had been one of my supporters, now hot, now cold. He worked at the Waltham Watch Company, was head of the watchmakers' union, and — when I was in his good graces — had thrown labor votes my way. Now it appeared that he was in a rage against Senator Taft — the Taft family money came from importing watch parts — and because I did not call off Taft he turned on Jim.

I had no intention of letting this pass and just at that moment the telephone rang; it was Cenerazzo wanting to speak to me. For the first and only time in my Washington experience, we linked up a recording machine with my telephone so as to have a record of what was said.

"Walter," I said, "I won't have anything more to do with you. You have no right to abuse my staff, calling them names the way you do."

"What did I say?" he asked meekly.

"You just called Jim Reynolds 'a goddamn son of a bitch.' "

"But that isn't calling names, is it?"

Jim was my appointments secretary and was very careful in preparing answers to the more personal and sometimes difficult letters, although he occasionally misinterpreted the nature of my acquaintance with the correspondent. When Mrs. Endicott Peabody wrote me regarding the United Nations, it came as a "Dear Leverett" letter. Jim prepared the answer and brought it back for me to sign. The letter commenced: "Dear Fannie," and then went on to describe our position. I punched the bell, Jim came in, and I said, "Jim do you know who this is?"

He said, "No, but she called you Leverett, so I called her Fannie."

I said, "Jim, my father would turn over in his grave if he knew that I was calling Cousin Fannie, the wife of the distinguished head of Groton School 'Fannie.' She has always been *Cousin* Fannie to me." So he rewrote the letter.

Jimmy was a very popular member of our staff and he was greatly missed when he left in 1948 to become the financial assistant to President Conant and then President Pusey of Harvard. He proved to be one of the most persuasive money-raisers in the university's history, and he will always be remembered for his advice to a solicitor approaching a difficult prospect. Jim, who owned a famous herd of Guernseys in Essex County, spoke from experience when he said, "A cow won't respond to a letter or a telephone call — you've got to sit right down beside her and go to work."

I had never realized what a demanding correspondence a United States senator is expected to carry on. In normal times I must have received from 200 to 400 letters a day; when a hot issue like the Taft-Hartley Act was being debated, or later when my colleague Sen. John F. Kennedy was in the hospital for a long period, we handled well over 500 a day. We had an early-bird secretary who arrived at the office at 8 a.m., opened all the mail, and directed the letters to staff members who were specialists — one girl, for instance, would handle letters from the veterans, another those having to do with welfare and appeals from senior citizens. John Jackson checked the answers and was expected to sign my name to what was routine. Serious letters bearing on legislation went to either Henry Minot or Jim Reynolds, and letters addressed "Dear Leverett" I read and signed myself. In this way every letter was processed within twenty-four hours of its arrival, with those which raised more difficult questions being referred to the proper government agency. Finally, I followed Calvin Coolidge's axiom, "Never write when you can speak, and never speak when you can remain silent."

Russell Gerould helped me with my speeches, as he had done throughout my governorship. He was extremely adept in looking up data for my historical references, and he followed my preference for short, succinct statements.

When I was governor the most interesting item which together we brought to the attention of the citizens of Massachusetts was the fact that the commonwealth had never adopted the first ten amendments to our Constitution, the Bill of Rights. Accordingly, I recommended that the legislature rectify this omission by voting a belated adoption of the amendments, and when the resolution was forwarded to the secretary of state, Mr. Hull formally acknowledged its receipt in a stiff parchment sealed with wax, which is now in the State Archives.

* * *

On Wednesday morning, Jan. 10, 1945, Sen. David I. Walsh, my senior colleague from Massachusetts, escorted me to the rostrum to be sworn in by Vice President Henry Wallace. I stood on the bottom step, listening to the clerk as he read the confirmation from Massachusetts, and then I repeated after Mr. Wallace my oath of office. There was mild applause from the senators, and with Walsh I retired to the anteroom where our picture was taken.

The visitors' gallery was well filled that day because it was known that Sen. Arthur H. Vandenberg of Michigan, the senior Republican on the Committee on Foreign Relations, was to make an important speech. (Vandenberg had been an isolationist. But the many Polish people in his constituency were angered by Russia's treatment of the liberated Polish government, and after rebuking the Soviet Union for this, Vandenberg went on in his speech to propose our cooperation with Russia against the revival of German militarism. This speech set him on a new course and resulted in his becoming a proponent of the United Nations.) But much as I wanted to, I was not permitted to hear him, since Senator Walsh had invited Alice and me to have an early luncheon in the Senate dining room, and obviously had no intention of listening to Vandenberg.

Luncheon passed agreeably, except when Walsh suddenly remarked to my good wife: "Mrs. Saltonstall, remember that Washington is the coldest town in the world and one that can forget you very quickly." I knew that Walsh had had some personal publicity that had hurt him, which was why he spoke with such feeling.

Luncheon over, Alice drove back to our new home, and as the Senate had recessed, Walsh led me around the basement, showing me the Senate Reading Room and the barber shop, where the senators get free service and where each is given a mug with his name on it. (I have mine today in my office. There was even one for Sen. Margaret Chase Smith. I know because when I was having my hair cut once she came to the door to claim it. This caused consternation among the three barbers, but finally a cup was found for her.)

In the days that followed I formed my first impressions, beginning with the senators of my own party. Wallace White, the minority leader whose father had been a senator before him — I liked him and appreciated his many courtesies to me. The actual leaders of the party were Senator Taft, the voice of the Midwest and the spokesman on domestic questions, and Senator Vandenberg, the spokesman on foreign policy and more toward the center than Taft. Senator White accepted this; he realized that Senator Taft, as chairman of the Republican Policy Committee, was the most influential Republican in the Senate.

On the Democratic side, Alben Barkley of Kentucky was the majority leader — attractive, courteous, and a good storyteller; he worked hand and glove with FDR on most issues. Sen. Richard Russell of Georgia was the most admired of the Southern group for his knowledge of military affairs and as an authority on the complicated and antiquated rules of the Senate. Sen. Kenneth McKellar of Tennessee, the chairman of the Appropriations Committee, was insistent on his prerogatives, vindictive at times, with a powerful voice in determining what bills came out of his committee. Sen. Carl Hayden of Arizona, the oldest senator, had served in Congress ever since Arizona had become a state, first as a congressman and later as a senator. Everybody loved Carl, and he usually got what he wanted; later when he became chairman of the Appropriations Committee, he and I became close friends. We worked together on many matters, and one of the greatest compliments I ever received was when he asked me to state the Senate's position in our conferences with the House on foreign aid.

I could see that Barkley and Taft respected each other. Taft did his homework and had the facts when he rose to speak — and when he spoke it was often a table thumping, bang-bang affair. Barkley was primed by the White House or the heads of departments, and he could be equally vehement. I remember one occasion when the debate over the Taft-Hartley Bill got so hot and temperatures rose so high that after the final vote was taken Barkley retired to put on a dry shirt and then came back and napped for the rest of the afternoon. (Barkley had an invalid wife and needed to supplement his salary by lecturing.)

Sen. Harry F. Byrd of Virginia, chairman of the Committee on Finance and a workhorse, was a quiet persuader. He would come to your seat, put his hand on your shoulder, his face down fairly close to yours, say what was on his mind, get your response, and move on. He was well liked on both sides of the aisle, and especially respected for his knowledge of taxation. He was always for keeping expenditures down. We became friends, and I always looked forward to attending the big Sunday luncheons which were held each spring when his apple trees were in bloom. Wives were included, and in addition to the Senate, there were high muck-a-mucks from Detroit, Pittsburgh and the Far West.

Senator Vandenberg's office was next to mine and on one of my first days in the Senate I stopped by to ask his advice on a problem that bothered me. Sinclair had suggested I would find him helpful. I called him "Senator." "The name is Van," he said.

Perhaps I did not approach him in the right way, but I found him uncommunicative. Either he didn't know the answer to the question or didn't want to give it to me, so I never tried that again.

H. Alexander Smith of New Jersey, who had thoughtfully called on me in the State House before I came down to Washington, was the colleague I got to know on the easiest terms. We were never on the same committees, but we enjoyed and trusted each other and would talk things out in our offices or on the floor of the Senate or at lunch.

The Republicans and the Democrats had adjoining dining rooms, and I lunched with the Republicans whenever I was free. Sometimes the table would be filled, and there would be serious conversation about questions that had just come up; sometimes the atmosphere was relaxed and the amusing storytellers like Bill Jenner of Indiana and Ken Wherry of Nebraska would hold forth.

* * *

The real work of the Senate is done in committees. Each

freshman senator was appointed to two committees, one of major and one of minor importance, and because of my late arrival I could not hope to be given top choice. Everyone, I am sure, put down Foreign Relations first, although not expecting to get it. At the end of January I learned my assignments, the major one being the Committee on Naval Affairs, and the minor, the District of Columbia.

I only served for one year on the Committee for the District of Columbia. Sen. Theodore Bilbo of Mississippi was the chairman, and he was quite a character — short, stocky, very southern in his dress and manner. His office was down the corridor from mine, and each morning as I passed the open door, there he would be with his feet on the desk, talking and joking with two or three very pretty girls who looked more like party girls than secretaries. We did not have many meetings of that committee, and when we did they reminded me of my days on the board of aldermen in Newton, the questions were so parochial. How close to a church should we permit a bar? What athletic contest should be allowed on Sundays?

Senator Bilbo was known to be very anti-Semitic, and I was troubled when I received a letter from a Jewish newspaper in New York City asking if I would release to them any letters that I had received concerning Bilbo and his attitude toward the Jewish people. This, it seemed to me, was an invasion of privacy and was so personal that I could not do it without Bilbo's consent. I showed him my file, which was not a large one. He thanked me, and asked me not to give it to the paper, and I did not.

A little later at a committee meeting when a professor from Harvard was testifying, I heard Bilbo growl in his gruff undertone, "He doesn't know what he is talking about. You can't believe those Harvard professors."

Of course I couldn't let that pass, and I interrupted: "Mr. Chairman, you know that isn't so."

"Oh, hell," he replied, "you know I didn't mean you."

In November 1946, Senator Bilbo was re-elected by the voters of Mississippi, but by this time there was a strong feeling in the Senate that he should not be seated. The possibility of a long wrangle on this personal issue, however, would have delayed the swearing in of all the newly elected senators whose names came after his in the alphabet, and as it was known that Bilbo was mortally ill with cancer, the oath was not administered and it was agreed to pay his staff on a pro tem basis. On Bilbo's death the governor of Mississippi appointed John C. Stennis to fill the unexpired term. Stennis was everything that

Picture, taken while Saltonstall was testifying at a hearing in 1963-64, won the White House photography award.

Winston Churchill speaks at Harvard graduation in 1943. Behind Churchill is James Conant, then president of Harvard.

Playing the bagpipes at Scotch Games in Boston in 1942.

N.Y. Governor Thomas Dewey meets with Saltonstall at Eastern States Exposition in Springfield, Mass. in 1947.

Placing a wreath during Memorial Day services in Newton in 1952.

Illinois Sen. Everett Dirksen, President Eisenhower and Saltonstall at the White House in 1959.

Associated Press

Adm. Forrest P. Sherman confers with Saltonstall during hearings in 1951 on the dismissal of Gen. Douglas MacArthur.

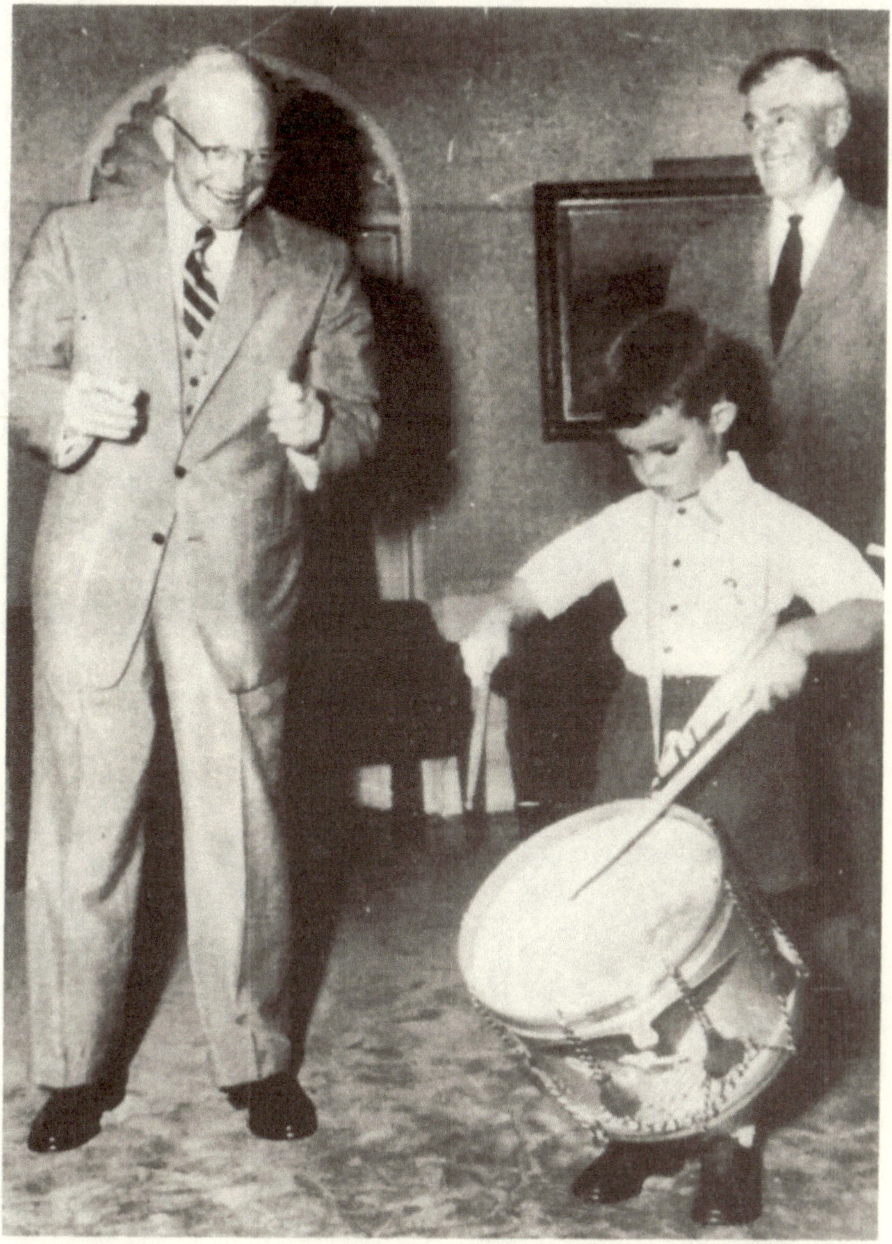

David Eisenhower rolls the drums to the delight of his grandfather, President Eisenhower, and Saltonstall.

In 1958, Saltonstall met to discuss Republican campaign strategy and issues with President Eisenhower, Vice President Richard Nixon and Illinois Sen. Everett Dirksen.

Harvard's second crew of 1914, during 50th reunion at Henley Regatta in 1964.

Queen Elizabeth, the Queen Mother, with Saltonstall at Henley in 1964.

Associated Press

Looking over government's 1957 budget with then Sen. Lyndon B. Johnson.

Associated Press

In 1963, Saltonstall and Sen. Hubert Humphrey, Sen. John Sparkman, Sen. John Pastore and Sen. George Aiken were in Moscow to watch signing of test ban treaty.

Bilbo was not — serious-minded, deeply religious, and immensely capable. We worked together closely on the Armed Services Committee, of which Stennis in time became chairman, and we are fast friends to this day.

I do not wish to disparage the work of the Committee for the District of Columbia, as I know that the problems within the district have become increasingly difficult in recent years. As a member of the committee, I was asked some years later to attend a controversial meeting that I shall always remember. It concerned public welfare: How much should Congress appropriate for the district and to whom should it be paid? Sen. Robert Byrd of West Virginia was then the chairman, and he was bitterly opposed to extending public welfare in the cases where the legitimacy of the children was in doubt. I remember one committee discussion of a group of six unmarried mothers who had sixty-six children between them. Byrd felt that assistance in such cases would lead to further delinquency, but the welfare group and the district's Public Welfare commissioner both were adamant. Still, Byrd insisted on cutting down the appropriation in this instance, and I supported him.

However, it needed only one more year to show that the real hardship fell upon the offspring, and at that time I told Byrd that while I sympathized with him in his view, I did not feel I could support him further along these lines because of the hardship involved.

Senator Walsh, who was chairman of Naval Affairs, ran his committee autocratically, but in a way that was respected and feared by the Navy high command. At the tick of 10:30 a.m., he would enter the committee room in the old Senate Office Building. Every naval officer present would spring to his feet and Walsh would say, "Good morning, gentlemen," seat himself at the head of the long committee table, bang the gavel, and announce, "The committee will come to order. The first bill is number so and so. Admiral, who is your witness?"

Knowing of his punctuality, I was careful to be there on time. Other members would straggle in, and by the time the morning hearings were nearing completion, there would be a quorum to act on the less controversial matters on the agenda. But the more important ones were generally held over, either for our aides to study, or at the request of a committee member who was particularly interested. Walsh could be rough on a witness but generally he was considerate. He was courteous to a fellow member, however bored he might be by his questions.

I noticed that he always wore a double-breasted blue serge suit, and if there were ashes on his waistcoat, one could assume that he had enjoyed a good evening the night before.

There are several steps leading to approval of a proposal that requires government funding. First, the proposal must be authorized by the appropriate committee, and the authorization approved by both branches and the President. An appropriation for the proposal is recommended by the President and must be approved — although not necessarily in the amount asked for.

Suppose, for instance, that the Navy Department, which during the time I am speaking of was under the leadership of Sec. James Forrestal, submitted a request for a new aircraft carrier to the director of the budget. If the latter approved of it, it would then be passed to the President, who would show his approval in a message to Congress for the necessary authorization. Then the request would go to the Committee on Naval Affairs, and in their consideration they would hear from the chief of naval operations, who would outline the condition of the fleet and discuss the need for the new carrier.

Out of these hearings would come the authorized bill, which the committee would send to the Senate. The House Committee on Naval Affairs would go through the same procedure; the two bills, which might differ in detail, would then be sent to conference, and when the conference committee, composed of members of both committees, agreed on a draft, it would come up before the Senate and the House for final confirmation, after which it would go to the President for his signature.

In a budget message or in a special message, the money to build the carrier would be requested by the President. If granted by the Congress, specifications would be drawn and sent out for bids, and in two to four years the ship would be put in commission for service in the fleet. Secretary Forrestal, a boxer in college and always trim, was very intent on cutting down the inventory of the Navy by correlating it with the other services. For instance, why should the Navy wear a different undershirt than the Army? No one, not even the secretary, knew how many hundreds of thousands of items there were, and how much variation existed in the inventory that had accumulated during the war. I remember one instance that involved the British Navy and ours. The American screw turned to the right; the British screw, on the other hand, turned to the left, and the separate parts were not interchangeable. Forrestal insisted that they should be, and finally a formal treaty was adopted to make the screws turn the same way.

The most important matter to come up during Walsh's last two years as chairman was the nomination of Edwin W. Pauley, an influential Democrat from Los Angeles and a prominent oil man, to be the undersecretary of the navy. It was well known that the Navy had large oil reserves in California, and the memory of the Teapot Dome Scandal was still in people's minds. Yet here was an oil operator, proposed for the position of undersecretary, who, if accepted, would be in authority over the oil reserves.

"In any other service," argued Sen. Charles Tobey of New Hampshire, "that might be all right, but in the Navy, no."

He took a strenuous interest in Pauley's record and questioned him at length, while Sen. Millard Tydings of Maryland, on the other hand, supported the President's appointment. Senator Walsh presided with dignity, but I could see that he was in the middle. The hearings went on for several days with the committee room filled with spectators and the press, and the opposition still strong. I was seated beside Senator Byrd of Virginia, and at length I whispered to him, "Ask Pauley if he will ask the President to withdraw his name, if we on the committee will clear him as an honest man."

Byrd gave his characteristic little giggle, poked me, and said, "You ask him."

I did. Mr. Pauley hesitated for a noticeable time, but his reply implied that he would think it over. I was surprised; Walsh was obviously hopeful. I wrote out a brief statement of what I had in mind, showed it to the chairman, and after some discussion, Walsh asked Tobey, Tydings, and me to his office. There we settled on a formal statement that was to be shown to the committee as a whole and that Tydings was then to show to Pauley. When he had seen it, Pauley asked Truman to withdraw his name.

During the 1946 session, which was Walsh's last, we worked together with a frank understanding; he was beginning to slow up and he relied more on me. I raised no objection to his recommendations for postmasters and other similar posts, for as a ranking Democrat, he was entitled to this patronage. He advised me that the speediest way to have the Senate act on a bill that had the unanimous support of the committee was to call it up at lunchtime, when there would be few senators on the floor and presumably no one would object to its being put through. I watched him do this several times. (This no longer became feasible under the leadership of Barkley, Lyndon Johnson and William Knowland, who made a point of giving advance notice of bills to be acted upon.)

I also learned a lesson from watching him in action. I recall one late evening session of the Senate when, not at his best, Walsh made a long, intemperate speech, "For God, for Country and the labor unions."

The chamber was well filled and it made me nervous just to listen to him; I knew if it came to a vote I was going to vote the other way. The next morning at breakfast I paged through the *Congressional Record* and was surprised to find only a single line stating that his talk would be reprinted in full in the final report of the *Record* due some three or four months later. Evidently a senior member of his staff had told Mr. Murphy, the chief reporter, to wait for a revised version.

In a debate some time later, I became so worked up over what I was trying to say that I sputtered and never finished my sentences. No reporter could possibly have made sense of my remarks. When I had sat down, I said to Henry Minot, "Henry, go see what Mr. Murphy made of all this."

He did, and Mr. Murphy said: "Mr. Minot, I could not make sense of what the senator said, so I had to start and build up his speech all over again from the beginning."

And so my remarks, clarified by Mr. Murphy, appeared in the *Congressional Record* the next morning.

The *Congressional Record* is really a remarkable publication. It is published every day Congress is in session, and it may be as short as 32 pages or as fat as a full-size book. For instance, the *Congressional Record* for Feb. 22, 1973, contains 55 pages of debate in the House of Representatives, 104 pages of the proceedings in the Senate, together with a so-called extension of remarks amounting to 49 pages more. Finally, at the very end comes the daily digest, which in this issue runs to 7 pages. Remember that all of this has to be proofread and published in one night and delivered to the members of Congress in time for their breakfasts.

When I first came to the Senate, the United States Chamber of Commerce sent to the senators each morning a precis of the preceding day's debates, a very handy guide for skimming through the fine print of the *Congressional Record* to concentrate on the topics in which one was personally involved. When presumably for financial reasons, the Chamber gave up this service, it seemed to Henry Minot and me that such a summary was indispensable and ought to be provided in each issue of the *Record.* So I drew up a resolution, which Senator Taft approved, as did his opposite number in the House, and thereafter the Daily Digest, this summary, became I daresay, the most carefully read pages of the *Record.* To give proper emphasis to the more important items calls for skillful and impartial editing, and the job has been well done to this day. We, all of us, needed such a time-saver, and thanks to the Daily Digest, I could skim the *Record,* the *Washington Post* and the *New York Times* before I went to my office.

* * *

As a loyal Republican, I had my private misgivings about Franklin D. Roosevelt. I always believed that he received credit for emergency measures early in the Depression that President Hoover would have put through had he not been faced with a hostile Congress. But I was for intervention; I thoroughly approved of the assistance he gave Britain, and during my governorship I worked closely with Washington on national defense problems.

I had my first meeting with President Roosevelt in 1939, when Gov. Herbert H. Lehman of New York was the host of the annual governors' conference. We all drove down from Albany to Hyde Park, where FDR and his mother gave us tea on the lawn outside the big house. I did not get as much opportunity as I had hoped to talk with the President as I was corralled by his mother; she was quite a talker and it was not easy to get away, much as I wished to listen to her son.

Shortly after that, I received at the State House letters from President Roosevelt and his wife Eleanor, written on successive days, expressing quite different views on the matter of welfare. My humor got the better of me. "Can't those two *ever* get together?" I asked Henry Minot.

Our next encounter was when he had a favor to ask during my last term as governor. We were sitting around the fire in Dover one Sunday evening when the telephone rang. Peter answered and came back very excited, saying that "a man who says he is President of the United States wants to talk with you." So I went into the other room and the President's secretary put him on the line. Roosevelt's voice held that soft-selling tone that he used when he wanted something. "Leverett," he said, "the Princess of Norway is coming to Massachusetts to stay on the Cape. We are sending up two Secret Service men, which is all the help we can give her, so will you please look after her?"

There was nothing for me to say except, "Why, certainly, Mr. President. We will take care of her."

Next morning at the State House I sent for the commissioner of Public Safety, John Stokes, who was in charge of the state police. "John," I said, "the President telephoned me last evening that he would like us to look after the Crown Princess of Norway when she arrives in Boston tomorrow."

He looked at me quizzically and asked, "Who are you going to take care of her with?"

"Why, some of your state police," I replied.

John was disturbed. "Governor, you realize that because of the war we're already some 200 men short in the state police? We have no extra men for duties of that kind."

"Well, John," I said, "I don't care how you manage it but do please look after her until she gets settled."

So he did and after a few days she settled in with friends and took care of herself.

Now, as a newly elected senator, I went with the other members of Congress to attend the President as he was sworn in by Chief Justice Harlan F. Stone in 1945, the beginning of his fourth term. The ceremony, very short and informal because of the war, took place on the balcony of the White House. The rain had only recently stopped, and as we stood in a semicircle on the lawn, most of us got very wet feet. Fortunately, FDR spoke briefly; then we moved around to the East Gate and formed in line to be received by Mrs. Roosevelt.

The last time I saw him was after the Yalta Conference, when he came to address a joint session of Congress, speaking to us from his wheelchair. He was wheeled in front of the rostrum with a loudspeaker at hand and make no pretense of getting up. I thought he looked exhausted, a very sick man, and shortly thereafter he went down to Warm Springs, where he died on April 12, 1945.

Congress was recessed the next day. The President's casket was brought to Washington by special train, and Henry Minot and I, from the terrace in front of the Treasury, watched the procession. Six white horses drew the caisson on which the casket lay, followed by a riderless horse with stirrups reversed; it passed slowly by on its way to the White House. The street was lined with spectators, many of them in tears.

Next day I was one of a committee of six appointed from the Senate to attend the funeral service, held in the East Room of the White House. It was a very modest Episcopal service, the room filled, but not crowded, with representatives from the leaders of many countries. As I sat there my thoughts went back to the beginning of FDR's long tenure, when his fireside talks on radio had had such a calming effect. "The only thing we have to fear is fear itself," he said in his first inaugural address on March 4, 1933, and repeated in a fireside talk. I listened to that statement of his, which brought confidence to me as it did to the many thousands of citizens throughout our great country.

President Truman, as vice president, was our familiar presiding officer in the Senate. He generally had a smile, was pleasant, and made a good presiding officer. On the afternoon of April 12, 1945, Sen. William Langer of North Dakota was sounding off on the floor of the Senate, the Vice President was in the chair, and I guess I was about the only other senator present. A page approached me with a pink slip in Truman's handwriting. "Governor, will you take this seat for a while? I want to see a soldier boy from home in my office."

I nodded and went down to sit on the dais. Truman said he didn't expect to be gone for more than half an hour. I asked what he would do to me if I ate the apple that someone had put on his desk. He told me he would have to fine me if I did. About an hour and a half later he returned and recessed the Senate, and I went back to my office. Sixty minutes after that he was sworn in as President of the United States. The next morning President Truman returned to the office of Leslie Biffle, secretary of the Senate. Word came down that the President would be glad to see any of his former colleagues if they desired to shake his hand. Sen. Forrest Donnell of Missouri and I went together to congratulate him and found him pacing up and down the little office with a drink in his hand. He always held a drink in the same manner as he walked back and forth. We shook hands with him warmly and asked him if there was anything we could do to help him. He replied, "If you really want to help me, pray for me, pray for me."

* * *

We had scarcely settled in Washington in 1945, before President Conant of Harvard telephoned, asking me to help him out of an embarrassing situation. Harvard had invited Admiral King and General Marshall to that spring's commencement to receive honorary degrees. King had accepted. But Marshall had declined. Harvard did not want to show preference for one service over the other. Could I do anything to change Marshall's mind? I told him I doubted it, but I would try. So I called the general's secretary and asked to see him on a subject not connected with the war. Almost immediately the word came back that the general would like me to lunch with him in his office.

At the luncheon General Marshall was most cordial, but unyielding. He said he could not accept a degree while the war was on; it was not right, the boys who were actually fighting were the ones to be honored.

He also spoke about his friend Gen. Sir John Dill, who represented the British joint chiefs in Washington. Marshall was devoted to him and said that Sir John was seriously ill. At the momentous meeting of FDR and Churchill in Quebec, where Marshall argued strongly against Churchill on the timing of the advance across the Channel and of not going up through the soft underbelly of Europe, General Dill had supported Marshall against his own boss, Churchill.

Now Marshall was worried that Dill might be recalled and he wanted Churchill to understand how much we respected him. Harvard, Yale, and Princeton were unwilling to grant a special degree in the mid-winter but General Marshall had persuaded the University of Wisconsin to do so and he was determined that the auditorium would be full of uniforms and VIPs when this degree was conferred. It was characteristic of his thoughtfulness.

He told me, too, all about our leap frog over the islands in the Pacific and produced maps for me to see. Aides came in and went out. Marshall must have talked for at least a half hour. I was so impressed that I was fearful I might blow it to someone. I did not even dare tell Mrs. Saltonstall. Naturally, I followed with close interest as General MacArthur carried out the advance that was planned; I wished that Peter could have lived to take part in it, and was proud that Lev Jr. was active in the New Guinea invasion.

So I made my negative report to Conant. The world knows that General Marshall did receive his Harvard degree after the war, when he was secretary of state, and when in a ten-minute speech he made the significant announcement of the Marshall Plan.

General Marshall—no one in the capital, not even the President, called him by his first name—was the most selfless and most revered of our military leaders. Victory was in sight that spring, and on several occasions both houses of Congress assembled in the auditorium of the Congressional Library to hear the general's off-the-record report of our triumphant progress. Marshall always spoke without notes, very ably and succinctly—he gave the impression that he was letting you in on a secret that you should not tell. Of course, he had thought it out ahead of time, but it appeared to be extemporaneous and highly confidential. I remember the time he brought with him General Eisenhower, who had just flown in from France. After Marshall's pleasant introduction, General Eisenhower tried to talk to us in the same easy, off-the-cuff manner, but he did not have Marshall's facility and took refuge in reading his notes, which were fresh from the front. He received tremendous acclaim from all of us.

* * *

By April, 1945, our troops had advanced far into Germany and were discovering the horrors that the Nazis had imposed upon the Jewish population and their brutality toward war prisoners. General Eisenhower, again at the front, cabled President Truman that he was going to leave everything "just as is" and that he hoped a committee of congressmen would fly over immediately to see things for themselves. The Senate committee consisted of three Democrats, Alben Barkley, Walter George of Georgia and Elbert Thomas of Utah; and three Republicans, Brooks of Illinois, Wherry, and me. Senator White of Maine was to have gone, but could not make it, and on twelve hours' notice asked me to take his place. His message reached me late one day at my home in Dover and I had to pack and be ready to leave Washington early the next morning. At National Airport we were joined by six congressmen, making a party of twelve in all; we boarded a C-54 and after stopping for fuel in Bermuda and the Azores, landed in Paris.

After a night's rest and a big breakfast, we were thoroughly briefed before taking off in a DC-3 to Buchenwald. There had been a few accounts in the press from the first correspondents to reach that dreadful camp, but nothing in print could be as gruesome or as shocking as the reality. We were first shown into the barracks, where the prisoners slept in three tiers of bunks—a bleak, unheated, miserable place. Many of the captives were so emaciated, so weak, they could not raise themselves from the bunks even for sanitary needs. From there we were taken to the incinerator. Here the prisoners were led into a chamber, ropes were placed about their throats and they were guided to a spot where the floor suddenly opened and they were dropped in the cellar, after which they were fed into the incinerator. Outside were several wagons with loads of bodies waiting to be burned. That was a picture one does not ever forget.

We were then divided into two groups. I found myself with Rep. Dewey Short of Missouri. We were detailed to visit and be briefed by General Patch and then go to the camp at Dachau near Munich. We reached General Patch's headquarters just as he was completing a long conversation with General Patton in which they were consulting about how Patton would make his way through the south. The Germans were in headlong retreat and, incidentally, it was on this advance that Patton captured the Lippizaner horses before the Russians got to them. After this telephone talk with Patton, Patch joined us for luncheon. Perhaps because his mind was on his talk or for some other reason, he made a preposterous remark that I was sure was not accurate, so I exclaimed: "Now, General, you know that is just not so." He looked at me and smiled, and from that moment on, the atmosphere was more relaxed. I had heard that Patch was depressed by the loss of his son in the war, and when he learned that I had also, he became easier. I hoped that I helped him.

What a ride that was in General Patch's car, up through the Sixth Army on the march—tanks, machine-gun units, amphibious vehicles, and all the rest of the vast equipment. He accompanied us on the drive to Dachau, and I recall our arrival at the gates, with woods to the left and in front of them, the bodies of dead German guards who had been shot while fleeing; and to the right, the railway yards with a freight train whose cars were loaded with corpses. General Patch would not get out of the car. But once they saw him, he became the center of thousands of cheering, pushing prisoners— Russians, Czechoslovakians, Poles—pressing forward to give him thanks.

Dewey Short and I visited the gas chamber, which inside was as clean as a showerbath, but outside we saw the pile of naked bodies stacked like logs to a height of six feet, gassed to death and now waiting to be buried. We saw the rifle pits where prisoners had been lined up and shot in the head. It seems incredible that such things could take place only a short distance from a great city like Munich, which, incidentally, had been captured by the Rainbow Division the day before our arrival.

We spent the night in Munich at the headquarters of the division in a doctor's house from whose bookshelves Dewey Short "liberated" a volume describing the birth of the Nazi Party and how it was destined to rule the world; and for my part somewhere along the line I came into possession of a German pistol.

After a visit to Heidelberg and a formal dinner at General Dever's headquarters, we were taken to the chalk mountain where in a tremendous cave the Germans had built the great V-2 rockets. We saw one all finished except for its head and ready to be shipped to Belgium. We interviewed some of the forced laborers who ate, slept, and worked inside the mountain.

On that day or the next we visited a muddy airfield with steel-strip runways where supplies were delivered in C-47s, which were then filled with repatriated American prisoners. What a happy bunch they were; the Massachusetts boys seemed especially glad to talk to me. The planes were landed, unloaded, and flown out with the repatriated prisoners at intervals of a very few minutes — an efficient, touching performance.

After a flight over Cologne and nearby devastated cities, we flew to Reims, where we were to meet General Eisenhower and be briefed by his staff. He invited us to lunch and talked freely, giving us a confident picture of the ending of the war, which did take place three days later. But it was the sight that greeted us when we stepped onto the street that will always be with me. The French people, men, women, and children, literally several thousands of them, when they learned that Ike was lunching in the cafe, surrounded the place clapping and cheering with affection for the general who had freed them. That gave me the first impression of the love and admiration our allies had for General Eisenhower.

We were taken into the famous Reims Cathedral. It was not badly damaged and it has long since been repaired. Then Gen. Alfred Gruenther, Eisenhower's chief of staff, guided us to the nearby airfield. He pointed out a C-47 filled with German general officers about to be sent to English prisons. He ordered them out of the plane for our benefit and his satisfaction. It was interesting to see their expressions when they learned who we were. Haughty, cynical, ashamed, if you will, but silent and obedient. Then at Gruenther's order they piled back into the C-47, and we returned to Paris.

As I recall, we stayed in Paris for several days of briefings and visits with our friends who were stationed there before we headed for home the morning the armistice was declared. The most memorable interview of the trip was with General DeGaulle; our ambassador had requested the interview and he was very pleased when DeGaulle discussed questions of policy with us for over a half hour. We were seated in front of him and to his side. He sat very straight at a large desk and the discussion was held through an interpreter, although I was convinced that DeGaulle understood our questions before they were translated into French. That, of course, gave him time to consider how to reply. The majority leader, Barkley, carried on most of the interview. I asked, with some hesitation, a question. I cannot remember what it was, but I do recall that DeGaulle answered very quickly and quite sharply. We found him very dignified, formal, and obviously feeling his importance, if you will, as the head of the government he had fought so long to rehabilitate. When we left, our ambassador remarked that it was the longest interview that any American or English group had had with DeGaulle since he had returned to Paris. In all, it was an unforgettable experience for a new senator of four months.

Earlier in 1945, on March 21, I had made my maiden speech in the Senate, concerning the importance of our supporting small nations like Poland, Czechoslovakia, and others to establish their independent governments without dictation from the Soviet Union or any of the European nations. It was important for the future peace of the world and for our international relations that we should advocate and support such a policy. Truly, I backed Senator Vandenberg in his opening talk on this subject. He was in the chamber when I spoke. He listened for perhaps a few minutes and then, satisfied that he knew where I was going, stood up and strode out, passing in front of me as I spoke from my rear seat. As he passed, he gave me a quizzical look, but I am sure he recognized that I was supporting his position.

Germany sued for peace in April, and Japan in August of 1945. A thorny question came up immediately before the committees on the military: How long should the draft be continued? There could be no immediate answer, for it was apparent that we could not secure through voluntary enlistments the men we needed for the armies of occupation and for reserves in the United States sufficient for any emergency. We would live with this problem for years, and in each discussion of the draft the biggest points were who should be taken and who could be exempt. We knew there was a shortage of doctors at home and were equally aware that the ablest young scientists were needed for research and development, but how to draw the line in a fair and practical way was so difficult that in the end we voted — always in a nonelection year — to continue the draft with little change.

General Eisenhower succeeded General Marshall as chief of staff in November, 1945, and thereafter he occasionally attended closed sessions of the Armed Services Committee to answer questions and to talk over problems of defense. I remember questioning him about the colored troops and the white, how they worked and lived together, and whether he thought integration could be worked out successfully in the Army. He replied in the negative. I was very much impressed by his frankness at the time and so, at a much later date, was Senator Styles Bridges of New Hampshire, who had read the record. Bridges was always very thorough in following the records of committees in which he was interested, and he was struck by Eisenhower's answer. Actually we were both afraid that it might be used against Ike in his campaign for the presidency, but it never was. Probably no Democrat took the trouble to read that particular exchange. When Eisenhower became President his point of view had completely changed, and his orders provided for full integration.

At the end of the war I received a good many letters from servicemen eager to get home or out of service, or protesting that they had not been paid what was owed them by the government. The Army, the Navy, and the Air Force each had representatives assigned to the Senate and House of Representatives to process the answers to such appeals as swiftly as possible. I recall a few emergency cases in which I intervened. In the 1950s there was a Massachusetts sailor whose father had died suddenly. We located him on a carrier that was on the point of sailing out of San Diego Harbor, for the Far East. The Navy sent a helicopter after his ship, picked up the sailor, brought him back to San Diego, and flew him home to Massachusetts in time to attend the funeral service. There was also the call from the sister of a serviceman who told me that their father had been killed in an automobile accident in Boston and could we possibly get her brother home in time to soothe their grief-stricken mother? This boy, as I recall, was actually in Japan but by delaying the funeral a couple of days we were able to fly him home in time to be with his mother when she needed him most.

One of the great personal satisfactions of being a senator is the opportunity to help constituents with their personal problems. We tried very hard in our office, when it was possible to do so, to assist veterans, elderly citizens, and young people wanting to get an education. Now when people stop me on the street to shake my hand, often they thank me for something I did for them as a senator or as a governor years ago. I have no idea what I did to help them with their problems, but it pleases me, and I always say, "I am glad if I was of a little help and hope all goes well with you now."

* * *

The social life in Washington is a strenuous one, as Alice and I soon discovered. We tried to limit our evening engagements to three or four a week, as we found that the dinner parties we gave in return were easier if we held them to five or six couples. While the war lasted, it was understood that the menu would be simple and that guests would leave early. We saw how well this was managed the first time that we dined with Lord and Lady Halifax at the British Embassy. That evening the ambassador seemed very preoccupied, the conversation was a bit formal, and the service was so brisk that at the dinner's end, the port, passed to the left in the traditional manner, went around the table in record time. By 9:30 the guests were taking their leave — to our embarrassment as we had told Pat Mulvihill, our driver, not to call for us until 10. We were the last to get into our wraps and we huddled in the shadow of the embassy entrance until Pat drove up. He always arrived ahead of time, so we weren't too cold.

The question of who is to be seated to the right and left of the hostess is a sticky one, and if in doubt one can settle it by a telephone call to the protocol department of the State Department. I remember one dinner party where I was seated across from the hostess. She had a Supreme Court justice on either side, and inadvertently she had not placed them according to their rank, Even before the conversation began, the justice on her right leaned across the hostess to apologize to his senior for being in the wrong place. I was surprised that such an outspoken excuse was called for.

One of our favorite neighbors was the French ambassador, Henri Bonnet. We grew to have a warm friendship with him and his charming wife, and there was never any danger of such embarrassment in their house. I always enjoyed the evenings we spent in their big mansion, which had formerly been the home of John Hayes Hammond, the mining engineer.

To one of our first parties came James Forrestal, secretary of the Navy, who seemed greatly impressed by the size of our rented home. "Lev, why did you ever get a place as big as this?" he asked me.

"Well," I answered, "we had to find a place for Pat to live, and this was the best available."

Pat Mulvihill had been with my family for more than thirty years, first as a coachman, then a chauffeur, and when we went to Washington he went with us and occupied the whole third floor.

At the time of which I am speaking, the wealthy widow, Mrs. Evalyn Walsh McLean, the owner of the Hope Diamond, was Washington's most bountiful hostess, and in the spring of 1945 she invited Alice and me to two of her parties. The first, she said, was to be a small affair, by which she meant ten couples. During the dinner, the conversation was pleasant, and I enjoyed it. But when we joined the ladies after coffee the hostess buttonholed me, and once we were seated in a corner she began to browbeat certain prominent figures in the government with such profane emphasis that I was embarrassed. My silence did not slow her down, but finally Sen. William Fulbright, sensing that I was having a hard time, came over and rescued me.

The second was a much larger dinner of at least a hundred people, and as Alice and I came up the line to shake hands with our hostess, Mrs. McLean said to me: "If you want to see the Hope Diamond — here it is," and she indicated the huge pendant that she was wearing under her chin.

We were seated at tables of eight, and I found that I had been placed between "Cissy" Patterson, the owner of the *Washington Times-Herald,* and Mrs. Joseph O'Mahoney, wife of the senator from Wyoming. She was a daughter of the superintendent of my grandfather's place in West Medford, so we were soon reminiscing happily together about our youth in Massachusetts. Then as conversational partners changed, Mrs. Patterson began to question me about my first impressions of the Capital. Thereafter, we seldom saw Mrs. MacLean, as she made it a point never to accept invitations from those she had invited to her house.

One of the invitations that Mrs. Saltonstall was glad to accept was when she was invited to join a Spanish class. Mrs.

Truman was a member, and they soon became good friends. When Truman became President, the class met in the basement of the White House on Tuesday mornings, and there Pat would drive her each week for the balance of that year. Security was tight at the time, as I found when Senator Walsh asked me to come with him to see President Truman on a matter concerning the Boston Navy Yard. We drove up to the gate in a taxi and the guard asked for our identification. Walsh mumbled something about our being senators, and I handed over my card identifying me as a member of the Naval Affairs Committee. The guard looked at it and grinned, "Okay, Senator Saltonstall, I'm glad to meet you. We know Mrs. Saltonstall and Pat very well."

Alice's and my visits to the White House were few and far between. I do recall that in 1947 Alice and I attended the reception that President Truman gave to the officers of the Army, Navy and Air Force. We were second in line behind Sen. Chan Gurney, chairman of the Armed Services Committee, and his wife, and after we passed by the President, we moved on into the dining room, where the Marine Band was playing "The Blue Danube." I said to Alice as we waltzed, "Did you ever expect to be dancing in the dining room of the White House to the music of the Marine Band?"

We agreed that we had never had that expectation, but were fully enjoying it. As Alice went forward to speak to Mrs. Truman, it was a pleasure to see Mrs. Truman smile. I think she was rather at a loss with all that military, and was relieved to see a friend she knew.

Chief Justice and Mrs. Harlan F. Stone gave a memorable dinner in honor of Gen. and Mrs. George Marshall on Feb. 6, 1946. Marshall had just returned from his mission to China, in the course of which he had tried to work out a peaceful settlement with Mao Tse-tung and Generalissimo Chiang Kai-shek. After dinner the general in his calm way told us of the difficulties of traveling in the cold winter weather and of the exasperation of trying to arrive at any agreement. As I recall it, Madame Chiang Kai-shek was present at one of the meetings he had with the Communist leader, but her husband would never confront Mao. Marshall's account gave me my first comprehension of the problems we would continue to deal with in the Far East, and of the difficulty in reaching an understanding with the Asiatic mind. Alice and I had hoped to have the Stones as our guests of honor a month or so later; they had accepted, but the party was cancelled on the sudden death of the chief justice.

* * *

In the summer of 1946 I was appointed to the committee established at the request of President Truman to report on the atomic bomb tests at Bikini Lagoon in the middle of the Pacific. Up to that time there had only been three atomic explosions; the first was the experimental one at Los Alamos, N.M., and the other two were dropped on Hiroshima and Nagasaki. At Bikini there were to be two explosions spaced three weeks apart. The first one was to be dropped from the air on a target of obsolete battleships and destroyers. The other was to be tested underwater. Sen. Carl Hatch of New Mexico was the chairman of our committee, the others being Karl Compton, president of MIT; Gen. "Vinegar Joe" Stilwell, who joined us in the Pacific; Bradley Dewey, the industrialist; Dr. J. Robert Oppenheimer, the ranking scientist at Los Alamos (who never came); a representative of the National Science Foundation, two members from the House, and me. We were told to bring light clothes and a bathing suit and that we might need a sweater on the seaplanes.

We flew in a C-54, an army transport, to Kwajalein Island, where we were quartered at the officer's mess, President Compton and I sharing a room together, and the next morning our party flew on to Bikini Lagoon in navy seaplanes. In all I was to make six flights in these sturdy seaplanes; on the first flight, which consumed only a couple of hours, I had the good luck to sit beside the pilot and heard him radio ahead that he had a number of VIPs aboard. The expression was a new one to me, and I asked what he meant. "You're one," he grinned at me and I realized that I was still a green senator. On later trips, I remember, I made one long run perched on a garbage can, and on another I stretched out among the mail bags in the tail — which was more comfortable. At Bikini we lived aboard a splendidly equipped hospital ship; the meals were good Navy chow, and of course there was much talk about the coming tests. By day we enjoyed swimming in the lagoon, the water temperature similar to that in Buzzards Bay. After supper we would sit on the upper deck watching a movie in the fresh, warm air of the broad Pacific.

"Vinegar Joe" Stilwell was a thin, short man who walked with a quick, long stride. He was a loner who kept to himself and was evidently skeptical of the value of our committee. His hours were unique, for he rose before the sun and was usually in bed and asleep by 7 p.m. I think I was the only one of us who tried to get to know him; I noticed that he took his exercise by walking the deck, so I made a point of falling into step with him in the late afternoon. The sailors would watch us and occasionally would ask Stilwell for his autograph — but not for mine.

As we walked, he became more and more talkative. He spoke of the many miles he had walked or been driven across China in that hardest of campaigns — perhaps it was then that he lengthened his stride — and he spoke with profanity about Chiang Kai-shek, for whom he had no respect. He was too reserved a man to encourage a swift friendship, but we came to respect each other, and on our return to San Francisco he invited me to stay with him at his home at the Presidio. I should have liked to do so, but I had to get back to Dover.

The first explosion was set off several days after our arrival, and we had been carefully briefed as to what to expect. On July 1 we were airborne in a C-54 about 9000 feet up and 18 miles away. A naval officer in the stern gave us the countdown. I was sitting in front of Compton and Dewey, all of us equipped with very dark glasses; both scientists looked away at the instant of explosion, while I with the innocence of a layman continued gazing out the window of the plane and saw the bomb explode. Afterwards, I was told that no matter how strong the glasses, I should not have looked directly at the explosion. We were well prepared for trouble, though none occurred. I had on a Mae West, which I knew how to inflate, and a parachute. I was sitting on a liferaft, whose mysteries I never did learn to solve. I figured if I inflated the Mae West, reached the ocean, and cleared myself of the parachute, someone would pick me up. Actually our plane shook a little when the bomb exploded, but that was all.

The bomb was aimed at the battleship *New York* and exploded near enough to kill or maim the goats that were tethered aboard her for the test. Later we went aboard the *New York;* it gave me an eerie feeling to climb up the side of the great battleship and find no one on the decks. We walked around following the officer with the Geiger counter — the count would jump as we approached a fallout — and we smelled the unfortunate goats. If the counter showed more than ten one-thousandths of atomic strength, we had to move on quickly. Just like any other gas, the strongest remains of the bomb were secreted in the passageways. On our return to the hospital ship, we learned that a team of doctors was analyzing material that had been brought back from the scarred vessel. I was impressed with the thoroughness of the research and the care that had been taken.

The second test was to be made with a bomb suspended beneath the bottom of an LST, and as the preparation for it would require three weeks, we VIPs were encouraged to go on trips. Part of the committee headed for Japan, but the President had promised Dr. Compton a free ride to New Zealand and Australia so that he might fulfill some speaking engagements, and Bradley Dewey and I accompanied him in the C-54. I went along because it seemed to me that a knowledge of that part of the world would be of much more use to me as a senator than what I might pick up in Japan.

After spending the night in the Fiji Islands, we flew on to Auckland, where I was instantly impressed by how far socialism had advanced — this was particularly noticeable in the public-housing projects, which at that time were virtually unknown in the United States. We drove to Wellington, the capital, where I called on Prime Minister Walter Nash, whom I had first met at a Tufts commencement, where he was the principal speaker and where we had been awarded honorary degrees. He received me very graciously in his office, and after the parliamentary session was over we were joined by the legislators, including two or three Maoris. We all had sherry and I made a few remarks about how much New Zealand meant to us, after which we joined hands and sang "Auld Lang Syne." At the end of the meeting the Prime Minister asked me what I'd like to do next.

I said, "I hope to visit a Mrs. Lyons in Hastings. I want to thank her for being so kind to my son Peter when he was hospitalized here during the war."

"Good," he said, "I'll send you up by plane."

The next morning he put a small Scout airplane at my disposal, and a scary ride it was as we flew cross-country so close to the hillsides that we frightened the grazing sheep, who scattered at our approach. We landed at a very small airfield, and there to meet me was Mrs. Lyons. She and her son, Ian, ran a large sheep and cattle station, where Peter had spent ten days while he was recuperating from jaundice. Next morning Ian took me on a tour of the station, where I saw how rich the pastures were. The cattle, of which they had some 200, were eating down the tall grass so that the sheep, above 5000 of them, could get at it. Mrs. Lyons was the last friend of the family to see Peter before he was killed on Guam, and it touched my heart to hear her talk about him and how much he had enjoyed riding about their place, Haut-au-Pai. By the second morning, when Mrs. Lyons and Ian drove me to the airport, we had become warm friends. We had breakfast before sunrise and departed when the fields were still white with frost, except for those dark patches where the cattle had lain during the night. At the airport I joined my companions, who had driven up from Wellington, and we flew towards Australia against a strong westerly. As we levelled off, we were buzzed by a New Zealand fighter pilot in training, and I confess I shuddered as the plane buzzed down within fifty feet of our wing, zooming underneath, roaring up the other side, and then repeating the performance.

Now it was Dr. Compton's turn to be in the spotlight. He gave his lectures, and afterwards Australian Chief Justice Owen Dixon, who had been the ambassador in Washington, entertained the three of us at a small dinner. Our host was also chancellor of the University of Melbourne, and at his suggestion I gave an informal talk to the students. I told them of how important Australia had been to us in the early months of the war, when the Philippines had fallen and when General MacArthur had escaped by submarine to Australia to begin the regrouping of our forces. Our boys took to the Australians, they gave us an openhearted welcome, and it was understood that if they were ever in trouble, we would come to their support, as they had supported us.

On my own I went out to pay my respects to Sir Norman Davis, the famous tennis player, who was captain of their Davis Cup team in the final matches against us in 1914. He was responsible for the buildup of tennis in Australia, and I liked him, although there were times when he seemed to be a little on his dignity. Dr. Compton had a lecture to deliver in Sydney, and after some sightseeing we were on our way back to Kwajalein and Bikini.

Immediately on our return we were taken to inspect the targets for the second test, first to the LST and then to a captured Japanese battleship that was anchored nearby. As we stood gazing at the complicated electrical apparatus that had been set up to control the firing of the bomb, the officer in charge asked me if I wanted to have the deck raised so that we could see the real thing. I thanked him but said I didn't think it was necessary. It was enough to know that we were standing about twenty feet above it.

Incidentally, the reason Robert Oppenheimer had declined to accompany our committee was that he thought the experiment would be a waste of time unless the bomb were exploded from the bottom of the sea. The Navy considered that to be too complicated an undertaking and settled for a bomb placed in close suspension — which in Oppenheimer's view would prove little that we did not know already.

On July 25 our hospital ship was anchored about six to seven miles from the LST. We were all given field glasses. I put mine on the rail of the ship, listened to the countdown, and watched a cloud go up from a geyser of water. The geyser must have risen about ninety feet or more in the air, then a great mushroom cloud soared above it and gradually drifted away. I have three pictures taken from the shore of Bikini with an automatic camera that showed the bomb at three seconds, six seconds, and nine seconds after the explosion. In one picture a large piece of metal, presumably a section of the LST, appeared in the cloud of spray perpendicular to the water, and then, of course, sank.

The Japanese warship that had been anchored close to the LST was severely shaken. As I said, we had been aboard it before the explosion and had seen the controls, the crew quarters, and the immense boiler in which all the rice for the crew had been cooked, so very different from the galley of the battleship *Massachusetts.* Now as we cruised near the Japanese ship we noticed that she was listing badly. Next morning when I looked out of my porthole, she was no longer there.

Since we had had several flights on Navy seaplanes, without too much comfort, I suggested to our liaison officer that it would be an agreeable change if our party could make the home trip to Kwajalein on a destroyer. He agreed. Next morning we boarded one at 8 a.m., had breakfast on her, and started for the island at 34 knots. What a day! I crawled up to the bow — crawled, I say, because I could not stand against the slipstream — and sat there in my shirtsleeves watching her plow through a calm sea. The commander put on his monthly tests that day for our benefit — depth bombs, 90 mm antiaircraft, and all the rest of it. It was pretty exciting to watch and to feel the ship shudder from the depth-bombing. We reached Kwajalein about 6 p.m. after a glorious experience, and from the bridge I watched the navigator direct the ship precisely to her designated berth.

Knowing that my son Peter was buried on Guam, I asked the Air Force commander on Kwajalein, General Powers, if I might thumb a ride on a plane going to Guam. The general, who later became chief of staff, told me to come with him in a B-29. He gave me a bunk in the radio section and off we flew at midnight, arriving in Guam for breakfast. It was fun to lie in my bunk and watch the radio operator guide us to the field.

That day I visited Peter's grave, then was driven to the spot where he and his patrol were ambushed, spent the night in Adm. Chester Nimitz's room at headquarters, and next day was back in the side gunner's seat in the B-29 to return to Kwajalein. Near the end of the trip the general invited me to the pilot's cabin. So I crawled up on my hands and knees through a tube, and after introducing me to the crew — one of whom proved to be a neighbor from Medfield — the general put me in the bombardier's seat forward. What a feeling as we descended! Nothing in front of me except Plexiglas — and the ground coming up to meet me! Then the wheels hit and we left the plane and headed for the guest house. I thought I had better claim a bed quickly, so I went to the room I had previously shared with Dr. Compton. Lo and behold, General Stilwell was in my bed snoring peacefully without a stitch on him or over him. I grabbed another room and after supper went to sleep.

We flew back to Honolulu, San Francisco, and home. The Senate had recessed before we left the Coast and so those of us heading East took our connecting flights. My own bed in Dover felt very good after three nights of lying without too much sleep on the floors of the B-54s.

We made no report because we felt the undertaking had been well carried out by the Navy. But witnessing the results at Bikini Lagoon certainly made a deep impression on me as to the future sea, air, and land forces that we might need for our security. Our mainstay at sea, the aircraft carrier — the battleship was obsolete — must not only be equipped to carry fighter planes, but to defend itself from air and submarine attack. Constant study should be made to improve the speed and the maneuverability, and the most up-to-date electronic gear must be installed on our fighter planes and bombers. How to train the land forces and what weapons to give them will also call for continued research.

Since 1945 we have built new-type submarines and equipped them with long-range missiles capable of being fired from under the sea. Our fighter planes are faster and more maneuverable now and have the most modern electronic gear. Our long-range bombers are constantly being modernized. On the ground the Army has learned much, but still we have far to go to make sure that we have the ability to counterattack devastatingly should we have to do so.

My reactions from my observations at Bikini Lagoon in 1945 made crystal clear the devastating destruction caused by the atomic bombs. Now we have to face nuclear bombs with a force a thousand times more destructive.

* * *

By the time of the off-year elections in the autumn of 1946, the war was behind us. Here, as in Britain, people were ready for a change: the reaction produced a Republican majority in the House of Representatives and sixteen freshmen Republicans in the Senate who provided a Republican majority of 49 to 47 in that body. It was a narrow margin, especially in view of the undependability of Langer of North Dakota and Wayne Morse of Oregon, but it was enough to give us a majority in the committees.

Senator Wherry was elected majority leader. He worked hard to get this post, and at the caucus of the Republicans in January, 1947, perhaps as an offset to a midwesterner, I was chosen to be the majority whip. It pleased me to be chosen. This office is a nebulous one. What it means is that I attended for the majority leader when he was absent from the seat on the floor. His absence is often when there is a long-winded speech with no particular vote or contest involved. Consequently, during the next few years, I sat many times practically alone on the floor of the Senate when a filibuster was in progress. In fact, I recall clearly the evening that I sat to listen to Senator Morse. He and I, with the various attendants required to be present, were the only senators.

I cite this as an illustration of many similar occurrences. Sen. Allen Ellender of Louisiana, who spoke once for twenty-three hours, told me that if you are going to filibuster, read from a book or a speech, but never try to speak extemporaneously because of the tiring effect. He also suggested orange juice as the best stimulant.

Bob Taft, who tolerated but often disagreed with Vandenberg on foreign policy, became the chairman of the Policy Committee and a decisive influence in domestic issues, as he was soon to show in his handling of the Taft-Hartley Act. Taft's attitude towards Henry Cabot Lodge and myself was one of reservation tinged with doubt. He had not seen eye to eye with us on preparedness or intervention, he had voted against arming American vessels before Pearl Harbor, against Selective Service on the eve of Pearl Harbor, and against lend-lease. And at the end of the war he was wary of foreign aid and voted against the reciprocal-trade treaties.

There was no open breach between us and I think that in time he respected my forthrightness. But when he was campaigning for the presidential nomination in 1948 and came to Massachusetts looking for support, he went out of his way to disparage my record, which was a really silly thing to do for it antagonized my friends. In the Eisenhower years, when illness cut down his activity, he appointed Senator Knowland as his deputy on the Senate floor, and that he did not oppose my being the Republican whip was, I think, in the interest of avoiding an internal conflict among the Republicans.

A freshman no longer, I knew that I would be assigned to two major committees in the new Congress of 1947, and the question was which to apply for. As my knowledge had been broadened by my two years' affiliation with Naval Affairs, I wished to remain on that committee, which shortly was to become part of the Armed Services Committee set up by the National Defense Act. The Foreign Relations Committee was always a desirable choice, but I doubted if Vandenberg and Taft would want me there. Instead, I applied for the committees on Finance and Appropriations. My friends in the Senate had warned me that Appropriations was one of the busiest committees in Congress, demanding many days of hearings and conferences, and that I could not expect to be on the floor of the Senate to any great extent while I was a member of Appropriations. But I stuck by my preference; after a brief tour on the Finance Committee, I shifted to the Appropriations Committee and have always been glad that I did, as that committee had to appropriate the funds for the operation of the entire government. Finally, through no request of mine, I was also appointed to the Small Business Committee. Senator Taft, whose duty it was to approve of the Republican committee appointments, had his needle out and wanted to know if I had asked for this third assignment. I said truthfully that I had not; I assumed the appointment had been made by the majority leader, Senator Barkley, without his consulting me.

The most important legislation before the Armed Services Committee then was the preparation of the National Security Act, the bill which brought together the Army, the Navy, and the Air Force under the Department of Defense. Now that the Republicans were in power, I had moved up toward the head of the table and I was intensely interested in the unification that Jim Forrestal had so strongly espoused. Sen. Styles Bridges of New Hampshire was entitled to be chairman of either Armed

Services or Appropriations; when he chose the latter, Sen. Chan Gurney of South Dakota assumed the chairmanship of Armed Services, and I became his deputy in the next seat.

It made sense to bring the three armed services together. The Army made no fuss, but the Navy and the Air Force differed sharply on the planes they needed for their respective missions, and each was too jealous of its air power to let go. Adm. Forrest Sherman and Gen. Loren Norstadt were the two officers assigned to work with the committee, and both were exceptionally able men; Admiral Sherman was later to become chief of naval operations, and General Norstadt, the commander in chief of NATO. Each had argued persuasively in behalf of his own service, and both realized that there must be an eventual compromise on the wording of the bill. At one informal conference, attended by Sec. Stuart Symington of the Air Force and Secretary Sullivan of the Navy, the argument became so violent that it was necessary for each side to revamp the minutes of the meeting. Privately, Secretary Sullivan came to me, still fuming, to say from the facts that he wouldn't change one word. (But he did finally agree to a revised bill.)

Sharp differences can be smoothed out in the give and take of a small group. Rep. Walter G. Andrews of New York was one of the ablest of the congressmen working on this problem. One evening he invited Admiral Sherman, General Norstadt, and me to have supper with him in his apartment, and after coffee and cigars we went to work and before eleven had blocked out our suggestions for a possible bill.

I knew that the conference committee's second meeting, over which I was to preside in the absence of Senator Gurney, was bound to be a tough one, and in advance I had a quiet talk with Rep. Jim Wadsworth, in whom I knew I had an ally. He was sympathetic to the Senate position though, of course, he could not say so. However, he did hint that when the compromise wording had gone about as far as he could expect the House to agree, he would give me a signal. When that moment arrived, he made a slight nod of his head. I had a few words with my confreres, Senator Byrd and Tydings, whom I knew were with me, and then said, "The Senate will agree to that wording." Rep. William Cole of New York, who was for the Navy all the way, would not sign our conference report, but there was a solid majority in favor. To get the Navy and the Air Force to agree was one of the thorniest problems we encountered in the creation of the National Security Act.

Not nearly as much tugging and hauling went into the establishment of the National Security Council, but the setting up of the Central Intelligence Agency in 1947 was a very different matter. The CIA was the offspring of the Office of Strategic Services which operated during World War II under Col. "Wild Bill" Donovan, and now it was to be our first organized effort for intelligence in foreign countries in time of peace. Its whole objective was to be overseas, and care was taken that it should not compete with the domestic duties of the FBI. For a brief interval at the war's end, the OSS had been put under the jurisdiction of the State Department, which did not want it. Then it was attached as a department of the Army, but here again this did not prove a satisfactory arrangement because so many members of its organization were civilians and it would be under the control of the military if the Army ran it.

The solution was to make it an independent agency, directly responsible to the President and the National Security Council. Its first director was Vice Admiral Hillenkoetter, and I have a clear picture of the admiral at a later date when the Appropriations Committee was concerned about the advance of the North Koreans towards Seoul. Why didn't the CIA know about this march? What had they done to keep the President and the secretary of defense informed? The admiral appeared before our committee and to our surprise proved conclusively that the CIA had done its utmost to alert our government but that its daily memoranda had been either ignored or discounted. Its findings had been forwarded to General MacArthur, who had no confidence in the CIA and relied upon his own intelligence service under General Willoughby, which did not take the Chinese threat seriously.

* * *

I took down with me to the Senate my concern for the industries in Massachusetts that I had been helping as far as I could during my years in the legislature and as governor. Massachusetts had long been famous for its clipper ships that sailed to the Orient, for the fishermen who made their living off the Grand Banks, and for the whaling fleet that sailed from New Bedford and Nantucket. The textile mills in Lowell and Lawrence and wherever there was good waterpower; the shoe factories in Brockton, Lynn, Beverly, and Haverhill; the manufacture of watches in Waltham — all held a commanding position until increasing competition from other parts of the country and too-prolonged dependence on antiquated machinery and the rising cost of skilled labor reduced the Bay State's advantage.

In the Forties, new industries, particularly the electronics plants to supply our war needs, sprouted like mushrooms along Route 128 on the outskirts of Boston. They were built up by the combination of local capital and the technical genius of MIT and Harvard, and they flourished. But the older trades like the Gloucester fishing fleet were in trouble.

In the last years of the war, fishermen from Gloucester, Boston, and New Bedford had been encountering increasing competition on the Grand Banks, which were closer to the commercial fishermen of Iceland, and one of my duties as a governor was to appeal to Robert Patterson, then the secretary of war. I told him of the conflict and hoped to persuade him to buy more fish from New England for our Army camps. What did he do? He decided to purchase from Iceland the fish needed for our armed forces in Europe; this kept the Icelanders happy and on the side of the Allies and also temporarily lessened the competition for the American market with New England. But it did not solve the problem.

By 1945, our fishing industry was in a bad slump. The tariff on fish was not large enough to protect our fishermen from the imports from Nova Scotia and Iceland. It takes a boat from Gloucester 15 to 20 hours to reach the banks; but it takes the Nova Scotian and Icelandic men much less time. In addition, by the 1960s, big trawlers were appearing from Portugal, Scandinavia, Poland, the Soviet Union, and even Japan. In all, I believe ships from 14 nations were fishing off the Grand Banks. It was obvious that the tariff on fish destined for the United States, most of it transshipped from foreign trawlers at St. Pierre and Miquelon, was no longer large enough to protect our home fleet.

In the winter of 1946 I paid my first call on Dean Acheson, who was then undersecretary of the Treasury — I recall it clearly because his office was a cold, vast room in the old Treasury Building — and I told him of our fishermen's dilemma. He was sympathetic, but gave me no encouragement that the tariff on fish could be raised. He thought it would come up for review as part of the general tariff revision, but that we would be lucky to keep it as high as it was.

A year later, with Senator Morse and Sen. Warren Magnuson of Washington (who were troubled about conditions on the West Coast, especially the action of Peru in the seizing of our tuna fishermen), we made another attempt. At the request of General Marshall, then Secretary of State, we called on his undersecretary, Bob Lovett, and again we were met with words of sympathy. Actually we arrived at an inopportune moment, for the news had just been received of Gandhi's assassination. Lovett told us that he got the word that morning while he was shaving. He said that he thought, as he went through the motions of shaving, "Twenty years ago we in the State Department would have said, 'Too bad! Too bad! Now let's see what England will do about it.' And some time after England had acted we would take our position.

"But now," he said, "It isn't what England will do about it, it isn't what we may do in two weeks, but what the hell are we going to do about it before lunchtime today. That's the trouble with our State Department — it isn't geared to act quickly!" Which was his way of saying that we couldn't expect any immediate help from that quarter.

As time went on and conditions worsened, Sen. John F. Kennedy and I, several years later, filed a resolution to establish a research commission of scientists to see what assistance could be given to our fishing fleets. Two laboratory ships were built and sent out to study methods by which the schools of fish could be more quickly located and the catch more efficiently processed. Naturally, senators from the farm belt were not eager to see funds diverted for research on fish. But the capital investment for fishing vessels continued to dwindle and except for the fishermen from New Bedford, who still find a ready market for whitefish in New York City, I think it is fair to say that over 75 percent of the fish now processed on the New England coast comes to America in foreign bottoms. The stock of cod, halibut, mackerel, and other seafoods will inevitably be depleted and the day will come when stiffer regulations of the catch on a quota basis will have to be respected internationally.

VI. Committees, filibusters and debates

I was learning the ropes, but on the question of public opinion I could be just as wrong as anyone. Looking back, it is clear that in the election of 1948 the Republican candidates for national office were overconfident. The hardest fighting the Republican party did that year was at the national convention, held in the wilting July heat in Chicago, where Stassen, Taft, and Dewey vied for the nomination.

The outcome was a bitter disappointment for Taft, who had been swept aside by Willkie in 1940 and this time was passed over for Governor Dewey. The selection of ex-Governor Earl Warren of California as Dewey's running mate assured us of victory in that pivotal state, and we were certain that Dewey would defeat Truman. Up until the very last week of the campaign, the polls showed Dewey with a comfortable lead, and this assurance accounts for the note of complacency in Dewey's speeches. He could be vigorous in attack, as he had proved as a special investigator of organized crime, when he earned the nickname "Racket-buster." But not now. We did not realize how the President was gaining in the home stretch — on a single day, Truman delivered eleven speeches to Dewey's one. We took victory for granted and did not appreciate until the morning after by what a narrow margin Truman had carried Ohio, Illinois, and California — a switch of a total of 30,000 votes in those three states would have made Dewey President.

In Massachusetts I, too, was overconfident. My opponent was John I. Fitzgerald, an elderly Democrat not particularly aggressive. When President Truman came to Boston to boost his campaign, I was told that Fitzgerald's son urged the President to say something disparaging about me in his speech at

Fenway Park. "Oh, but I couldn't do that," said the President, "Mrs. Saltonstall is too good a friend of Mrs. Truman."

Fitzgerald was not a compelling speaker, but the week before election day, in a series of front-page advertisements in the newspapers, he accused me of being in favor of birth control. True, a bill in favor of birth control had come up in the legislature during my last term as governor and I had taken a neutral position. It was a touchy issue to Roman Catholics in the commonwealth, and Fitzgerald's attack cut into my expected plurality. I won with a majority of 125,000, but it wasn't what I had hoped for.

* * *

At the beginning of my new term, my committee work became engrossing. The Committee on Armed Services met on Thursday mornings at 10:30, and I rarely missed it. The Committee on Appropriations demanded all the time I could give it, and then some. It was the largest committee in the Senate and it needed to be, as it surveyed the entire financing of the government. There were twenty-eight members, each of us being assigned to four or five subcommittees that met constantly, sometimes in the morning, sometimes in the afternoon. Each member devoted his attention to those subjects in which he was most interested. In my case I asked for the subcommittee on defense, as I knew it would dovetail with my work on Armed Services; I also worked on the subcommittees on state and justice, the treasury, the post office, and independent offices, under whose jurisdiction so many commissions receive their appropriations.

I am sometimes asked how any member of Appropriations can vote intelligently on bills involving so many billions of dollars, and the answer is of course that he learns to trust the judgment of his fellow members who have become knowledgeable in their fields, just as they come to trust him. For instance, when I rose to be the senior minority member of the defense subcommittee and had determined how I was going to vote and what I believed was best for the department, I would then consult the Republican and Democratic members who did not expect to attend the executive session. I would explain the problem and what I thought the answer should be and would ask the senator, if he agreed with me, to give me his proxy. If I thought there were going to be sharp differences of opinion, I might ask for his proxy in writing, although this was seldom necessary. Generally, members would simply say, "Lev, you vote for me," and then when the roll call was called of the full committee, I would respond, "Senator so-and-so votes "Yes."

Of course in every instance a quorum had to be present. Let me add that the hearings were so lengthy and and the decisions so difficult that only twice in my twenty-two years (each time when the Republican were in control of Congress) was the total appropriations bill completed before July 1st, which is the start of the fiscal year. Senator Taft, as the Republican leader, must be credited for that accomplishment.

While many of us were immersed in our committee rooms, the regular business of the Senate went forward on the floor according to schedule. But when an emergency arose, a warning would be given; bells would ring in every committee room and every senator's office — one long ring indicating a vote, two bells a call for a quorum and three bells signaling a recess or adjournment.

In 1947, one of the first bills to come up before Appropriations was that to establish the National Science Foundation. When the bill defining the scope of the NSF first came out of Appropriations to the floor of the Senate, it was severely criticized. Knowing of our interest in the matter, Senator Thomas of Utah, the chairman, urged three of us to get together: Senator Magnuson of Washington, who took a broad view of the development of air power, Senator Smith of New Jersey, and myself, who wanted the foundation to play a constructive part in the universities, particularly in the advancement of doctors and scientists.

Thomas said, "You three look over the language of the bill and see if you can't get a satisfactory compromise." So in the Senate Reading Room we went over the proposed bill, line by line: how to set up the foundation, what type of scientist or professor should be the chairman, how the funds should be distributed — how much to the universities, to the government laboratories, to the hospitals — how much Congress might be willing to appropriate, and whether it should be an independent agency or put under an existing department. Our bill created an independent agency, and some senators shook their heads when we proposed an initial appropriation of $7 million. After further readings, the bill became law.

Over the long run, the National Science Foundation has been very well managed. Indeed, it is an indispensable source for medical research, for testing and innovations in aviation, for the studies that are made in environmental protection, and, last but not least, the financial aid that it extends to young scholars and scientists. It pleases me to think that the annual appropriation of $7 million we struggled so hard for in 1947 has now been increased to over half a billion.

The hearings on foreign aid were conducted by the full Committee on Appropriations in executive session, and after General Marshall's famous speech at Harvard, the extent of the appropriation became of international consequence. Practically speaking, I favored the recommendations of President Truman, not always in the full amount, but generally on the higher side, as opposed to my isolationist colleagues like Senator Taft, who wished to cut taxes and consistently voted against continuing a large appropriation for military and economic assistance to Europe.

* * *

My coming to the Senate in 1945 had given me the opportunity of renewing my friendship with Justice Felix Frankfurter. At Harvard Law School, as I have mentioned, I was a member of the first class which he taught on criminal law, and later, when I was governor, he came to the State House occasionally to pay his respects. Now we began to catch up with each other over lunch. When I lunched with him in his chambers at the Supreme Court, it was always a tasty and elaborate affair with a salad for which he made the dressing. I am afraid the meals which I served him on trays in my office were a lot less stylish. After lunch it was his habit to go through all the rooms shaking hands with my assistants and secretaries. They liked it, and I liked to have him do it. On one of those rare occasions when it was snowing hard, he remarked in that high, carrying voice of his, "I think a good executive would let his help go home early in this snowstorm." So I acted on his cue.

At one of our early luncheons, Felix said he had made an appointment for both of us to call on Chief Justice Stone. Well, that morning my assistant, Henry Minot, had shown me a report of the Army Corps of Engineers recommending that a channel be dredged between Kimball's Island and Isle au Haut in Maine. As I have said, the chief justice spent his summers on Isle au Haut, which is the next island to North Haven, where Henry and I had summer houses. So we knew it well. Henry laughingly called the proposed channel one of the biggest boondoggles he had ever heard of. So after greeting the chief justice, I began to lead up to what Henry had said. But when the chief justice remarked, "I have been working on that prop-

Saltonstall with President John F. Kennedy and Sen. Edward M. Kennedy at Boston College centennial observance in 1963.

With son William in 1941, photo at left; and in 1972, photo below.

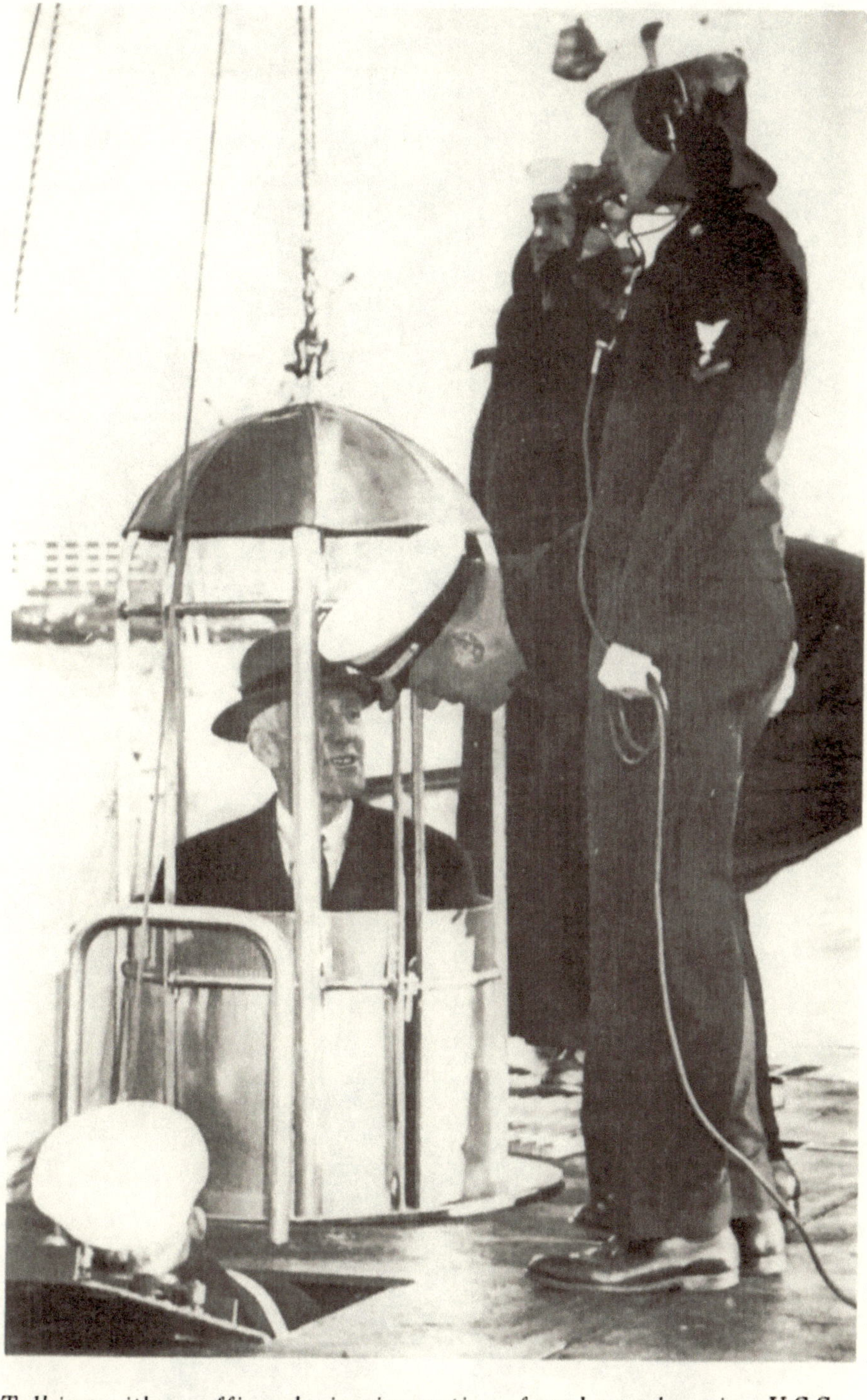

Associated Press

Talking with an officer during inspection of nuclear submarine, U.S.S. Edison, at Norfolk, Va. Naval Base.

With pony at his Dover farm in 1963.

osition for several years and am glad that the engineers have at last seen the light of day," I changed the subject quickly.

Felix and his charming wife, Marian, dined with us several times, and we had dinner with them. At one dinner party, among the guests was that very distinguished Frenchman, Jean Monnet, who was the founding father of the Common Market. Frankfurter was a wonderful conversationalist and as he questioned Monnet, the talk became an exciting forecast of the future.

Felix and I had an amusing encounter at the time when Truman's appointment of Dean Acheson as secretary of state was up for confirmation. Acheson and the justice used to meet each morning and walk from their homes in Georgetown to the State Department, where Frankfurter's clerk would pick him up and drive him to the Supreme Court. (The Frankfurters never owned an automobile of their own, and I am not sure that Frankfurter ever had a driver's license.) One day when Henry Minot and I were walking to my office on the Hill, Frankfurter spotted me and had his driver stop the car. He jumped out to ask, "How is Dean's appointment coming along in the Senate?" I replied that I was confident that he would be confirmed. As we were talking, Senator Wherry, the majority leader, who for some reason bitterly objected to Acheson, drove by in his car. He saw us, and he was well aware of how close Acheson was to Frankfurter. Later that day when I met Wherry in the Senate I said to tease him, "Ken, did you see who I was walking with this morning?"

"I certainly did," he replied. "Oh, hell, all you Harvard men stick together." It never occurred to him that Acheson had graduated from Yale. As it happened, Acheson was confirmed overwhelmingly with Wherry one of the three in opposition.

There was one special project in which Justice Frankfurter and I shared a personal interest. When Justice Oliver Wendell Holmes died in 1935, he left the residue of his estate, approximately $350,000 to "the United States of America," but with no word about how it was to be spent. For what purpose should it be put and who was to decide? A commission was appointed consisting of Chief Justice Stone and two members of the Supreme Court — Frankfurter being one of them — two members of the House of Representatives (of which Richard Wigglesworth, Holmes's nephew, was one), and two members of the Senate. There was a vacancy on the commission when I was elected to the Senate, and possibly because of Felix's prompting, I was selected to fill it, my colleague being Sen. Paul Douglas of Illinois.

In the ten years since Holmes's death there had been a number of suggestions — a rose garden behind the Supreme Court, a statue of the donor — but none which seemed the most appropriate way to memorialize this brilliant American, a soldier who had been three times wounded in the Civil War, an able, eloquent lawyer, a fine teacher at Harvard Law School and a judge who had served for seventeen years on the Massachusetts Supreme Judicial Court before being appointed to the US Supreme Court by President Theodore Roosevelt.

Meetings of the commission had been suspended during World War II and Chief Justice Frederick Vinson took no action in the matter despite my efforts to rouse him; but later, when Earl Warren of California became chief justice, I saw my opportunity. We had been fellow governors, and I wrote to him describing Justice Holmes's will and expressing the hope that at last some definite action could be taken. He asked me to come to see him, and at our meeting I proposed that the fund be used to finance a series of lectures by distinguished lawyers and scholars from different parts of the country, each talk having as its background Holmes's philosophy of the Constitution and its application to current questions. The chief justice approved of this, but it was his desire that the fund also provide for a review of the major decisions of the Supreme Court from its beginning. He felt that this could be done in a series of volumes, each to be edited by an eminent professor or member of the bar. The commission adopted our two proposals to use the principal and the interest of the fund until it was exhausted.

So I prepared a joint resolution for the approval of Congress. The value of the bequest from 1936 to the present was figured out at compound interest, and an appropriation was asked for the total amount. The bill also set up a committee, headed by the Librarian of Congress, to select the authors for the books and the speakers from year to year. Sen. Claiborne Pell of Rhode Island, chairman of the Rules Committee, brought in the bill, and I remember the tense moment in the Senate when he ran up to me excitedly to say that he had a speech all ready to go. "So have I," I replied, "but, for God's sake, let the vote be taken without starting a debate, and afterwards we can put our speeches of explanation in the *Record.*" He sat down and we both stayed quiet until the resolution passed. What a pleasant surprise! I had never really believed that Congress would permit the fund, plus interest compounded over thirty years, to be used for such a scholarly purpose, but they had, and without a murmur. I might add that the lectures have been given in various sections of the country year after year; the first two volumes of the series have been published, and eight others are in progress. I like to think that Justice Holmes would approve of this way of using his bequest to "the United States of America."

* * *

Even to one who is familiar with parliamentary procedure, the rules of the Senate are difficult to comprehend. The rules were first created in 1798, and since then they have been amended and amended and amended, and the amendments have been amended. Perhaps the most controversial while I was in the Senate was Rule 22, Section 2, which provided for "cloture" and was supposed to stop filibustering and bring the matter to a vote. Yet, there was a loophole, and I take credit for making the first move to fill that loophole.

The Senate can do just two things: it can talk, or it can vote, and once it stops talking, it must vote or adjourn. Up until 1917, there was nothing in the rules of the Senate that provided the means for closing debate. That year a very controversial matter about the arming of merchant ships came before the Senate, and a cloture rule was adopted. That rule specified the way in which a motion "to bring to a close the debate upon any measure" would be handled in the Senate.

I had become interested in the problem when I was Speaker of the House in Massachusetts, where the way of closing a debate *was* established. When I came to Washington, I was convinced that it was imperative to close a debate after a full discussion and to vote on the important bills rather than let them be killed by endless discussion.

But in 1945, when I first came to the Senate, the cloture rule was inoperative because it provided for closing a debate only in order to vote upon a "measure," which meant a bill. There was no provison for ending debate in order to vote on other business before the Senate.

Legislation on civil rights was the most sensitive of the many issues to come before the Senate in my time, and a sticking point was always reached when a senator from the South began to filibuster. I remember very clearly when a debate on civil rights was interrupted by a motion of Sen. Clyde Hoey of North Carolina, who typified what the traditional senator should look like. He always appeared in a gray cutaway with wing collar and a crimson carnation in his button hole to match his tie. He had a full head of beautifully combed gray hair, and he could speak eloquently and easily on any subject, with a beautiful vocabulary. (I occasionally went over to his seat and ribbed him if his tie and flower did not match.)

A day came in the late forties when Senator Hoey clearly did not approve of the civil rights measure that was before us. Now, each session opens with a prayer by the Senate chaplain, and customarily this is followed by the majority leader asking unanimous consent to approve the minutes of the previous session. So on the occasion when the majority leader asked for consent, Senator Hoey said, "I object, and I move to amend the chaplain's prayer by inserting . . . "

Well, we debated his motion to amend the prayer for the next two weeks, when it was generally agreed to drop the civil rights bill. Whereupon Senator Hoey arose and said, "I believe we thoroughly understand my motion to amend the chaplain's prayer and I ask unanimous consent to withdraw my motion." Everyone laughed. But in effect his diversion ended the civil-rights measure for that session, and that particular bill was never voted on.

Such a trivial discussion, endlessly pursued, continued to stir me as a former Speaker, and with the assistance of Parliamentarian Watkins, I filed a bill to amend the cloture rule so that it would be possible to invoke cloture upon "a motion or other matter pending before the Senate." Had this amendment been in existence, it would have been possible to invoke cloture on the fortnight's discussion of the chaplain's prayer.

The Senate Rules Committee was then under the chairmanship of Senator Byrd, and it included Senator McKellar, Senator Ellender, and a number of others. They were very polite, they listened to my remarks and saw at once my purpose — and nothing came out of the committee. I remember Harry Byrd smiling at me as if to say that the members wanted no change in the rules that would permit cloture to be broadened.

The year following I filed the bill again, but this time I discussed the matter with Senator Taft, at that time chairman of the Republican Policy Committee, and it was at his suggestion that the words, "or the unfinished business," were inserted so that our amendment now read: "Motion, or other matter pending before the Senate, or the unfinished business." For me the key word was still "motion," for it was the "motion" that had to be acted on, but the Taft clause broadened the interest and enlisted the support of more senators. Ultimately, Senator Wherry, who had become the majority leader, called a meeting in his office on a Sunday morning, attended as I recall by Senators Russell, Hayden, Taft, and myself, and perhaps one or two others. After a long discussion it was finally agreed that the Saltonstall-Taft wording should be accepted, providing that the constitutional two-thirds of the whole Senate voted to invoke cloture. In short, at least 64 senators would have to vote affirmatively to make cloture stick. This change, which became known as the Wherry Amendment, was accepted by the Senate on March 17, 1949.

Throughout the 1950s efforts were made to impose cloture, and they failed. Some of the senators from the East and Midwest felt that the rule was too stiff, so finally in 1959 at the instigation of Lyndon Johnson, then majority leader, the so-called Johnson Amendment to the rule was adopted. This change enabled cloture to be invoked "by two-thirds of the senators present and voting," always assuming that a quorum was present.

In 1975, a further amendment was passed stipulating that three-fifths of the Senate, or sixty votes, can compel cloture.

I have gone to some length in this discussion of the rule because of my spade work that led to the Wherry Amendment. I think that I voted in favor of cloture on every occasion when cloture was involved throughout my term in the Senate. In fact, the presence of the Wherry Amendment made filibustering more difficult. The Senate is no longer often in session day and night. I have dozed in my capitol office while filibusters were droning on through the night, and when the bells rang I debated whether I should put on my trousers over my pajamas or come as I was. (Margaret Chase Smith, I knew, would be on the floor.) During the protracted discussion of civil rights the effect of the Wherry Amendment was to caution senators that a compromise might be acceptable.

Some years later, there was a movement sponsored by Sen. Joe Clark of Pennsylvania and Sen. Paul Douglas and others to have each new session of Congress regarded as a new Senate rather than as a continuing body, their aim being to rewrite the rules for each new session, discarding those considered obsolete. I opposed this and argued strenuously that the Senate was a continuing body, as it was historically intended to be by the framers of the Constitution, that any amendments had to be based on the existing rules, and therefore that any change would require a two-thirds vote of the Senate, instead of a simple majority, as the reformers wished.

The argument that each session provides a new Senate that should be free to set new rules is an appealing one. When Richard Nixon was Vice President and our presiding officer in the Senate, it was my belief that he was attracted by this argument, and I went to see him with a brief because I felt so strongly opposed. We discussed the matter in his office for half an hour and I came away with the feeling that if the matter had come to a tie vote, he would have ruled in favor of the Senate being a *new* rather than a *continuing* body. In my judgment that would not have been a wise decision.

* * *

To return to my committee work. I had one brief encounter with the subcommittee on public works, which handled appropriations amounting to about two billion a year — and one was enough. To this day I smile as I recall my meeting with Sen. Robert Kerr of Oklahoma, the oil man and the powerful chairman of the subcommittee on public works, and Senator Ellender, his ally, who was chairman of a subcommittee on appropriations. Both men had a special interest in the Mississippi River, its floodgates, and its depth, Ellender having in mind the facilities of the Port of New Orleans and Kerr the building of channels for merchant ships upstream to Missouri and all the way to Oklahoma. Because of the spring floods in western Massachusetts, I came before the subcommittee to request funds for building dams in North Adams and Worcester County, estimated by the Army Corps of Engineers at a cost of about $1 million. When my appeal had been granted, my two colleagues, who were seeking appropriations of well over $100 million, said to me, "Lev, you have your dams in Massachusetts; now we need your help in Louisiana and Oklahoma." This tit-for-tat business was too much for me, and thereafter I confined my activities as much as possible to committees that did not involve "You scratch my back and I'll scratch yours."

My work on the Appropriations subcommittee on defense was of steadily increasing interest to me for as long as I was in the Senate. One of our recurring problems was to agree on the essential appropriation for military hardware. To approach a realistic figure, we had to take into consideration the construction of aircraft carriers, destroyers, and submarines, and to compare these estimates and the logistics with those of the long-range bombers like the B-36 and the B-52. We studied the development of new tanks, new helicopters, and improved bazookas; we agreed to replace the old Garand rifle with a more modern weapon, and in all these developments there were sometimes sharp differences, not only among the military experts but also among the senators.

I naturally did what I could to protect Massachusetts industry; a rifle plant in Worcester County, I remember, was something of a headache because it had difficulty in living up to the terms of its contract. Again and again I would defend the maintenance of the rope walk in the Boston Navy Yard although I knew it was becoming a museum piece and that most of my colleagues had no idea what a rope walk was. Of course it did not occur to me at the time that the Boston Navy Yard itself would ultimately be phased out of existence. From our Massachusetts standpoint, this was a sad event.

I was also very concerned about the St. Lawrence Seaway. That question had been simmering on the back of the stove since the days of FDR and was to continue to do so until the Eisenhower administration. New England congressmen had unanimously opposed the project in the House and in the Senate in the belief that the Seaway would be of greater benefit to Canada than to the United States and because it would hasten the deterioration of the ports of Boston and Portland. But we were in the minority, and a resolution in favor of the seaway was adopted by the Committee on Foreign Relations and came up for debate in the Senate in February of 1948.

I suppose I must have researched this problem, with Henry Minot's help, more thoroughly than any other subject affecting New England. Officials of the railroads and of the various steamship companies were interviewed, and I talked to members of the Boston Port Authority. I made my carefully prepared speech on Washington's Birthday, 1949. It was a holiday, so the gallery was empty and there were only the presiding officer and myself on the floor of the Senate — an indication, if I needed one, that the minds of most senators were made up. Still, I wanted to get my talk into the *Record.* I based my opposition in part on the impossibility of navigating a fully loaded, oceangoing freighter through a twenty-seven-foot seaway and into harbors on the Great Lakes, where a ship of the newer type with a draft of as much as thirty-four feet could not dock. (Those statistics were supplied to me by the chief of the Army Corps of Engineers.) I also pointed out that the complicated system of locks would be closed by ice for certainly four, if not five, months of the year, necessitating a probable transshipment to rails in Montreal. And I observed that a Brookings Institute study in 1929 had estimated the cost of the harbor and channel improvements at $340 million, but that construction costs had risen sharply since then and that no accurate survey had been made to determine how much. Finally, I seriously questioned if the Seaway would ever pay for itself.

The project continued to be pushed until ultimately President Eisenhower came out in favor of building the Seaway. I believe that the President was influenced by Secretary of the Treasury George Humphrey, who as a resident of Cleveland and a former officer of the Hanna Steel Company, was much interested in moving iron ore from Labrador to his home port. Perhaps the only opposition of mine that President Eisenhower ever recalled came when he said to a group: "I believe we should advocate the Seaway. I realize that Lev (looking at me) is opposed to it, but I think he is the only one present who is."

I replied, "Mr. President, as a summer-along-the-shore sailor, I have never understood how you can get a thirty-four-foot-draft steamer up a twenty-seven-foot channel."

And that was the problem that had to be faced if the Seaway was to be able to take ocean-going steamers. Actually, I believe that there has been much transfer of cargoes to steamers of lesser draft at Montreal, where the harbor was deepened to make such transfers possible. In any event, the Seaway was authorized, with an agreement signed with Canada as to its share of the cost, and the locks were dedicated in the presence of Queen Elizabeth and President Eisenhower. But I believe my economic arguments are just as sound today as they were when I made them. The Seaway, to my knowledge, has not yet operated in the black in any year.

* * *

Probably the most emotional hearings during my twenty-two years were those conducted jointly by the Senate Foreign Relations and Armed Services committees triggered by President Truman's recall of General MacArthur from Japan. The recall by Truman was, in my opinion, an act of courage and wise judgment.

MacArthur had grown to be a national hero as he drove the Japanese out of the Philippines, New Guinea, and the various islands they had captured. He was the dominating figure when the treaty with Japan was signed on the deck of the battleship *Missouri* and he then became our proconsul, restoring our relations with the Japanese. He was given broad powers that he exercised with discretion at the beginning, but gradually he came to do this on his own without seeking approval or advice from Washington. He arrogated to himself more and more authority.

In the early stages of the Korean War, President Truman flew halfway around the world to meet MacArthur at Wake Island. The general kept him waiting forty-five minutes at their first appointment; after apologizing for his rudeness, he reassured the President that the Chinese would not enter the conflict — in which he was dead wrong. The trouble came to a head in 1951 in a politically inspired letter that MacArthur wrote to Rep. Joseph Martin of Massachusetts, the Republican leader in the House. The letter was made public, and in it MacArthur indirectly challenged the judgment of the President. Truman finally ordered him home. In this he exercised his authority as the civilian leader of our country and the commander in chief of our armed forces.

The admirers of General MacArthur openly and loudly objected. MacArthur's leave taking from Tokyo was a ceremonial occasion in which the Emperor took part. The Japanese were upset, and MacArthur made the most of it. When he came to Washington, there was a parade in his honor similar to the parade that General Eisenhower had enjoyed upon his return. Before a joint session of Congress, General MacArthur made an emotional speech, ending with those moving words, "Old soldiers never die; they only fade away."

The country was stirred and sympathetic, and there was a public demand for Congress to investigate the alleged improprieties by MacArthur. A resolution was adopted in the Senate for hearings to be held by the Foreign Relations and the Armed Services committees sitting jointly. Senator Russell of Georgia, chairman of the Armed Services Committee, was selected to preside.

The first question that the committees had to decide was whether the hearings should be open or closed. After considerable discussion, it was agreed that the hearings should be closed, but should be conducted in such a way that the stenographers could appear for short stretches and then be replaced by others in order that they might quickly type out their notes and turn them over to an admiral and a general who stayed in a room nearby and were assigned to review the transcripts immediately after they were typed. These officers would then decide what, if any, of the testimony would be struck out for security reasons before the press had an opportunity to see it. This method of conducting the closed hearings worked out most satisfactorily. There were only one or two differences between members of the committee and the officers as to what testimony would be available to the public, and there never was an appeal to the membership of the committee for a final decision.

MacArthur was, of course, the principal witness, and sat with the committee — with only short luncheon breaks — on May 3, 4, and 5 of 1951. MacArthur was followed by General Marshall, General Bradley, and others. The hearings were held periodically until June 28; I attended them all and asked questions when my turn came.

Senator Russell received much acclaim — and properly so — for the manner in which, with dignity and fairness, he conducted the hearings; he confined the questions to the matter at hand and kept the thirty-odd senators within the time limits established for questions, from three to five minutes in each go-round. At the conclusion he prepared a factual and thoughtful statement, sustaining the President, which the majority of the committee, myself included, signed. There was a minority report led by Senator Bridges that was more favorable to General MacArthur and that Sen. Bourke Hickenlooper of Iowa hoped I would sign. But I went along with the majority of the committee because fundamentally I considered that President Truman was justified in recalling a commander who had been difficult and almost insubordinate and who was dabbling in politics. The joint committee voted 18 to 5 not to file a formal report. At the time I felt that much of the public and the press sympathized with the general, but in the long view the conviction has grown that Truman was right.

* * *

The member of the House with whom I was most closely associated was Christian A. Herter. Chris, who graduated from Harvard in the class behind me, had gone straight into our foreign service. He was born in Paris and was an attache at our embassy in Berlin on his twenty-first birthday in 1916 — a good start for a future secretary of state. He took part in the peacemaking at Versailles, and for five years thereafter was a special assistant to Secretary of Commerce Herbert Hoover, whom he greatly admired. I really came to know him when he moved back to Boston and when in 1932 Henry Shattuck recommended that Chris take his place in the Massachusetts House of Representatives.

You could always spot him, for at 6-foot-5 he towered over everyone. In time he became the chairman of the important Ways and Means Committee and was very helpful to me when I was the Speaker. One of his great assets was his ability to work out practical legislation with his colleagues, who respected his judgment. When in 1934 I had intended to retire, it was Chris who collected the signatures of the majority of the Republicans, urging that I stand again for a fourth term as Speaker. (He always made light of this, which was really a turning point in my career.) When I became governor, Chris was the Speaker of the House; we worked together as a team — he was very good on finance and the budget — and in those years I came to admire him and his attractive wife.

In 1943, Herter was elected to Congress, where he quickly gained the support and friendship of members of the House. When I took my seat in the Senate, Chris was about to file legislation defining the ways in which the United States could aid the European countries that had been devastated in World War II. He asked me to file an identical bill in the Senate, and I was glad to do so. Our bills did not become law, but the wording of President Truman's famous Point Four, which was the starting point for the Marshall Plan, was almost identical with this bill of Herter's. At the war's end Chris became chairman of the committee of the House that was sent abroad to study the financial plight of the various countries and how they could best be helped. It was a conscientious, hardworking group that came to be known as the Herter Commission, and Chris was its most influential adviser all the way. This spadework and the confidence that it generated in Congress helped President Truman gain essential support for the unprecedented Marshall Plan, support even from those states that had once been cool to foreign aid.

While Chris was making his reputation in the House, Republicans back in Massachusetts were more and more disturbed about the way Governor Dever was conducting the state government in his second term. They wanted a strong candidate to oppose Dever in his bid for a third term in 1952, so Henry Shattuck, Mike Farley, and three other Republicans came down to Washington to get me, Cabot Lodge and the delegation from Massachusetts behind a strong candidate for governor. Governor Dever was going to be very difficult to defeat. We hit on the idea of getting Chris Herter to be the candidate, but I never really thought he would go along with the idea. We all went to lunch with Herter and everyone put the bee on him.

At the time, Herter was enjoying his work in the House of Representatives and had made quite a reputation for himself as chairman of the subcommittee on foreign relations. His re-election to Congress was a certainty, while a bid for the governorship against Dever was far from a sure thing. But to my surprise and great joy, Herter accepted the draft, and his candidacy was announced. And back in Massachusetts the man who had expected to be the Republican nominee, State Sen. Sumner G. Whittier of Everett, graciously stepped aside and agreed to run for lieutenant governor as Herter's running mate.

The national election of 1952 was critical for the future of the two-party system. The Democrats had been in power for twenty years and under FDR and Truman had put together a powerful coalition of independents, labor, and ethnic minorities. If the Republicans were to elect a President in 1952, it would have to be done with a candidate who was nationally known and popular enough to attract independents, and even Democrats, to what had become a minority party.

We had twice lost with Dewey — I once told him that I thought he was too young when he first ran — and from a New England point of view, I felt that we could not win with Taft. Eisenhower with his great prestige and attractive personality had returned briefly to civilian life, making his residence in New York as president of Columbia University before being recalled to Europe as the supreme commander of NATO.

The question was, could he be induced to stand for the highest public office as a Republican, and in time for the Republican convention? Lodge was the first to sound him out, and he secured Ike's tentative pledge. Chris Herter must also have talked to him in Paris. But Eisenhower took his responsibilities at NATO very seriously; he was willing to have his name entered in the New Hampshire primary but would not himself take part in it and stipulated that he could not withdraw from his command until June of 1952. Cabot Lodge became his campaign manager; he, too, was convinced that Taft's isolationism was wrong for the country and that Taft could not be elected. Lodge himself would run against John F. Kennedy for re-election to the Senate in the autumn, but this became secondary to his unsparing planning and speaking for Ike's nomination.

Gov. Sherman Adams asked if I would speak in New Hampshire before their primary in March, and I was happy to do so. On my first appearance, the governor, who was to introduce me, took me to dinner in the nearby Treadway Inn, which we found swarming with Fred Waring's "Pennsylvanians."

The band leader was an ardent admirer of Ike and had volunteered to lead his orchestra at the meeting after I had spoken. Seeing the enthusiasm of those attractive boys and girls made me realize that the tide was beginning to turn toward Eisenhower. When Bob Taft came up to woo the New Hampshire voters, he was politely listened to, but the polls showed how strongly they favored the general, and from that time on the Taft forces knew they had a formidable opponent.

The 1952 convention in Chicago was a hot affair. The convention hall was stifling and although the Massachusetts delegation had only five delegates in favor of Taft, they never quit fighting for him. We had to have a roll call on everything. Chris Phillips was our secretary, and when the first vote came up on rules, he was busy hanging up signs for Ike and hadn't had time to finish polling the delegation. By the time Massachusetts was called, I had to say we passed. I got hell from the Eisenhower people because it was an important vote for them. I went to Chris and said: "You'll either be our secretary or else you'll be a spoiler. You can't do both." After that we got our votes on time. But the five Taft delegates led by New Bedford publisher Basil Brewer never quit.

One big fight at the convention came even before the delegates had been called to order by Joe Martin. The issue — and it was a very intense fight — was over the seating of the Texas delegation. The Republican State Convention in Texas, like others in southern states, had been rigged for Taft, but such strong-armed methods had been used that the delegates for Eisenhower were not given a fair chance.

As a result, two slates of delegates presented themselves in Chicago, one for Ike and the other for Taft. The Fair-Play Amendment, which was the first piece of business when the convention opened, stated that no delegate could vote until he had been properly seated, and when this was carried by a resounding majority in the roll call, it gave a great psychological lift to those delegates who were in favor of Eisenhower.

When the balloting for the nomination took place on July 12, General Eisenhower received 595 votes to 475 for Senator Taft. The delegates from Minnesota were among the first to change their vote to Eisenhower, and although Earl Warren, the favorite son from California, would not release his delegates, Ike's nomination went over the top on the first ballot.

The next day the vice president was to be nominated, and to my surprise and without consulting me ahead of time, Wayne Morse put my name in the ring. Before the nominations were made, Richard Nixon came over to where I was sitting with the Massachusetts delegation, and leaning down beside me, asked me what my thoughts were about the vice presidency. "Why," I said, "with Eisenhower registered in New York, I don't see how there could be two easterners on the ticket."

I got the impression that I was being sounded out, but I didn't take it seriously, and, with a little hemming and hawing, he left. If ever there had been an elusive aspiration to be the vice president, it vanished on that hot night.

As the campaign for Eisenhower went into high gear, the Republican National Committee sent me to the Pacific Coast, where I spoke — I don't know how many times — at Olympia, Seattle, Portland, and Eugene and worked my way down the length of California to San Diego. Ike was up the coast as I was going down, and occasionally our paths crossed and I had glimpses of Sherman Adams and of Robert Cutler, who with others were helping with Ike's speeches. There was the feeling of victory in the air.

I always remember Ike's long-distance telephone call to me at midnight on election day. He wanted to know how Lodge was doing against John Kennedy and how Herter had finished. Cabot had devoted most of his attention that year to Ike and he wasn't around Massachusetts as much as he should have been. He also made a television talk in Fall River that was ineffective because he hadn't prepared enough for it. Kennedy had been campaigning actively throughout the state. Until the final week of the campaign I was of the opinion that Cabot would prevail. But in the closing days I felt Kennedy had forged ahead. Basil Brewer, who was so strong for Taft, had hurt Lodge in Bristol County. So when Ike called me, I had to tell him that the news was not good and it looked like Cabot would be defeated by Kennedy. At least it wasn't a total loss in Massachusetts because Herter was going to squeeze in, and Eisenhower seemed pleased by that development. Cabot's defeat was partly because of his sacrifice for Ike, his 16-hour-a-day devotion to him, and also because Kennedy proved to be a most attractive and worthy opponent who had worked hard during his campaign.

VII. Overseeing the CIA and censuring McCarthy

I really think the most enjoyable event in my senatorial career was the opportunity to sit down with President Eisenhower in the Cabinet Room on Tuesday mornings when Congress was in session.

To these meetings the President invited the Republican leaders, four from the Senate and four from the House, to talk over pending legislation informally with himself and his advisers. We met at 8:30 and were welcomed with a cup of hot coffee. I secured a good seat by coming early for the first two meetings and standing right behind the chair I wanted, opposite the President, who sat at the center of the oval table. This shortly became my place for the eight years. I was to the left of Vice President Nixon, and Senator Bridges was on his right; Taft sat at the right of the President, and Joe Martin, the Speaker of the House, to the left.

The agenda was usually prepared by General Persons. Specialists were present to give their views on matters, and as we were a small group the give and take was often fast but never furious. Those meetings gave us the President's reactions to the issues before Congress, and I took many notes, which I kept hidden in my office, but since the discussions were off the record, I eventually tore them up. I wish now that I had not.

Simply stated, President Eisenhower's principal concerns were for the welfare of our people, for national security, and for peace in the world. It was clear that he disliked politics and that political criticism, either of the executive or of the various agencies, bothered him. I doubt that he was ever really at ease in his press conferences, for he had a quick temper, and a loaded question would cause him to flush and to stumble as he sought for the proper answer.

Although they never became close friends, Eisenhower and Taft had a good working relationship that was clearly in evidence during the Tuesday meetings. Ike had great respect for Taft. As for Joe McCarthy, Eisenhower had a very low opinion of the Wisconsin senator. I never had any conversations with Ike about McCarthy, but it was well known that he did not like him. Eisenhower was never overly friendly with Joe Martin, who was very political. Ike was so unpolitical that he had trouble dealing with politicians who were totally political.

The filling of subordinate positions, outside of Civil Service, with Republican appointees, Eisenhower gladly delegated to others. Once Joe Martin remarked plaintively in the hearing of us all, "I only asked the President for a postmaster in one of my little towns, a man well qualified in Civil Service, but I didn't get him because someone else had already been appointed." Of course, the President didn't really know anything about it; he had simply accepted a list that had been given him. Everyone laughed, and Ike remarked soothingly that "Congressman Martin must be listened to more carefully.".

This was just one small illustration of Ike's reliance on the chain of command. Some have termed this a weakness in his administration; but President Eisenhower's strength came from the confidence he gave to the people of our country. Certainly if he had not advocated the constitutional amendment limiting a president to two terms and had instead chosen to run for a third term, even after his illnesses, he would have been re-elected.

One of the first problems in the new administration was in having Charles Wilson, then the president of General Motors, confirmed as secretary of defense. Senator Taft, who was the majority leader in the Senate, called me up to say that Wilson wanted to talk to him. He said he could not go at that moment and that it was my job anyway as the senior Republican on the Armed Services Committee and would I please see what he wanted. I met with the secretary-to-be in his apartment in the Wardman Park Hotel; we talked for an hour or so, in the course of which he read me what he had prepared to give the press that afternoon, stating in substance that he would not give up his shares in General Motors in order to become secretary of defense. It was a very firm statement.

Wilson's confirmation was at the moment a top priority and I was called to the White House by General Persons at five p.m. on that same day. As I walked into his office, he said, "Wait a moment. Wilson is in with the boss now," and with that he departed for the President's office at the other end of the White House. In half an hour back he came. "It's all right," he said, "Wilson is going to sell all of his stock. It's all okay."

Some weeks later I happened to sit beside Mrs. Wilson at a dinner party. I said to her, "Mrs. Wilson, your husband changed his mind between twelve o'clock, when I left him, and five o'clock that afternoon. I think you must have persuaded him to do so."

She smiled. "Well," she said, "Charlie and I were talking that afternoon and I said, 'Charlie, we just can't go back to Detroit now!' "

"I knew you had something to do with it," I said. She laughed and that was the end of that conversation.

At one of our first Tuesday morning meetings the proposed budget for the Pentagon was submitted by Secretary Wilson. The Korean War was simmering down, with an armistice likely, and Bob Taft considered that a budget of $50 to $55 billion, which Wilson was proposing, was excessive. He intended to have it cut and in that emphatic way of his raised his voice, banged on the table, and declared, "It's too big!" There was dead silence.

As the chairman of the Armed Services Committee, I had gone over the figures, and I quietly remarked that the budget could be reduced by using the "unobligated funds," that is to say the money that had been previously voted but not spent. Using the unobligated funds, I said, would have the effect of reducing the new budget. Treasury Secretary Humphrey backed me up. The meeting ended shortly thereafter, and as we were leaving, as if to explain his forcefulness, Taft said to me, "I thought I had to make it absolutely clear that the time has come to cut down our defense budget." I agreed, but again pointed out that the sensible way was to use those unobligated balances, which were very extensive and had been carried along in several different categories. It should be understood that when the Korean War ended, the contracts for new aircraft or submarines were canceled, but the money that had been voted for them was still available for the Department of Defense without further authorization.

At those Tuesday meetings we all had the opportunity to speak. I wanted to be very sure of my subject before I raised any questions, and naturally mine concerned either appropriations or defense, and occasionally a matter affecting Massachusetts. On rare occasions I asked General Persons if a subject in which I was keenly interested could be put on the agenda, and he usually agreed to do so.

In his last month of office, President Eisenhower gave a farewell luncheon for those senior Republicans who had been meeting with him on Tuesday mornings in the cabinet room. After the coffee Ike began to present boxes of a dozen golf balls with his name on them, and he passed me by. "Don't I get one?" I asked, I guess a little plaintively. "Why, Lev, I didn't know you played golf!" he said with a smile as he handed me a box. It did not take me long to give them away, though I did keep two for myself; the one I gave to my caddy at Dedham he treasured, and just recently his father told me that he still had the ball, mounted in a little case.

* * *

My good health, which for so long I had taken for granted, began to creak a little in the fall of 1953, when I noticed a soreness in my right shoulder. That something was wrong occurred to me while cruising to North Haven on the *Fishhawk,* my mother's boat. I had had a bad cold and was so tired that we finally put in at Boothbay, where I went to see a doctor who had been recommended by a friend. I was anxious to try out a new inhaling gadget which the doctor had just installed in his office. I may have taken more penicillin than he intended; but in any event, not long afterward my right shoulder became very sore indeed. Dr. Streider, whom I consulted at New England Baptist Hospital in Boston, removed practically a full glass of liquid from my shoulder, but X-rays showed that there was still more in my lung, and he advised an operation that would involve removing part of a rib in order to tap my right lung.

They shaved and cleaned me up early in the morning of the operation, and finally the little attendant said, "Now, sir, will you please give me your teeth," to which I replied, "If I had to give you my teeth, it would require another major operation," which made him blush. The doctor wanted to ease me out with a sleeping pill before giving me the anesthesia, but I didn't like the idea and went on reading the newspaper. Streider seemed surprised at my lack of nervousness.

The publisher of the old *Boston Post* must have picked up a leak in the hospital, as we were careful to give out no news of my illness; he published a boxed story to the effect that I was in a serious condition and might not be able to continue my duties in the Senate. The first get-well flowers I received came from two persons interested in my job. Anyway, I fooled them, and when the Senate reconvened I was back in my seat as good as new.

* * *

The Republican majority of 1953-54 caused a reshuffling of committee chairmanships. Senator Bridges, the senior Republican, became chairman of Appropriations, and also the senior member of Armed Services. Since he could not preside over both, he left the chairmanship of the Armed Services Committee to me. We met regularly on Thursdays, and very shortly I had my first encounter with Adm. Hyman G. Rickover, a thin, wiry, short man, very determined and a dynamo. He was dedicated to the task of building better submarines, and this has been his objective from the very first Nautilus submarine to the Poseidon submarine of today.

I first met him at an Armed Services hearing, after the Naval Committee of Admirals, whose job it was to recommend promotions to the rank of admiral, had passed over his name. The Armed Services Committee wanted to know why, since this would mean retirement with the rank of captain — and Rickover did not want to retire. One of the admirals on the Naval Committee was testifying about promotions and being severely questioned as to why Rickover had been passed over. His answers were vague. Suddenly one of our staff whispered to me, "Secretary of the Navy Anderson is in the back room and would like to see you."

I stepped out and he came right to the point. Did I think that the committee would recommend promotion for Rickover even if the admirals' committee refused to do so? I replied that the chances were that it would. He left, I went back to the committee, no action was taken, and we adjourned with Rickover's fate undecided. The next morning I learned that overnight he had been made an admiral on orders of the secretary. That was in 1953, and he remained in active service until he was retired at the age of seventy-two.

Rickover was dedicated to the task of putting submarines together. The nuclear-power plant, the electronic system, the clean air required for long stays underwater, the modern navigation instruments, the communication system, the gates to be locked for emergencies, the mess and galley arrangements — all these facilities and the equipment for them had to be brought together from various subcontractors and installed, and a sub had to be launched on the day planned for its christening. Rickover was the one who had overall charge of the plant at New London, and he brooked no excuses. I can think of no other admiral who had such complete charge of the building of American warships. The Navy bureaucracy in Washington backed him as time went on; they really had no choice. He was also a loner. He was boss, he made the decisions, he saw that they were followed. He was not a popular officer, but he was a most efficient one at the job of building better and more efficient subs for the United States Navy.

Some years later, when I was inviting distinguished leaders of government to speak on a televison program for a Massachusetts station in 1960, I invited Rickover. He accepted. Then, as we were discussing what we should talk about, I asked him if he had any special questions I should ask. He said, "Ask me if I have any aide."

I asked, "Have you?"

"None," he replied forcibly and made a big zero with his thumb and forefinger. "Ask me if I have any publicity men?"

Again I asked, "Have you?"

Again he said loud and clear, "None," and made the same gesture with his fingers. "Ask me if I have a secretary." Again, the same reply and gesture. It was most effective when he did it on the air.

I came away with a deep respect for Rickover as a man and as an admiral with a record of accomplishment. Arrogant, if you will, but beneath was a deep confidence in his ability to accomplish the task for which he had fitted himself.

When each new submarine was ready to make its shakedown cruise, the admiral went to sea in it, and on a number of occasions he wrote me. I have perhaps a half dozen letters from him written from these different cruises many fathoms under the surface, and there is one in his handwriting, one for which I am particularly grateful:

U.S.S. Skipjack (SS (N) 585)
Care of Fleet Post Office
New York, New York

at sea, submerged
10 March, 1959

Dear Senator Saltonstall,

We are returning to New London, Conn., from sea trials of the U.S.S. Skipjack, our first nuclear-powered, streamlined, single-screw attack submarine. The ship successfully met all her trials, surfaced and submerged, and attained the highest speed ever achieved by any submarine. We were at sea for two days, during which the Skipjack steamed 192 nautical miles on the surface and 510 miles submerged.

I am writing you because I know how interested you are and how much help you have given to our program. I want you to know that your understanding and help are just as important in creating these revolutionary submarines as the efforts of the designers and builders.

Respectfully,
H. G. Rickover

The bane of any committee meeting is the speaker who insists on creating a diversion from the matter about which he is invited to testify. This happened a few years later when General Gruenther was speaking before Armed Services on the strength and stability of NATO. Sen. Herman Welker of Idaho was a confirmed isolationist, and his questions led the general further and further afield. 'I've got to get this back on the tracks,' I said to myself, and I asked if the senator would yield. He did, as courtesy required him to do. In my nervousness I put one hand on the table and the other on the knee of Sen. Margaret Chase Smith, who was sitting beside me, as I leaned forward to question Gruenther. Quietly but firmly she lifted my hand and with both of hers, put it back on my own knee. Her reproof, if you want to call it that, was seen by everyone, and the laughter that followed cleared the air. I did not have to ask anything further of the general. When I returned to my office after the session, I found on my desk a bottle of Scotch and with it this longhand note from Al Gruenther:

Supreme Headquarters
Allied Powers Europe
Office of the Supreme Commander
March 27

Dear Senator Saltonstall:

You were exceedingly helpful at the hearing, and I am most grateful to you.

The Washington spring is going to be a very cold one — so I hear — so please take a dose of this tonic as needed. It will fill the bill in a bit of a way, I hope.

I promise to keep that knee slapping episode in a top secret category, well almost top secret. I may tell a few "special" friends!!!

Sincerely,
Al Gruenther

I came to know and admire Adm. Chester Nimitz, who was the chief of naval operations at the Pentagon and prior to that commander of our forces in the far Pacific. He carried out his far-flung operations during World War II with skill and determination from his headquarters on Guam and later in Honolulu. We owe much to him for his leadership of the Navy in those activities in the Pacific that were ultimately concluded when General MacArthur signed the treaty of peace on the deck of the battleship *Missouri.*

In Washington we exchanged hospitalities with the Nimitzes, and I was always amused by Mrs. Nimitz, a former Massachusetts citizen whose sister had a place on the Cape and who feared that the beaches of Cape Cod would be ruined by what she called "the national shrine" that Senator Kennedy and I advocated. We had many pleasantries, and she added some rather cynical retorts concerning the future of the National Seashore Park. Her husband, the admiral, always remained discreetly silent during these skirmishes.

For Gen. Omar Bradley I had great admiration, and I considered him a friend. I recall that as chief of staff he testified in reply to a question of mine before the Korean War broke out that the total expenditures of the armed forces should not exceed $15 billion a year. They are now nearer $90 billion a year.

Never shall I forget the day that General Montgomery was present in Washington and was my guest at a luncheon with the Armed Services Committee in the Senate. He was not too easy to entertain. On that same evening General and Mrs. Bradley and Mrs. Houghton Metcalf dined with us at our house. Across Mrs. Metcalf I told General Bradley about our luncheon. Mrs. Metcalf said, "Who is Monty?" I replied, "Ask the gentleman on your right."

General Bradley replied: "I have never forgiven Monty for what he did to me in the Battle of the Bulge."

How quietly he said it, and how deeply he meant it! And yet, I remember how many thousands of men on both sides were involved in that battle and how much the event contributed to the winning of the war. General Bradley made it such a personal issue that I have never been able to forget it.

Alice and I were honored to be his guest in the commander in chief's quarters at Fort Myer on several occasions. Truly, General Bradley was a leader who meant much to the men under him in our armed forces and to every American citizen for what he did to build our success in World War II.

* * *

Allen Dulles, who had been responsible for some remarkable intelligence work in Switzerland during the war, became deputy director of the CIA under Gen. Bedell Smith in 1952, and director a year later, and by then I really felt that I knew quite a little about its activity.

Allen Dulles was more approachable than his austere older brother, John Foster Dulles. He had made a notable record in the OSS and from his listening post in Switzerland had played a decisive part in taking Italy out of the war. During his administration, the CIA became our counterpart to the British and French intelligence services; it worked in close collaboration with them and its purpose was to acquaint us of any dangers posed by Communists outside the United States (within our own borders the FBI was our watchdog). It was the responsibility of the CIA agents posted abroad to secure intelligence essential to our defense. From their incoming reports Allen Dulles collated each day a memorandum which he submitted to the White House, the secretary of state, and the secretary of defense.

In its operation the CIA had to work under cover. This was particularly true in the assistance which it gave to the leaders of those countries which were leaning toward us. With the approval of the National Security Council, such aid might take the form of cash or arms, but the details of such operations were not invariably disclosed to our legislative committee — perhaps we should have been more inquisitive. When the presence of the CIA was detected, as, for instance, in Guatemala, there would be a screech from Moscow, usually in *Pravda.*

Senator Russell created a "hush-hush" committee from members of the Armed Services and Appropriations committees. I believe there were five in all. The House had a similar hush-hush group, and we met informally. The annual appropriation for the CIA was then running at about $500-$600 million and was completely hidden in the Defense Department budget. Only a couple of times did we go to the CIA administration building to have this analyzed for us — so much for administration, so much for offices in the various countries overseas, so much for assisting those governments who were in trouble and in whom we had confidence.

Bob Amory, an old friend of mine in Massachusetts, was Allen Dulles's budget-control officer. He and his deputy would attend our hush-hush meetings to explain how the appropriations they needed came from various parts of the Army and Air budgets. With a few members of the Senate this concealment did not sit well. Eugene McCarthy, Mike Mansfield, and others offered resolutions to bring the CIA into the open, but they were defeated by Russell and Barkley, then the majority leader, and I tried to help on the Republican side. It was clear to me that if the activities and the budget of the CIA were made public, it would cease to be of value, and other countries would have the full knowledge of what we were doing.

Naturally we wanted to work with our counterparts in other countries: the English helped us, the French and the Italians were not so reliable. We trusted the English to clear their own agents, not always successfully — one thinks of that Englishman who worked here in America with us on the atomic bomb and fed his information to the Russians.

In 1954 when the Democrats regained their majority, Senator Russell became the chairman of our hush-hush committee, Lyndon Johnson and Harry Byrd being the other Democrats, and on the Republican side, Milton Young of North Dakota, and myself. We met regularly with representatives of the CIA who were frank in answering our questions, but we rarely knew enough to get at the whole truth. Dick Russell trusted me as we had worked together for years on problems of defense. When a new CIA project was in the air about which we wanted precise information, he would sometimes say, "Lev, you do it." I would call up Allen and he and his security man would stop at my house at the day's end or I would go to his home in Georgetown. We would have a little hospitality; I would ask him questions, and he would tell me what the CIA was up to, and the next morning I would pass on the information to Dick Russell in his office.

In this way he and I learned about the U-2 planes before one of them was shot down over Russia. Some years later the pilot who had been captured returned to Washington, and I remember how intently the Armed Services Committee listened as he testified before a crowded hearing. Those overflights told us how the Soviets were protecting Moscow from possible air attacks and, more immediately, of the building of missile sites in Cuba. There were, as I said, senators like Eugene McCarthy who wished to bring the CIA into the open, but

I can say categorically that the agency could never operate effectively with full publicity, and that I believed we needed it if we were to preserve our national security. Can anyone believe for a minute that the Soviet Union is about to recall its agents from Africa — or indeed those operating in the United States?

Although we knew about the U-2 and other CIA operations before they became public knowledge, we didn't know enough about them to ask perceptive questions. Our difficulty was in not knowing what to ask. Dulles and his CIA operatives always were very candid with us whenever we made inquiries here or on trips abroad. We did think the U-2 was impregnable and couldn't be shot down.

One time in the Senate the question of what the CIA was doing came up and Henry Dworshak of Idaho, a deep-voiced fellow on the Appropriations Committee, wanted to know what the CIA was doing, where the money was coming from, etc. After the committee meeting adjourned, I went up to him and said: "Henry, if you really want to know where that money is coming from, there's no reason why you shouldn't know." But then in his deep tones he said: "No, I don't really want to know." And that was the end of that.

We never had any conversations with President Truman about the CIA. Through Vice Admiral Hillenkoetter, he did have accurate information on the Chinese crossing the Yalu River during the Korean War. As I said earlier, Hillenkoetter had given notice every morning to the President, to the secretary of state and to the secretary of defense. The CIA had the correct information on that, and General MacArthur did not.

MacArthur, who was receiving bum information, was getting his data from General Willoughby and wasn't paying any attention to the CIA information. MacArthur didn't get along with the CIA.

The guiding principle behind the formation of the CIA was to retain ~~our intelligence~~ with relation to our national security in other countries. We had reached a point after World War II where we had very much in mind our own national security, and so we had to know what was going on in other parts of the world. The events leading up to Pearl Harbor had demonstrated the need for a more coordinated intelligence service.

Despite the fact that the act which created the CIA in 1947 appears to some people to be a blank check for the CIA to do anything it wants to do, I have always felt it was a good piece of legislation. We were putting our confidence in the CIA to give us intelligence that might not come through ordinary channels.

When the CIA was organized, J. Edgar Hoover was very careful not to have the CIA come into the United States, so to speak, and interfere or cross up the FBI. He was very clear on that and I think the language of the act spells out in specific terms that the CIA was not to conduct any particular intelligence in this country.

As I indicated before, we may not always have known enough to ask intelligent questions. But we always had cooperation from Dulles or Bedell Smith and John McCone. We knew everything we thought we ought to know.

The problem with the issue of over scrutiny of the CIA is one of loss of effectiveness if there is too much congressional oversight. The minute you open up this thing wide — I believe Defense Secretary James Schlesinger stated it well — the whole CIA is spoiled and ended. Because if you do, how much will England trust us? How much will France? And how much will Italy put its faith in our operations? We get much information from these countries and their intelligence systems. But that would come to a halt or at least be seriously scaled down if they felt they couldn't trust us. The CIA is a very important force for our national security. To have it ruined, to have its influence and authority in other section of the world and its ability to get good information from these areas reduced, would be very damaging to our own security. That would be a sorry development.

Publicity from the Ellsberg case and the Watergate investigation has generated the impetus for the push for more scrutiny of the CIA. I do hope that the reports that the agency has been responsible for looking into the private lives of many of our citizens have been exaggerated. I don't know because I am not down there now. But there's no question that such abuses, if they exist, must stop. It is difficult to draw the line between morality and strategy. Each case has to be judged separately. You cannot say: "that is a covert operation and this is not a covert operation." I believe you have to leave this decision to those in authority, and I firmly believe that as a whole we have had very responsible leaders in the CIA command.

As a former member of the hush-hush committee on the CIA, I don't pretend to convey the idea that I knew everything that was going on. I didn't. That's the weakness of members of Congress. But I can say that on a trip abroad in the mid-fifties, every CIA agent in every city and every country I visited had been given instructions from Dulles to answer all questions that I asked and to give me any information they felt was pertinent. With the exception of Israel, I saw every CIA agent in the countries I visited. The agent in Tel Aviv was out of the country at the time. All the others answered every question I asked.

I don't think any of us on the hush-hush committee ever thought that the CIA would get as big as it obviously is today. By the time I retired, I knew we had a great many operatives in many nations of the world, in Russia and in other Iron Curtain countries. And I was aware that we were losing some of these men every year. Some of them were captured and some just disappeared.

If the CIA has spied on Americans, that is a sad turn of events. A very sad situation. But I do hope that out of all of this publicity and scrutiny of the CIA, the agency's authority for protecting the national security of this nation won't be lost.

We must be able to deal effectively and cooperatively with the intelligence network of England and with the intelligence system of France and all of our other friends throughout the world. We have to trust them and they must be able to trust us and our men in the CIA.

* * *

In 1954 it became apparent to all of us on the Armed Services Committee that either the academies at West Point or Annapolis had to be enlarged or a new academy for training officers in the Air Force must be established. Actually the young officers themselves forced this decision, as each year 25 percent of those graduating from the point volunteered for service in the Air Force. Our committee was unanimous in believing that we needed a separate academy for the airmen. But where, and how much would it cost?

Harold Talbot, Air Force secretary, was asked to designate a commission of five members who were to select the site. If the commission was unanimous, the secretary was obliged to accept its choice; if it were not, he could choose one of the top three. The commission examined over 700 sites and selected three, and the secretary made the final choice of the location near Colorado Springs. Of course, there was some disappointment among Senate members who favored their own states, but no attempt was made to alter the decision.

But a big headache did arise over the architecture, and especially that of the chapel. In the ensuing argument, everyone became his own architect. Although no quotas were set, the academy was expected to have about 75 percent Protestants, 20 percent Catholics, and 5 percent Jews. I was just as astounded as the other senators and congressmen who studied the first sketches. Even with revisions, the projections gave a new look to the churches I was used to seeing in New England. The senators shook their heads, and once more the plans were modified. Finally a Catholic chapel seating 500 and a Jewish synagogue for 100 occupied the lower level, and above was the Protestant chapel with a capacity for 900 and a large choir. I made a point of visiting the chapel when I inspected the academy some years later, and after my first look — still with a little amazement — I felt we could be proud of it as a church for universal worship. Incidentally, the furniture and the decorations were provided from private subscriptions.

The ultimate cost of the Air Force Academy was about $150 million, and in keeping with the Air Force desire, it is a self-contained unit for the training of our youngest service. I was happy to be chairman of the Armed Services Committee when it became a reality.

* * *

I have referred to a Southern demagogue, Sen. Theodore Bilbo of Mississippi. It was our misfortune to be plagued in the early 1950s by a more aggressive demagogue from Wisconsin, Sen. Joseph McCarthy. He won his seat after a bitter primary battle against Sen. Robert LaFollette, and he had served with some competence as Stassen's floor manager at the national convention of 1948. He was ambitious, egotistical, and determined to be of influence, and he seized the opportunity to lambaste the Democrats for being soft on communism.

In February, 1950, in a speech before the Women's Republican Club of Wheeling, W. Va., he brandished what he said was a list of 205 persons in the State Department who were "members of the Communist Party." He spoke without documentation, and for a time was encouraged by his Republican seniors in the Senate. This was a stick too good not to use. "Whether Senator McCarthy has legal evidence," said Senator Taft, "whether he has overstated or understated his case, is of lesser importance. The question is whether the Communist influence in the State Department still exists."

McCarthy's attack came a month after Alger Hiss had been convicted of perjury; the British shortly announced that their atomic physicist, Dr. Klaus Fuchs, had confessed to spying, and in the United States the Rosenbergs were found guilty of espionage. McCarthy continued to make wild allegations in his public talks as well as on the floor of the Senate. I remember his saying to me in the Senate dining room one day, "Lev, I'm going to make a speech this afternoon, and I hope you'll listen to it." I told him I would be there, and I was. But his talk turned into such a tirade that I returned to my office with a feeling of disgust. The attacks spread, to the Army, to those of the left wing in radio and Hollywood, and to scientists as highly trained as Dr. J. Robert Oppenheimer.

In September of 1950, when the name of Gen. George Marshall came before the Senate for confirmation as secretary of defense, the vituperations hurled at him by Senators Welker and Jenner were revolting. I was absent at the time, at home in bed with a bad cold. As a ranking member of Armed Services, I was scheduled to be heard in support of the general, and when I learned that my turn would come directly after Senator Jenner had delivered what was expected to be a bitter attack, I put on my clothes and drove to the Senate, which was then meeting in the old Supreme Court room. From longhand notes I had written at home, I spoke as follows:

> Mr. President, I wish I had the words and the voice to express how strongly I disagree with many of the statements which have just been made by my colleague the Senator from Indiana (Mr. Jenner). If there is any man in America who is decent and clean it is General George C. Marshall. If there is any man whose public life has been above censure, and whose public actions have been for the public interest, during my span in public life, it is George C. Marshall. Whether we disagree with some of his judgments or not — and I do — I believe from the bottom of my heart they were made for the best interests of our country, regardless of himself.
>
> I wish I had the vocabulary to answer the statement that General Marshall's life "is a lie," because if there ever was a life spent in the interest of our country, a life that is not a lie, it is the life of George C. Marshall.
>
> Mr. President, I shall vote for the bill which will permit one man, General Marshall, to hold temporarily the office of secretary of defense even though he has been an officer of our armed forces within ten years. . . .
>
> I am against military control of our defense establishment. I want it to be in the hands of a civilian. We argued that point at length in committee when we considered the

Unification Act. But the general has now been a civilian for five years. He has held the highest civilian office in the land, with the exception of the President. Because he has held the office of secretary of state, it can be said truly to have emphasized his change to a civilian status, and thus to have reduced the waiting period of ten years.

But the point we must keep actively before us is that General Marshall is the President's choice to fill a most difficult assignment in his cabinet in a critical moment in the nation's affairs. Whether or not, Mr. President, you or I would have chosen General Marshall had we the responsibility is not the question. The President has the responsibility, and he has chosen the general. . . .

It has been argued that General Marshall, first as special ambassador to China and later as secretary of state, has taken positions that are not to the country's best interests today. When he was ambassador, he was given a special mission to perform. He tried to fulfill it. That effort undoubtedly influenced his point of view when he assumed the office of secretary of state. That is only human. Maybe it still does color his judgment with respect to China. I do not know his present views on the problems of that great country. But I do know that he is sufficiently cool and reasoning to change his point of view, and I am confident that he is sufficiently unprejudiced to form new judgments if his earlier ones have proved unwise.

Furthermore, he has been long enough in government service and is wise enough to get the judgment of those who have been intimately connected with recent events. He can, and, I am confident, will make new decisions on the new facts as given to him. His long experience and his ability to grasp a problem quickly give him a unique chance to adopt a course that will meet the needs of national defense. Perhaps in these ways he is more ideally suited for the office than any other man the President could have chosen. . . .

The vote of confirmation came later that day. I, of course, voted for General Marshall, and when Bob Taft opposed him I felt dismayed. Soon after the general had been confirmed by a large majority, I received from him — he was then serving as president of the Red Cross — a letter which I treasure:

THE AMERICAN NATIONAL RED CROSS
NATIONAL HEADQUARTERS
Washington, D.C.

Office of the President September 23,1950

Dear Senator:

I have just this moment received a letter from [Adm.] Dick Byrd and was very gratified to learn that you had left your sick bed to go to Capitol Hill to support my nomination. You have been very kind and gracious and I am most appreciative.

I do hope that by this time you have been able to rid yourself of whatever physical disturbance you had.

Mrs. Marshall joins me in warm regards to Mrs. Saltonstall and yourself.

Faithfully yours,
George C. Marshall

Honorable Leverett Saltonstall
United States Senate
Washington, D.C.

After listening to McCarthy's speeches for quite a while, Sen. Ralph Flanders of Vermont filed a resolution to have the Senate censure McCarthy on the grounds that his conduct and remarks were injurious to the Senate and derogatory to its influence as a responsible body of the government. Senator Fulbright of Arkansas joined Flanders in seeking the censure. It is hard for an ordinary citizen now to realize the abuses to which Flanders was exposed, abuses which caused him to change the number of his telephone almost daily and even to worry about the safety of Mrs. Flanders in their home in Washington.

Eventually the Senate appointed a committee headed by Sen. Arthur Watkins of Utah to determine whether the evidence warranted a censure of Senator McCarthy. Senator Ives of New York and I were both up for re-election in 1954, and we each decided that we would await the report of the committee before stating our position. By now McCarthy had accused Harvard University of being a hotbed of communism and President Pusey of condoning the utterances of a couple of radical instructors. Pusey replied with a stout affirmation of Harvard's faith in academic freedom, in which he was supported by the corporation and a majority of the alumni.

But McCarthy had his supporters, many of them in Massachusetts, and I caught hell from both sides. Mrs. Dwight Morrow, who was one of my ardent friends shook her finger at me for not coming out for censure; and when I spoke to General Electric Company workers in Pittsfield, who were as strongly for McCarthy as were the Boston Irish, I caught hell from them for not coming out in opposition to the censure.

In the thirty-six televised hearings before the Senate committee, Senator McCarthy met his match in the repeated exchanges with the Boston lawyer Joseph Welch. Welch in his quiet way exposed the extent of McCarthy's exaggeration and the damage he inflicted with his charges of "guilt by association." Public opinion began to swing against the senator, and after the election in November of 1954, the Watkins Report recommended that McCarthy be censured by the Senate. The Republicans were split, and I was surprised when the three top Republicans, Taft, Bridges and Knowland, opposed censure, while Homer Ferguson of Michigan, Margaret Chase Smith, and I were among the majority who voted for it. After this vote McCarthy's influence dwindled, he lost his power, and before long became mortally ill. But he had been the agent of a very serious and damaging division in the nation; he had driven some good men from office, men who were later exonerated, but only after years of suffering, and he had created an atmosphere of fear, especially in the Department of State, which lingered on long after his death.

The McCarthy era was a very difficult time for Republicans. I was up for re-election, as I said, and I had an awful time of it. The people were divided on McCarthy. I took a very sound position on the McCarthy issue, but it was greatly misunderstood. I felt that while a committee of honorable senators was sitting to decide whether to censure McCarthy, I should make no judgment until they returned a decision and recommendation based on the evidence presented to them. It was similar to a jury being out and I still believe it was a very moral position. But I caught a lot of flak because of it, particularly, as I said, from Mrs. Morrow, who was acting president of Smith College at the time.

I never knew why Taft, Bridges and Knowland were supportive of McCarthy in the censure vote. They never told me. Taft probably felt the issue of freedom of speech was involved. In addition, his own personal feelings must have motivated him. The Republicans never became involved in any discussions about the morality of McCarthy's actions, which certainly raised some serious questions. Most politicians who were

Saltonstall talks with Mrs. Eleanor Roosevelt in 1960.

Susan Saltonstall takes her father for a ride around the Dover farm.

The Saltonstalls and William and Susan go for sleigh rides at Dover in 1964.

Saltonstall tastes the frosting of a cake at dedication of Boston's Saltonstall Building in 1969 with Mass. Gov. Francis Sargent.

Tipping his hat during St. Patrick's Day parade in South Boston in 1965.

from areas where McCarthy had some following were reluctant and even too nervous to talk much about the controversy. Sen. Stennis was very much against McCarthy. I always had great confidence in and respect for Stennis.

When he was campaigning for the presidency in 1952, General Eisenhower was restrained by his advisers from defending General Marshall when he spoke in Milwaukee. I know that Ike was made indignant by this caution and regretted that he had accepted it. The McCarthy scourge was nothing to be proud of. In the long run it may have established one distinction between a loyal citizen and a security risk. A man could be loyal to the country and yet be a security risk because of his reckless talk or writing; in which case he could be transferred from a position of trust to one involving less responsibility. But this was never an easy distinction to make, and at the time, men of proven trust and great ability like Dr. Oppenheimer and John Patton Davies of the State Department were smirched in the overemotional hunt for Communists.

* * *

In 1954, Senator Ferguson of Michigan was having a hard fight on his hands for re-election, and, wishing to help him, Bob Taft came to me to suggest that I let Homer have the prestige of being the Republican whip. It was certainly unusual to request a senator to step down from a post he had held for some time. But Ferguson was a friend of mine, so after thinking the matter over, I told Taft that I would agree to do so after the year was up. I heard some time later from Taft's assistant that Bob himself had been surprised by my acquiescence — he said he had never before heard of a politician being willing to relinquish an office he valued. However, Taft died before the matter came to a test. Senator Ferguson was defeated and was later appointed ambassador to the Philippines.

For all of our differences, Bob Taft and I had, I believe, a mutual respect for each other, and in time he came to trust me. I knew he did not approve of my voting to support some of President Truman's nominations for office, but I felt that the President was entitled to have the men he wanted, unless, as in the case of Edwin Pauley, there was a good and sufficient reason why he should not be confirmed.

But certainly one of the most difficult decisions that I made very early in my Senate career was when I supported President Truman's nomination of Henry Wallace to be secretary of commerce. My vote created a tie, so that Wallace was confirmed over the strenuous objections of Senator Taft and most Republicans. Wallace had made an unsuccessful run for the presidency as a progressive at a time when his views had turned to the left. But I voted for him on the assumption that he could do less harm if he were in the cabinet of government, and also because I felt that the President should have the man he wanted. In this decision, I was vindicated, for the differences between Wallace and the President soon became so sharp that Wallace was asked to resign, and did so.

We all knew that Senator Taft was unwell as he grew thin and was no longer his customary aggressive self on the Senate floor or in committee. When he went to a New York hospital he did it without any publicity and under an assumed name. In accord with his personal philosophy, he designated Senator Knowland of California to be in charge of Republican policies. Then, shortly before his death in July, 1953, we senators knew that he did not have long to live and there was sadness on both sides of the aisle.

In Bob Taft, the Senate and the country lost one of the most conscientious, hard-working senators of the 20th Century. He spoke not only for Ohio but for the entire Midwest and as a dedicated patriot. In his devoted wife, Martha, he had an intelligent partner who helped him in many ways until the stroke which resulted in her death. I did not support his candidacy for the presidency in 1940, 1948, or 1952 because I felt that he could not get the support of Massachusetts and most of New England. Whether or not he would have made an effective President had he been elected is something that we can always debate, for he was an isolationist and was reluctant to give foreign aid through the Marshall Plan or other assistance, not only to Europe but to the Far East.

Taft was one of the few senators ever to be given a memorial service in the rotunda of the Capitol; there was an honor guard, and President Eisenhower, the diplomatic corps, and cabinet members attended. The eulogies — well deserved for a man who had given so much for his country — were delivered for the Senate by William Knowland and Taft's colleague from Ohio, Sen. John Bricker. Later, Taft's friends raised funds for a tower to be placed on the Hill near the Capitol with chimes to tell the hours, and I, despite our differences, was glad to join with his friends in this final tribute.

* * *

From time to time senators are sent on trips to freshen

their knowledge of government activities far from Washington. In the fall of 1953 I was one of three members of the Armed Services Committee appointed to visit Alaska. My companions were the quick-witted Wayne Morse of Oregon and the more reticent Sen. Lester Hunt of Wyoming. We flew from Washington in FDR's famous plane the *Sacred Cow,* with its elevator, which was a most comfortable way to travel, and after our arrival at Anchorage were the guests of the armed forces. Our objective was to examine the military bases, those in existence and those that were being constructed, and to estimate the possibility of defense against invasion.

Before the days of flying, transportation to Alaska was by ship, and the only railroad ran from Seward, the main seaport, north to Whittier and then to Anchorage. This short line depended on many timber trestles, spanning deep canyons, and it was dangerous and expensive to operate. We made the trip in reverse, from Anchorage to Seward; it took the better part of a day and there were times when my hair stood on end as I looked at the rocky torrents below us. The whole thing was obsolete; the Whittier terminal was in the hands of a caretaker, the harbor at Seward was no longer used, and I recommended that the line be abandoned.

Our next stop was Nome, and General Kepner insisted that we fly in his personal plane with pilots who knew the terrain. It was bumpy as we came into Nome in a rainstorm with a heavy wind blowing the sea up the narrow channel that enters the city. I thought the water felt salty when I washed my face and hands in our quarters, and I soon learned that when the wind blew strongly from the west, the authorities had to shut off the fresh water supply and the drains, as the sewage was all blown back into the city channel instead of out to sea, a peculiar arrangement for one from old New England, where everything went down to the sea rather than having the sea back up the wrong way. Senator Morse at that time was an independent, Hunt a Democrat, and I a Republican, and as I recall the many meetings — one was organized for us by the Democrats, and others by the Republicans in Anchorage and in Fairbanks — politics was forgotten as we listened to the natives express their anxiety about the strength of their defenses in case of an invasion. I did not believe that there was any likelihood, but it was recognized by all of us that if the Russians did gain a foothold in Alaska, it would make the defense of the Northwest very difficult and would expose its industries to bombing.

We flew through ugly weather to Fairbanks, and it was a relief to get on solid ground, where our pilot gave us a certificate that we had flown over the Arctic Circle. Here we were briefed on the Ladd and Eiels Airports and their needs; both of them seemed to me excellent, as did the University of Alaska, which I visited on my own. With my long experience as an overseer at Harvard, I had a yardstick with which to measure, and in my talk with the president I was favorably surprised by the educational opportunities that were available in this remote but sizable campus.

Back in the air once more, on our way to Juneau, we flew over Whitehorse and Haines, high above a mountain range and a glacier, and for the only time in my life I was at the controls, for about thirteen mintes; it seemed longer than that and I was very relieved to have the pilot take over. Dinner that evening was in the executive mansion, where we were the guests of Gov. Ernest Gruening and where we met the admiral of the Coast Guard and staff officers; they gave us their version of the defense of Alaska in much more pessimistic terms than what we had received from members of the Air Force.

The probabilities of statehood were then in everyone's mind, but what struck me was that approximately 96 percent of Alaska was owned by the federal government. This was important in my thinking, for if statehood were granted to Alaska, the pressure for financial aid from the federal government would be considerably larger than if it were to continue as a territory. So, as you might say, I came home a skeptic: I did not feel that we had anything like an adequate defense for this huge, valuable, unsettled territory, and I questioned if it were yet ready to become a state. This, of course, was almost twenty-five years ago.

One picture lingers in my mind. I remember standing on the shore at Nome and looking westward to the islands that are populated by the Eskimos and under the religious guidance of a Roman Catholic priest. From those islands on a clear day one can see Siberia. I am not a warmonger, but this was a sobering reminder of the closeness of that great Communist country, and I am sure it had something of the same effect on my companions.

The flight home in the *Sacred Cow* was uneventful. We dropped off Senator Morse in Portland and Senator Hunt in Casper, and before the pilots could set their course for Washington, I persuaded them that it would not be much out of their way to fly me to Boston. So there I sat, in President Roosevelt's comfortable chair near the elevator all through a lovely autumn afternoon, listening to various football games below, and at last picking up the Harvard score after we had crossed over the Appalachians.

* * *

Alice and I went on a more far-reaching trip in the autumn of 1955, when I was the lone Republican on a Senate committee to visit our overseas defense establishments and examine the alliances on which they were based. I was included because of my position on the Appropriations and Armed Services Committees and my consistent interest in foreign aid. The Democrats were Sen. Dennis Chavez of New Mexico, our chairman, who planned the itinerary; and Senators John McClellan of Arkansas and Harley Kilgore of West Virginia, and my good friend John Stennis of Mississippi.

Alice and I crossed the Atlantic ahead of the committee to spend a few days with the Conants, Jim then being the U.S. high commissioner in West Germany. They met us at the Berlin Airport, which in 1948 had become our vantage point when the Russians imposed the blockade that led to our airlift, and that afternoon in the high commissioner's car with the American flag flying on the fender, we drove into the Russian zone in East Berlin. There we sampled some of the stores, which seemed very shoddy in contrast to those we had seen in the American sector. That evening we enjoyed the performance in the beautifully restored opera house, where Conant was warmly greeted as we took our places in what in other times would have been the royal box. Then with our luggage we were driven to the railroad station and shown into a most comfortable compartment in the high commissioner's swank train. We felt we were traveling in state, had breakfast with the Conants the next morning in their special dining car, and enjoyed the glorious scenery along the Rhine on our way to Bonn.

It was from Jim that I first learned of President Eisenhower's heart attack in Denver, and I was so worried that I telephoned my office in Washington to ask if they thought I should return. But I was assured that the President was making a good recovery and told to continue our trip.

We joined the committee in Bremen and flew with them to London, where Ambassador and Mrs. Winthrop W. Aldrich entertained us at a beautiful dinner in the new embassy, formerly the home of Barbara Hutton, and invited Alice and me to spend the night in one of their comfortable guest rooms. As I mentioned earlier, Allen Dulles had alerted the CIA agents in the countries I was to visit to provide me with information that would clarify my understanding of their missions. Accordingly, I had a thorough briefing in London before we flew on to Scotland for a look at the airfields, both the British and our own in that northern area.

Dublin was our next stop; we had no military bases there, but our ambassador, Bob Taft's son, William Howard Taft III, described the economic problems of Eire, Ulster at that time not being in eruption. In the afternoon Alice and I rented a car and drove out to Bective in County Meath, to meet old friends with whom we had hunted in the U.S. before the war.

At each stop protocol was observed. Senator Chavez would lead us off the plane, and we would file after him according to our seniority as he presented us to the American ambassdor and his aides. John Stennis came at the end of the line and was always insistent that I precede him.

Paris was a one-night stand, but in Rome the committee had several conferences with Ambassadors Clare Booth Luce, who told us with a smile of how distracting it was to play host to some 400 congressmen who were descending on the embassy shortly. She knew that I was to have a meeting with our CIA agent and was very firm that the three of us would have tea in her living room. The Italian Communists were then making a strong bid for power, and by her questioning it was clear that Mrs. Luce knew a good deal of what the CIA was doing and wished to be sure that I had no private information.

From Rome we flew to Naples, passing over Mt. Vesuvius and the abbey of Monte Cassino, which our troops had captured at such bitter cost in 1944. Admiral Fechtler and his staff showed us the naval setup in Naples before we embarked on our flight to Istanbul. Over the Gulf of Corinth we were caught in a thunderstorm, and our plane was struck by lightning, the flash scorching the roof of the cabin. One of our engines stopped and I remember Alice saying, "Something awful has happened!" She seemed composed, but not I, for I was being airsick into a ripped paper carton that had no bottom.

It was an enormous relief to us all when in the howling rainstorm the pilot made an emergency landing in Athens. A glass of brandy at the airport and another at the hotel brought me back to life. Of course, we were not expected in the hotel that put us up; it was so new that the walls still smelled of fresh plaster. When the weather cleared we resumed our journey to Istanbul, and there we left our wives to shop and see the sights while we senators flew on to the Turkish capital of Ankara, where we lunched with the ambassador and heard his off-the-record account of the Greece-Turkey antagonism in Cypress. It was an acute problem even in 1955. On our return to Istanbul we passed over several air bases, our own and the Turkish, with the planes on the ground. The next day the lot of us were given an enjoyable excursion on a Navy launch up the Strait of the Dardanelles until we reached the submarine nets at the mouth of the Black Sea. The landscape, the large mansions, and the beautiful lawns reaching down to the water are a memory that will always be with me.

Then we were confronted with the troubles in the Middle East. In Beirut, we learned a lot about the flare-ups between the Israelis and the Arabs and of Eric Johnson's plan for the development of the Jordan River. In Damascus Alice and I visited the Street Called Straight, with camels going in one direction and ourselves in the embassy car creeping along in the opposite, through the narrow way. In Jordan we visited the refugee camps so crowded with the Palestinian refugees, and in Jerusalem we walked along the Wailing Wall and carried our bags through No Man's Land to the Israeli side and drove on to Tel Aviv, a distance of seventy-five miles, on a modern highway whose width and traffic lights reminded me of what we had at home. And in Tel Aviv we heard some very frank talk from the head of the military and his staff.

Egypt would not permit a plane from Israel to land, so to reach Cairo we had to retrace our way to Adana, where we had stopped en route to Jordan, and make a fresh takeoff. Ambassador Henry A. Byroade had arranged for us to pay a courtesy call on Nasser, and an attractive, self-assured person he seemed to be. I remember that he had three telephones on his desk, two of which he paid no attention to, but when the third rang, he answered promptly with the single word, "Nien." He probably knew of our visit to Israel, and we knew that Egypt at this time was receiving aid from the Russians, but we skirted those touchy subjects.

On our way out, we passed a small dwarf shaking a tambourine into which we threw a few coins. I didn't have anything less than a five-dollar bill, which I wasn't going to put in, so I borrowed some coins from Stennis. He never would let me pay him back and said he wanted to hold it over me that I owed him some money. I think it was ten or fifteen cents.

That was the end of the trip for the rest of the party, and they went home via Rome, but my wife and I were going around the world in the other direction.

The next day the Paris edition of the *New York Times* came out with an editorial saying that if we didn't know better than to support the Egyptian army, we should be brought home. I knew it would be all right with the other congressmen, so I held a press conference to explain that we didn't know that the dwarf was collecting the coins for any cause. I pooh-poohed the whole thing and told the *Times* man that the dwarf reminded me of the little man that had been put in J.P. Morgan's lap at a congressional hearing. That ended the incident.

The CIA agent in Cairo filled me in on everything I had to know about Egypt. That has been so long ago that I don't remember the specifics, but I do recall that I received a complete briefing.

Alice and I then continued on our journey to the Far East, accompanied by Francis Hewitt, a staff member of Appropriations who took care of our reservations and who picked up quite a bit of information on his own. Our first stop was Karachi, where we landed in a torrid afternoon and where, since I had not been briefed about our aid to Pakistan, I was given a difficult time in the questioning. New Delhi was more pleasurable, for there I resumed my friendship with John Sherman Cooper, the former senator from Kentucky and now our ambassador. He loaned us his car to see the Taj Mahal by moonlight and by sunrise. What a dusty ride, and what an unforgettable sight of an historic spot! The next night we said good-bye to the Coopers and drove around the cows asleep in the streets of the capital to the plane that carried us via Calcutta to Bangkok.

Bangkok, Saigon, Laos, Hong Kong, Taipei, Manila, Guam, Honolulu — places where Alice and I had never dreamed of visiting — always on the run, a bit of red carpet, welcoming hands, and never enough time to see all we wanted; and then home, in fifty-six days from our takeoff.

Much was made of us in Taipei. We were given a dinner by the Harvard graduates in Taiwan; there must have been twenty-five of them, and the subject they kept harping on was, "When we go back to the Mainland."

My talks with Chiang Kai-shek were carried on through an interpreter, although I was perfectly sure that the generalissimo understood every word I said in English. He and Madame Chiang received us in their town residence, where there were plenty of guards in evidence. She was very beautiful — and she knew it, too — and artful in the way she kept filling my glass with Fu-Ki at the same time that she was filling her own with tea. Alice and I had entertained her at Dover on one of her visits to her alma mater, Wellesley, and she had that in mind when she said in parting, "Remember, Senator, I am almost a constituent of yours."

At Manila we were the guests of Homer Ferguson, then ambassador to the Philippines and earlier my associate in the Senate. Homer proved to be a good guide and generous host. We had a round of golf together to loosen me up and then early one morning, the ambassador and I flew by helicopter to Sangley Point, the naval headquarters, and after touring the base went on by seaplane to Subic Bay, where our warships were repaired and where I learned of the difficulties of working out the boundaries with the nearby township. From Subic Bay an Air Force plane took us to Clark Field, where we inspected that large base and the important hospital located there.

The high point was a luncheon given for us by President Magsaysay in his palace. We came by automobile and arrived just as our admiral was landing from his launch. One of the best pictures I have of Mrs. Saltonstall was taken as the President was leading her on his arm into lunch. Magsaysay was a man to remember, a man of the people who had risen from a humble background and by his courage had united the Philippines and suppressed the rebels. They told me the story of how he had gone to meet a rebel leader up in the hills, where there had been a plan to assassinate him. But Magsaysay escaped, in part because the assassin's car broke down and he did not arrive in time. Magsaysay was a leader in the best sense of the word; he was, if you like, a prime example of democracy, which we had helped to install in the islands, and we were much taken with him. It saddened me when I learned later of his death in a plane crash.

Guam had a special meaning for both of us, and here I am afraid we disappointed the wife of the admiral in residence, who had arranged a ladies' breakfast in honor of Alice. But I think they forgave us when I explained that during our short time ashore, I dearly wanted to fly Alice to the spot where our son Peter was killed.

VIII. Working with John F. Kennedy

I had a warm friendship with John F. Kennedy despite the difference in our ages. It used to make me smile to think that at Harvard he was in the class behind my eldest son. He always called me "Senator," even when he was President, and I called him John — not Jack as he was known to his friends and neighbors — and, of course, "Mr. President." I was told by someone that the only other person who called him John was his mother. If this is so, I was in good company.

We first met as members of a special committee, of which I was chairman, appointed by President Conant to recommend an appropriate memorial for the Harvard men lost in World War II. It was difficult to know what to do; Memorial Hall, which commemorated those killed in the Civil War, had been a white elephant. So instead of a new auditorium or a university theater, the corporation finally proposed — and we approved — a tablet holding all of the names, including those few in the German forces, to be placed on the wall of the chapel. I have often looked at that beautiful plaque, as I daresay John had; it lists his older brother, Joseph P. Kennedy Jr., Class of 1940, whose plane was lost in the English Channel, and my son Peter, Class of 1943.

When John was elected to the Senate in 1952, I escorted him down the aisle and presented him to Vice President Alben Barkley to be sworn in.

The relations between a senior senator and a junior are not always helpful, especially if they belong to different parties. I remembered the responsibility that Senator Walsh had entrusted to me in Naval Affairs, and out of my liking for John I wanted to be even more helpful to him. Very early he came to me with the proposal that we bring together the twelve New England senators for monthly meetings, he and I to be the hosts of the kickoff luncheon. It was a good idea, for we did have problems in common — flood control on the Connecticut River, depollution of the Merrimack, the enlargement of local airports as rail transportation thinned out, and the location of the first nuclear-power plant in the Northeast. We followed protocol and invited Senator Bridges to preside; an agenda was prepared for each meeting, and to speed things up the hour was soon shifted to 8:30 in the morning, when we discussed matters over coffee and doughnuts or, in Senator Flanders's office, flapjacks and maple syrup.

Kennedy and I were friends and never had any serious disagreement in the Senate. Often he would come over to me on the floor and ask me how I was going to vote on a particular issue. The only major difference we ever had came when he was preparing to run for the presidency and became the first New England senator to vote in favor of the St. Lawrence Seaway. He never told me that he voted that way because he needed the Midwest vote, but I felt this was the situation.

And one time he opposed a nomination I had made for postmaster of Worcester County. It was during the Eisenhower years. The usual practice was for the Republican State Committee in Massachusetts to pick a nominee for such a post and forward the name to me. The late Ralph Bonnell was national committeeman, and he submitted three names to the state committee for consideration. One of them was a member of the committee from Worcester and he broke a tie vote in committee and voted for himself. There was quite a furor over the appointment. I can't remember his name but I do recall that I didn't think him especially fitted. Anyway, he left the postmaster's job not long afterwards.

When the Senate voted to censure Sen. Joe McCarthy, Kennedy had been hospitalized with a serious back ailment and was the only senator who was not recorded. He had sustained the injury when the PT boat he commanded in the South Pacific was sunk during World War II. The ailment remained with him throughout his life and required frequent treatment.

I never talked with Kennedy about his feelings on McCarthy or the fact that his aide, Ted Sorensen, never had him recorded one way or the other on the controversial issue. In his book about the late President, Sorensen said he felt that he could not have Kennedy recorded on such an issue because Kennedy was absent throughout the censure debate. Had he been present, Kennedy would have voted for censure, Sorensen said. But due process and civil liberties prevented Sorensen from recording Kennedy's vote, the senator's aide said. The issue plagued Kennedy for years because he was accused of ducking on the vote.

Kennedy's illness plagued him severely during the next two years and he had to undergo critical back surgery which almost cost him his life; he was even given Last Rites. During his subsequent convalescence, he wrote his famous book, *Profiles In Courage.*

While he was recovering, I handled many bills concerning Massachusetts in which I knew he would be interested. I would first consult with Sorensen, before acting for the two of us. During this period I had only one disagreement with Sorensen and I have to say with a smile that Ted was quite disagreeable to me.

One time I left Kennedy's name off a piece of legislation because I thought it would be an unpopular position for him to take. But Sorensen got mad at me because I hadn't consulted him first, as I usually did. When Kennedy came back to the Senate, I told him about the incident and he smiled and said: "Oh, you mean you were doing business with Senator Sorensen?"

Incidentally, I was in New York while he was still recuperating, and so I called up the hospital to ask his nurse if he would care to see me. On the telephone, instead of the nurse, came his father, Joe Kennedy, who thanked me but said that Jack was seeing no one except members of the family, and so I sent my best regards and that was that. But it interested me to think that Joe had enough leisure time, or was so concerned about his son, that he was in the hospital answering the phone when messages like mine came for John. After his spectacular career, Joe Kennedy's principal occupation in his later life seemed to be to keep up with his family.

When he was active, Kennedy was a very effective senator on those matters in which he took deep interest. I remember clearly his very strong position on the modification of the Taft-Hartley Law into what became the Landrum-Griffin Law. He was chairman of the subcommittee on labor and industry, which reported this bill with amendments. He had Archibald Cox, the Harvard professor, sitting beside him as his adviser, but John's original speech and his answers to questions over nine days of debate were both clear and forceful. On that bill and others where he was in charge of the committee report, he really did a remarkable job not only in defending the position of the committee but in appealing for modifications in favor of labor with very considerable eloquence.

He was also chairman of a committee to determine what portraits should be painted to fill the empty walls in the large outer chamber where senators receive visitors. Every senator had an opportunity to make recommendations, and I recall that Webster, Clay, and Taft were three of the five choices of the committee. I happened to have an engagement with Kennedy in his office to have my picture taken with him for some purpose, and he apologized for having kept me waiting. We had our picture taken, and meanwhile he scanned the draft of the speech that had been prepared for him to deliver at the dedication of the portraits. I watched him look this over very quickly, make some illegible pencil changes, and put the notes in his pocket. I preceded him into the lobby room and listened to him make a short address, very pleasant, very well informed, from the notes that had been presented to him, pointed up with his own observations. It was my first impression of Kennedy's ability to speak effectively from notes that he had improvised on the spur of the moment.

John and I were usually in agreement on the necessity for foreign aid, and on every case but the St. Lawrence Seaway we cooperated on legislation protecting the interests of Massachusetts. I have already referred to the efforts I made in my first year in the Senate to find relief for the fishing fleets of Gloucester and New Bedford, which were getting a dwindling catch of cod and halibut on the Grand Banks. The Saltonstall-Kennedy Act of 1954 made available to the secretary of the interior money from customs levied on imported fisheries or agricultural products and specified that a certain proportion of those funds be used to promote the domestic fishing industry and technical research. For this purpose, $3 million a year was realized. Also in 1954, I submitted a program asking for a subsidy for construction of trawlers (fishing vessels that could be integrated as minesweepers in an emergency), and two years later I sponsored a program to set up a revolving fund of $13 million with which to provide loans to the owners of fishing vessels. Such legislation, as I said before, got little support from the senators of the Middle and Far West who were concentrating on farm subsidies.

I was surprised when early one Sunday morning, Nov. 9, 1959, I got an urgent long-distance call from on old friend, George Olson, the president of the Ocean Spray Company. He told me in dismay that the government food and drug authorities were about to condemn the crop of cranberries then being harvested, having found that it had been poisoned by a dangerous pesticide. On inquiry I found that most of the cranberries had been damaged in Wisconsin and only to a small degree in Massachusetts. But it did constitute a danger, and that condemnation, when broadcast in the press, kept housewives from buying any cranberries that autumn and the next. Massachusetts produces about 85 percent of the total cranberry crop in the United States, and this loss of two years' crops was a body blow, especially to Cape Cod.

Rep. Hastings Keith of the Cape, Sen. Alexander Wiley of Wisconsin, John Kennedy, and I investigated the situation. Once we were assured that the damaging spray would no longer be used, we had to restore the confidence of both growers and consumers. We met with General Persons and appealed through him to President Eisenhower to agree that $7 million should be allocated to the cranberry growers for the loss they had suffered during the ban. Actually, in the long run, the ruling by the Food and Drug commission did more for the cranberry industry than they realized: it not only cautioned management about the careless use of pesticides, but it stimulated the whole industry to advertise its product and consumers to use cranberries in a way they had never done before. Today one hears of cranberry juice cocktail, cranberry and apple compote, cranberry muffins, and that juicy sauce without which the Thanksgiving turkey would not be at home.

* * *

The most sensitive and perhaps the most worthwhile project that John Kennedy and I sponsored was the Cape Cod National Seashore Park. Early in my governorship I was amazed to learn that taking care of tourists was the second biggest industry in Massachusetts. As Cape Cod lies within a day's drive of almost a quarter of the nation's population, one can imagine the astronomical number of visitors who are attracted to its sandy beaches, picturesque dunes, and warm sea water in the open months. The Cape has a unique character; the neat saltbox houses are indigenous, and the native Cape Codder takes pride in his way of life. But in the mid-1950s, it became evident that large sections of privately owned waterfront and some of the finest coves were no longer accessible to the public, and, at the same time, that real-estate developers had their eyes on salt marshes that ought to be preserved as they were.

In order to safeguard the outer Cape for the enjoyment of future generations, John Kennedy and I began in the mid-fifties to smell out the possibilities of a national recreation area to be created by federal law and administered by the federal government. This had never been done with land enclosing so many communities — Eastham, Chatham, and Provincetown to name but three — and so many landowners, some of whose property titles reached back to the 17th Century, and we knew the opposition would be strenuous. When I went down to speak at a town meeting in Eastham in 1957, the questions fell into Various categories: some asked what the obligation of the various communities should be, how much responsibility should be left to the selectmen, and who would pay for the maintenance of the roads; and the landowners, some of whom were bitterly hostile, wanted to know whether their property would be included in such a park and whether they could will it to their descendants, or sell it.

It took many meetings; Kennedy sent up a man from his staff and I one from mine (Jonathan Moore); they were tactful, they listened to all the grievances, and after many hearings, modifications, and amendments, the draft of a bill began to emerge. Rep. Keith, who represented the Cape Cod area, was of course greatly concerned and subject to more objections and abuse than we senators who covered the whole state.

The three of us, with our aides, had a final meeting in my office. I knew that Keith was in a difficult spot and at last I said to him, "Hastie, Senator Kennedy and I are going to file this bill in the Senate. We hope you will file it in the House, but in any event we must decide now and we hope you will join us so that we may go forward together." Keith vacillated for a few minutes, but finally said yes, and his assistant, a large, pleasant woman, winked at me across the table in satisfaction that her boss had made up his mind.

So in 1959 the Saltonstall-Kennedy Bill was introduced into Congress. It created, in effect, a national seashore park and authorized the expenditure of $16 million to purchase land within the boundaries, extending forty miles along the outer coast from Provincetown to the tip of Nauset Beach. Two years later, the bill went through both bodies without changes of consequence, and its passage was facilitated by John's driving enthusiasm. He was President when the bill was signed on

Aug. 7, 1961, and he gave me one of the pens.

The park today embraces about 29,000 acres, including miles of sand cliffs and dunes overlooking the Atlantic, the sand spits of Nauset, the salt meadows, and a large cross section of Wellfleet plain—in all,land belonging to six contiguous towns. The initial purchase money was used up by 1968, but additional funding bringing the total to over $25 million was appropriated before the big developers could get into the act.

There are still over 500 houses in the park system. Residents who were living within the boundaries before 1959 may keep their homes, will them, or sell them, but any modifications to the house or land must be approved by an advisory commission, in 1959 chaired by Joshua A. Nickerson, whose ancestors were among the first settlers and who was himself at the outset a leading opponent of the whole project.

Each year Alice and I try to think up appropriate Christmas cards to send to our family and many friends, and when the clamor about the Cape Cod National Park was beginning to subside, we looked over various pictures of the sand dunes and the water beyond, chose one that seemeed to us typical of the Cape, had it printed with our Christmas greetings, to which we added the words: "The Cape Cod National Seashore: Massachusetts contributes her history to the nation." It was an attractive picture; people told us they liked it, and there was only one criticism — from the future governor of Massachusetts, Francis W. Sargent, then the commissioner of conservation. He asked, "Lev, why did you send me a picture of the Indiana dunes and a portion of Lake Michigan as your Christmas Card?"

I replied, "Sarg, shucks, no one has noticed the mistake but you — don't get me in wrong with those who love Cape Cod."

He didn't, but he still likes to remind me of my love for the Indiana dunes.

* * *

My campaign for re-election in 1960 against Tom O'Connor, a former mayor of Springfield, was not as difficult a fight as I had had six years earlier when I defeated Foster Furcolo.

Furcolo had hoped to run against me in 1960 but O'Connor defeated him in the Democratic primary as a result of the corruption charges against the state Department of Public Works and the MDC during Furcolo's two terms as governor from 1957 to 1960.

In the 1954 campaign Furcolo was state treasurer and had

been lured away from Congress in 1952 by Gov. Paul Dever, who wanted to give the Democrats some ethnic balance on the ticket.

During the campaign between Furcolo and me, Kennedy gave Furcolo the freeze on a television program at which he was supposed to endorse the entire Democratic ticket. Kennedy arrived late for the TV appearance and was given a prepared script which had been approved by Furcolo. After he took a quick look at it, he refused to read it and said he would handle it his own way. Tempers flared a bit, I understand, and then Kennedy made a pitch for the other Democrats on the ticket but slighted Furcolo.

There have been many rumors over the years about the animosity between Kennedy and Furcolo. The only substantial thing I ever learned about it was that when the two of them were congressmen in the late forties, Furcolo once arranged for a meeting of all Democrats in the Massachusetts delegation with President Truman. Furcolo talked Kennedy and the other Democrats into attending this meeting, which was planned to present a unified front on the part of the Massachusetts congressmen. The bill in question was supposed to be a controversial one and it was with some reluctance, as I understood the story, that Kennedy and some of the other Democrats went to the meeting with Truman. Well, all of the congressmen showed up, except Furcolo, who had made the appointment with the President. That annoyed Kennedy no end and I don't think he ever forgave him for it. But it sure helped me in my campaign.

On election night in 1960, after I defeated O'Connor, the telephone rang and when my daughter Susan answered it, she called to me: "President Kennedy is on the line. Come quick." It was close to midnight and I said, "Oh, pooh, some drunk."

"No," she said, "I recognize his voice." She was right; it was John, who asked me if I had won and congratulated me when I told him. It pleased me to have him think of me at a time when he himself had just been elected by the narrowest of margins.

He was inaugurated on a bright, very cold and windy day in January, 1961. The night before, Washington had had one of its larger snowstorms. I had attended a reception at Fort Myer and was driving home but had to leave the car and walk the last half mile because of the tremendous drifts. By early morning the streets to the Capitol were pretty well cleared, but it was so cold you could see your breath. I sat in the front row of the platform, fairly close to the President, and beside me was Dick Russell of Georgia, who had come without any gloves and was shivering. To keep his hands warm, I loaned him one of my gloves and kept that hand in my pocket — so Massachusetts and Georgia shared gloves on that very frosty morning.

Cardinal Cushing opened the ceremony with a long prayer. Robert Frost rose to read a poem he had written especially for the occasion. He was shivering, his hands trembled, the wind blew his paper so that he could not follow the lines, and as a last resort he recited one of his old poems that he knew by heart. Then President Kennedy, after being sworn in by Chief Justice Earl Warren, gave an eloquent oration in which the memorable line was: "Ask not what your country can do for you; ask what you can do for your country." It set a high ideal at the start of his administration. He had taken his coat off, he wore no hat, and why he did not freeze to death I shall never know.

After the inauguration ceremony was over, Mrs. Saltonstall and I were invited by the Kennedys to a luncheon in the old Supreme Court Room. It was a small affair, about forty persons, and at the head table were the President and his wife, his parents, and former President and Mrs. Truman.

After the luncheon, we were given very strict and clear instructions as to where we would find the cars to join in the trip to the White House in order to watch the inaugural parade. Mrs. Saltonstall and I went down to the Capitol plaza, where we were supposed to find a car with a driver — number and all. Of course, there was no car there. Sen. Hubert Humphrey and his wife were in the same predicament. One of the sergeants-at-arms came up and said, "Sir, former Vice President Wallace isn't here, so why don't you take his car?" It was a Chevrolet with a Marine driver.

So I got into the front seat beside Sen. Humphrey's aide and in the back seat were the senator, Mrs. Humphrey, and Mrs. Saltonstall. We moved forward, and to our surprise we found ourselves right in the front of the line. Perhaps if we had gone a little further ahead we would have been ahead of the President himself. We held up our driver and let the President and Vice President go through. Then we followed along very closely. To our amazement, as we went up Pennsylvania avenue the guides would say over the bullhorns, "Here comes the President," and name the people in his car, and then the Vice President, and perhaps one more car. Then they would come to us. At that time we had taken Henry Wallace's sign off, and there was dead silence as to who was in our car as it went by.

However, Humphrey loved it. I rather shrank into my seat as we went up the avenue until we reached the old Willard Hotel, where somebody waved to Humphrey out of a window. He stood up and waved back heartily. After that, even he became a little nervous about our position in the line, so I said in no uncertain terms to our driver, "Go through that rope — get a policeman to pull it aside, and we will go up behind the Treasury and get out and walk," which we did. I learned later that Wallace did appear, looked for the car assigned to him, and was miffed.

* * *

During 1959-1960 a group of anti-Castro Cuban exiles carefully chosen and finally numbering over 1,000 was trained in Guatemala under the leadership of a retired marine colonel. This movement was carried out secretly under the general guidance of Allen Dulles. He was confident that with the air support of some old B-26s flown by Cuban pilots the invaders could be landed safely on the coast of Cuba at the Bay of Pigs, where it was anticipated they would be joined by natives eager to throw off Castro's yoke. It was expected that Castro's meager air force could be wiped out before the invasion, permitting the supply ships to land the necessary ammunition and support.

Dulles received a letter from the marine colonel in early 1961 stating that the Cubans were trained and eager to fight. In Guatemala there was heavy pressure to close the camps. I have always compared the readiness of these men with a football team trained and tense on the night before a game. If their assault was held off, the morale would quickly die.

President Kennedy, when he took office in January, 1961, learned of this force and its training. Perhaps he had known of it before? I did not know. I did know as a member of the CIA subcommittee that the training was proceeding and that the group had arms.

Ambassador Adlai Stevenson at the United Nations was under heavy pressure to make it clear that the armed forces of the United States would take no part in any such attack. President Kennedy, apparently with the approval of Secretary of State Dean Rusk, had given him his word, and Stevenson so stated to the UN.

The attack, which was launched on April 17, 1961, went badly from the start. Castro preserved at least one fast plane, which was not put out of commission and sank one of the supply ships and drove the other away. Meanwhile, there were two of our bombers in Georgia ready to go, but the word of our government had been given that we would not participate in any way, so they never got off the ground, even though last-minute appeals were made for our air-power support. So, the Cuban exiles went to their deaths, or were captured.

That things were in a desperate state I knew that evening when Alice and I dined as the guest of Gen. and Mrs. Wade Haislip and found one of the guests to be the former ambassador from Cuba, whose son was on the beachhead. The ambassador was called to the telephone repeatedly, and it was clear that the news was not good. There was no uprising such as had been anticipated and no supplies or ammunition for the assaulting troops, since the supply ship had been sunk.

The next afternoon, I recall, President Kennedy called the leaders of the Senate and the House to consult about the situation. He was clearly our President, but seemed nervous and excited. He asked Allen Dulles to read the marine colonel's letter, which I have referred to previously. He read the letter and then explained about our planes being grounded in Georgia and the sinking of the supply ships. I don't recall that Kennedy asked us to give him our support. I think he merely wanted us to know how he found the situation.

Altogether, it was a mighty unfortunate undertaking. I believe that President Eisenhower knew about the plan. I doubt if he had agreed to the use of American armed forces, but it is certain that both the Cuban exiles and the CIA were misinformed about Castro's strength, his personal appearance as the leader of his land forces, and the fear of internal resistance to him. The failure raised, really for the first time, the question of the CIA and its participation in international affairs.

* * *

The situation in the autumn of 1962 when the missile sites were discovered in Cuba was fundamentally different. President Kennedy acted decisively and with complete assurance. Through August, mist and cloud cover prevented accurate observations, but when the weather cleared in early September, it was obvious from the pictures taken from the U-2 planes what the Russians were building. These pictures were shown to the members of the Armed Services Committee, and when we met with the President he told us calmly the steps he was taking to convince Khrushchev that he was in the wrong.

Our Navy kept close watch on the Russian ships that were

bound for Cuba until they stopped and turned back, and meanwhile our tanks and armored infantry were pouring into Florida, just in case. The rocket emplacements were subsequently dismounted without a shot being fired, and President Kennedy deserves full credit for the firm, swift orders that brought this about. Incidentally, at that time, John McCone, who had replaced Allen Dulles as the head of the CIA, was in Europe on his honeymoon, and the full responsibility for our action devolved on the President. If the Bay of Pigs was a failure, on our part, the abandonment of the missile sites was a failure on the part of the Soviet Union, and it may have been responsible for Khrushchev's removal from office.

* * *

In late July, 1963, the Nuclear Test Ban Treaty was to be signed in Moscow. I was glad to accept the invitation of Secretary of State Rusk to be a member of the group from Congress that was to accompany him.

The purpose of the treaty was to limit the competiton between the Soviets and ourselves in designing new nuclear weapons. But it also gave us an opportunity to learn more about Moscow and the Kremlin. We paid a courtesy call on Gromyko. We met with Khrushchev in the Kremlin and were his luncheon guests prior to the signing. It was the typical Russian menu, from caviar to coffee, nuts, and fruit with toasts following one another in quick order. I found myself beside Mrs. Gromyko. She spoke good English with a fine sense of humor, and we had a pleasant time. After the luncheon, Adlai Stevenson and I visited a much-decorated chapel several floors above us in the Kremlin. It was beautifully adorned and impressive, but shortly we became lost in the maze of rooms so that I was afraid we would miss the ceremonies for which we had traveled 4,500 miles; indeed we returned just in time to see the treaty signed in Catherine Hall. It was a comparatively narrow room with a long table on which were placed three copies of the treaty. Gromyko sat in the center and on his right was Secretary Rusk and on his left, Lord Home. Five television cameras were located to cover all angles, and the photographer and reporters were on a raised platform directly opposite the table. We from the United States, the British, and the Russians all stood behind the table. There were speeches by the three foreign ministers and the secretary general of the United Nations. Afterward we filed into the Grand Georgian Hall, where there were long tables covered with drinks and food.

Again Khrushchev talked of the importance of peace and how the Soviets wanted a more peaceful world. More toasts were drunk. The spirit of the occasion was one of hope and optimism carried out in a most dignified and ceremonious manner.

But underneath all the talk and hospitable gestures I never lost my sense of feeling that we at home and in the free world must be watchful and alert as to the real intentions of the Kremlin and its leaders toward the free world. We must be determined to maintain our armed strength and our everlasting research for modernization of all sorts of our material. If not, our negotiations for a more peaceful world may well be weakened and jeopardized.

* * *

I have already referred to President Kennedy's ability to memorize quickly the substance of something that he might have read and wanted to utilize as the basis for a speech. This was brought home to me after Kennedy's death when I was serving on a committee to try to settle a railroad strike. The other members of the committee were Mr. Kappel of American Telephone and Telegraph Company, George Meany of the AFL-CIO, Senator Morse of Oregon, and a professional negotiator. We were preparing our report one Sunday in New York City, and while the report was being typed, George Meany began to reminisce about a conversation he had had with President Kennedy at the time of the President's triumphant visit to Berlin. Meany told of being escorted down the Friedrichstrasse (the principal shopping center — two miles long — crossed by Unter den Linden, which runs in the inner city for a mile from Brandenburg Gate to the old royal palace) with motorcycles screaming on either side and of arriving at the hall, from the balcony of which Kennedy was to speak.

This hall, given to the city of Berlin by the Quakers of the United States, had a plaque at the entrance in German and English saying in substance that we must all work together toward a peaceful world, with a better understanding of each nation's point of view and problems. Meany wrote down the words on a small piece of paper because he considered them so significant. At that moment, President Kennedy arrived, and as they were going up in the elevator together, Meany handed him the slip of paper. Kennedy looked at it, put it in his pocket, took it out, looked at it again, and when the time came for him to speak, he departed from the prepared text and quoted with dramatic effect the words Meany had shown him, ending with the sentence which was to echo throughout Berlin:

> "All free men, wherever they may live, are citizens of Berlin. And therefore, as a free man, I take pride in the words 'Ich bin ein Berliner.' "

That statement was greeted with tremendous enthusiasm, not only in Berlin but also in the United States and around the world. Meany was much impressed at Kennedy's ability to look twice at that scrap of paper and then be able to quote it so accurately. I said, "George, did you ever make a recording of this for the Kennedy library?" and he said he had not. So when I reached my office the next day I wrote to an official of the Kennedy library, told her the story, and urged that she ask Meany to do a recording of it. Several months later in came a letter from Bob Kennedy, thanking me for this valuable addition.

* * *

As I remember, my last meeting with President Kennedy was in the Cabinet Room of the White House, with a few of the senior senators, in 1962, at the time when he was discussing what he should say in his State of the Union address to the Congress. The talk came around to civil rights, and Sen. Everett Dirksen questioned how far the President should go in the message. I listened and then questioned whether he should go the whole way on integration in the schools, instead of taking a step forward and then perhaps a further step when the time was right. In short, I thought he could go forward with further recommendations, but it would be impossible after making them to pull back. After the meeting was over, he walked out to the automobile with Dirksen, and as I caught up with them he saw me and remarked, "There's Saltonstall trying to get us together again on something to which we can all agree."

On the day Kennedy was assassinated in Texas, Friday, Nov. 22, 1963, I was lunching with some friends at the Alibi Club in Washington. I had counted 13 at the table and had made up my mind that I would not get up until we all rose together. I am a superstitious person. So that day at the club I waited until we all rose together and as I went to the door with

Sam Spencer, I told him of my superstitions: "I am always afraid of thirteen at meals and particularly on a Friday." As I got into my car my driver said word had just come over the radio that Kennedy had been assassinated. Sam Spencer reminded me the next day of our conversation.

John Kennedy was the youngest President in our history. His youth, the idealism with which he spoke, and the young administrators he brought to Washington created an image of American vitality more widely appreciated around the world than anyone realized until his death. I have often wondered whether, if he had lived, he would have reversed his buildup in South Vietnam and pulled us out instead of increasing the size of our activities there as LBJ did.

* * *

Lyndon Johnson in my judgment was more adroit and successful as a majority leader in the Senate than as President. He first served as the minority leader in 1948 and two years later became majority leader, a post he held until he assumed the vice presidency. He made a shrewd estimate of every senator and of how to solicit his support when he wanted it. Some he would hit over the head and whack into line, you might say, but to others he would say, "Bill, I did you a favor at such and such a time (he had a good memory), and now I really need your vote on this matter." His third method was to begin with some pleasant conversation, including a little flattery, and this was the one he always used with me. As the Republican whip, I would occasionally talk with Johnson's capable aide Bobby Baker, before he got into trouble, and Bobby made a point of knowing how everybody stood, both Democrats and Republicans. When Johnson called for a vote at a certain hour or threatened to shut off debate in order to vote, you could be sure he knew where the votes were and that he had them on his side.

I recall President Eisenhower's nomination of Secretary Strauss to be secretary of commerce. There was a long debate and vehement opposition led by Sen. Clinton Anderson of New Mexico. We all knew it was going to be a close vote. No one knew where Sen. Margaret Chase Smith stood. Finally, when Johnson called for a vote at three o'clock on a certain day, we felt that he must have known that Mrs. Smith would vote against Strauss. I was never sure why she did. Strauss's nomination was turned down, and Johnson won.

We served together rather closely on two committees. The first was an investigation in connection with the future of the B-36s, and the second was the subcommittee of Armed Services that created NASA, where he presided and I was the senior Republican.

On the NASA subcommittee, the question of the rights of the inventor of a patent came up. What rights did an inventor have in a patent that had been developed with government funds? I always took the position that if the incentive for creating a new gadget was taken away from the creator, there would be fewer inventions; while other senators, notably Russell Long of Louisiana, argued that since the government provided the funds, the invention that resulted should be available to all and would thus produce fewer royalties for the inventor. It was a sticky problem. Senator Johnson and I drafted a bill that gave a share of the rights to the creator.

One of the remembrances that I carried away from Washington was a remark of LBJ's when we were attending a meeting of the full Committee on Appropriations. It concerned an amendment to a bill that President Eisenhower wanted and which LBJ favored. As the time approached for a vote, I whispered to Tom Scott, Appropriations clerk, "Tell Lyndon to propose the amendment. I don't want to seem to double-cross him by offering it."

So, Tom whispered to the senator what I had said, and Johnson replied, in an aside, "Lev wouldn't know how to double-cross anyone."

Tom came back and told me what Johnson had said, and I have never forgotten it.

I am embarrassed to recall the day when Lyndon, as majority leader, invited me to a luncheon in the secretary's dining room — and I forgot! I was halfway through my luncheon in the Senate Dining Room when I received word that Johnson was waiting for me, so I rushed up and with apologies took my designated place between Lyndon and Henry Ford II. It was a lucky seat because I had the chance to talk with Ford and to tell him of my impressions of Bob McNamara as secretary of defense, of how he operated and kept much of the control to himself. Ford, incidentally, said that was one of the problems they had had at the Ford Motor Company; none of the heads of the various departments would make a decision without getting the final word from McNamara, the president. Certainly over the years I felt that he led the Department of Defense in much the same manner and determined many of the decisions concerning the military efforts in Vietnam even though the President was the civilian head of the armed forces.

I believe that Johnson was at his peak as a majority leader and that the legislation on civil rights would not have advanced as far as it did without the pressure he exerted on other southerners. He was at his best in working toward a compromise. When he became President and had to initiate ideas, he was neither as confident nor as successful as he had been in pressing forward with policies that someone else had originated. We did not see so much of him in the presidency, although he was intimate with the minority leader, Everett Dirksen. When LBJ called the senior Republicans into the Cabinet Room, it was to tell us what he was going to do rather than to ask our opinions. I don't suppose that in the six years that Johnson was in the White House I was "consulted" more than half a dozen times.

But Alice and I were invited to several social affairs. I remember one occasion when we attended a show in the Rose Garden depicting various historical events. I had intended to leave early, but found myself sitting beside Lady Bird Johnson, and I could not excuse myself from the President's wife. So I surprised her by telling her that I had met William Jennings Bryan and heard him speak on the Chautauqua Circuit when I was in school in Arizona. She turned to me with a look and said, "I did not realize you were that old."

* * *

Many years earlier, Justice Felix Frankfurter soon after he came to the Supreme Court began to take a personal interest in the National Archives, a product of FDR's regard for history; it was Felix who suggested that I be appointed to the National Historic Publications Commission when a vacancy occurred. The commission is, in effect, a scholarly secretariat that supervises the collection and arrangement of papers of national interest. It is composed of one member of the Supreme Court, who was, of course, Felix Frankfurter, one member of the

House, one senator, and at least six distinguished historians. So in 1959 I was chosen for the place vacated by Sen. Wallace Bennett of Utah. The discussions were usually way over my head, but I found two congenial scholars, Arthur M. Schlesinger Sr., professor emeritus of Harvard, and Lyman H. Butterfield, who had been working on the Jefferson papers at Princeton, and they helped to orient me.

For many years the archives and its commission were hamstrung for lack of funds. The Woodrow Wilson papers were in the Congressional Library, Jefferson's papers were at Princeton, the Adams papers in Boston, and an indefinite store of valuable documents elsewhere. But in 1950, when the first volume of the Jefferson papers, edited by Julian Boyd, was published, a copy was sent to President Truman, who read it and wanted more. The Jefferson papers included not only Jefferson's correspondence but letters to him, and the editing of them set a new standard. The commission prepared a report in 1954 listing a number of American leaders whose papers seemed worthy of similar treatment, and in 1963 a request for congressional funds had the strong backing of President Kennedy. I suggested that I file the request and ask for an annual appropriation of $500,000. Personally, I did not believe that Congress would agree to as much as that, and I was pleased when we were voted an appropriation of $300,000. But not so the historians: they were disappointed, for they felt they really deserved the full amount.

However, the commission got a substantial boost from the Ford Foundation, which came forward with a grant of $2 million, to be spread over ten years, for the editing and publication of five "priority" projects—the papers of Jefferson, Franklin, Adams, Madison, and Hamilton. President Kennedy wrote a review of the first four volumes of the Adams papers, which was published in the *American Historical Review,* and under his stimulus the congressional appropriation for the commission began to go up.

Today the National Historic Publications Commission is operating under a ceiling of $2 million a year for a limited number of years. The Daniel Webster papers are being edited and arranged in Hanover, New Hampshire, and the Andrew Johnson papers at Rice University; the papers of Henry Clay, John C. Calhoun, and Jefferson Davis are likewise in process. The government funds are used both for letterpress editions and for microfilm publication. I can take credit for only a modest part in all this—helping the commission get the appropriation that first put them in business.

* * *

I was lunching one day at the Harvard Club in Boston when David McCord, the poet, stopped by my table and asked, "Why doesn't Congress give a medal to Robert Frost?" I said I wasn't sure there was any precedent. "Oh, yes," said Dave, "Congress gave a medal to Irving Berlin," and he named several others. A little later, shortly before the inauguration of President Kennedy, Robert Frost was in Washington, and his friend Sen. Ralph Flanders of Vermont, invited me to dine with them at the Sulgrave Club, just the three of us. It was a very pleasant evening and afterward it seemed to me that Dave's suggestion was right and that it would be appropriate for Congress to award a medal to Mr. Frost in recognition of the fact that he was the best-loved and best-known living American poet. I sounded out the two senators from Vermont to see if they would make the first move, but to my surprise they hesitated, perhaps because Frost was not a native Vermonter; anyway, not hearing from them, I decided to go ahead on my own. I filed a resolution in the Senate to authorize the striking of a gold medal to be presented to Mr. Frost by the President of the United States; the idea was an appealing one, and it was adopted without opposition.

On March 26, 1962, President Kennedy made the presentation with some graceful, amusing remarks that had us all laughing. I soon learned that a number of people wanted to own bronze copies of the Frost medal, and I was told that another bill would be necessary, authorizing the secretary of the Treasury to coin the bronze duplicates and make them available to the public. Since they were to be sold at a price sufficient to cover the expenses, no additional appropriation was necessary, which suited my Yankee economy.

* * *

The event that I treasure most clearly of my four years at Harvard College was the winning of the Grand Challenge Cup at Henley in 1914, the last regatta before the war. I have spoken earlier of this and recall it now because of its happy aftermath. In late autumn of 1963, our crew was honored by being invited to Syracuse, N.Y., to be inducted into the Rowing Hall of Fame. So we all gathered there to participate in this honor. We had met and rowed together twenty years after 1914, then twenty-five, thirty, thirty-five, forty, and forty-five. At each of these reunions in Cambridge, we gathered at the Newell Boat House, went on the river, had our pictures taken with Robert Herrick, our coach, and afterwards enjoyed the successors to the two bottles of champagne given us in 1914 by the Leander crew at Henley. On each occasion after our spin on the river, we dined together with our wives, a happy dinner of reminiscences, toasts, and affection. But that day in Syracuse, we decided to celebrate our 50th anniversary by going back to Henley, if the Henley authorities would permit us, to row on the Thames at an hour that would be convenient. Louis Curtis, through his association with Brown, Shipley and Company, started the negotiations that led to an invitation. We were informed that we would be welcome and that we could go on the river either Friday or Saturday evening at tea time, when there was a pause in the races. We chose Saturday.

We stayed in a hotel near Henley big enough to take care of the nine oarsmen and our families, although the quarters were somewhat cramped. In fact, my daughter, Susan, had to crawl under a half door to get in and out of her room, which happened to be partitioned off for some reason or other. Alice and I had the manager's room, and all I can say is I should hate to sleep every night in that bed.

Prior to our sailing we had selected a new replica for the Grand Challenge Cup. The old cup was about 130 years old. There was no room for new names, even on the stand, and the cup was no longer solid. The replica on its polished oak base cost us $3000, and we were happy to give it in return for the pleasure that had been given us. At the annual stewards dinner, which was given in our honor, the old cup was formally retired with proper toasts, and the new cup accepted for the regatta. We were very proud, happy, and excited to be there. Only two members of the Leander crew that had rowed against us were still alive, and one of them was present.

The Queen Mother, her daughter, Princess Margaret, and her husband came to Henley to watch the finals, the first time in many years that royalty had been present, and as a representative of our crew I was invited to escort the Queen Mother aboard the launch that followed the race for the Challenge Cup. It was not close, as the crew from the Soviet Union, an impressive bunch, handily defeated the Harvard second varsity of 1964, which meant that our new cup would spend its first year in Russia.

Then, after the Queen Mother had inspected the various

prizes, I had the honor of presenting to her each member of our crew. We and our wives were lined up in accordance with our seating in the shell, and as she went down the line, the Queen Mother gave to each oarsman a medal commemorating the event. "Waddy" Bush, who had been our substitute for the fifty years we rowed together, was present with his wife, "Hatsie." He, of course, had been awarded his Harvard letter although he had never had the chance to row in a race, and now he received his medal too. Then came the introduction to our wives, all of whom were present, as were Robert Herrick's two daughters, Mrs. George Mumford and Mrs. Houghton Metcalf. The Queen Mother had a pleasant remark for each one and when she reached Mrs. Metcalf she asked, "And what was your part in the crew?" Mrs. Metcalf, who remembered the Victorian tradition that one should always address the Queen as "Mam," replied, "Oh, I am the daughter of the coach, Mam." Her sister could hardly suppress a giggle, and later said, "Why in the dickens did you say you were the daughter of the coachman?"

By now it was tea time, and the Queen Mother was due to leave, but she insisted on staying until she had seen us perform. I had had the idea that when the loudspeaker announced that we were rowing again fifty years after our victory, the English would give a mild handclapping and say to themselves, "Get those old fogies off the river," as there were still races to come. But they didn't. We started at the finish line and rowed upstream by the grandstands for about a half mile, backed water, turned around and at a leisurely stroke returned, receiving to our utter surprise a tremendous applause from the people in the punts and those lining the banks. A photograph taken of us after our cox, said, "Let 'er run," showed me with my hand raised, waving to the Queen Mother.

When we returned to our boathouse the float was so crowded that we had a hard time clearing a way to get our shell out of the water. After our finish in 1914, as I have said, members of the Leander crew had greeted us on the float with two bottles of champagne. Now we found Lawrence Coolidge and several other good Harvard men with two chilled bottles and glasses waiting for us. So I toasted the crowd and told them we would be back again at our 75th anniversary. That evening there was a big dinner at the hotel, a happy affair for our families and friends — three score of us — with much reminiscing and pictures taken of us all.

As the Senate was still in session, Alice and I had reservations for the flight to Washington the next day, but we had not allowed for the density of the Sunday traffic, and by the time we checked in at the airport, we found that our seats had been sold. When the clerk saw how concerned I was, he said, "Are you a member of that Henley crew?"

I replied, "Yes."

"Okay," he said, and stamped our tickets.

Then the stewardess, who escorted us in double time to the plane, asked the same question, and when I said yes, her comment was: "Well, you gave my boyfriend and me the best afternoon yesterday that we've had in a long time."

* * *

It had come as a pleasant surprise when, in the spring of 1949, by resolution of the Senate, I was appointed a regent of the Smithsonian Institution. The origin of the Smithsonian is an unusual story. James Smithson, an English scientist, was the natural son of the first duke of Northumberland. He deeply resented the circumstances of his birth, and in his famous will made in London in 1820, he left his entire estate to a nephew; if the nephew should die without issue (as he did) the inheritance was to be given to the United States to found in Washington an institution bearing Smithson's name, ". . . for the increase and diffusion of knowledge among men." So far as is known, Mr. Smithson had never visited America, but the seed he planted here has certainly grown.

The Smithson property converted into gold sovereigns was shipped to New York in the summer of 1838, and when recoined in American money at the Philadelphia mint, it amounted to just over $508 million. Congress at first was undecided as to how this sizable gift should be used, but finally in 1846, President James K. Polk signed the act that established the Smithsonian Institution under the administration of an executive secretary with a board of regents to be headed by the chief justice of the United States and including as a member, the Vice President. Then as now the board consisted of three senators, three representatives, and six private citizens, two of whom are residents of the District of Columbia.

The original building, designed by James Renwick, with towers and turrets as much like an English castle as possible, was erected on Independence Avenue not far from the White House; in it was the tomb of James Smithson and spacious galleries for exhibitions, and to it flowed an increasing collection of historic and scientific objects, such as the manuscript of "The Star-Spangled Banner," the desk on which Jefferson wrote the Declaration of Independence, Eli Whitney's cotton

Saltonstall stands below his portrait in the Massachusetts State House.

With officials of Plymouth, England, in 1970 during 200th anniversary of the sailing of the "Mayflower."

Henry Cabot Lodge talks with Saltonstall in 1960.

With former Speaker of the House of Representatives John McCormack in 1973.

United Press International

With Everett Dirksen at Republican convention in 1968.

The Saltonstalls in 1971.

gin, George Catlin's portraits of Indian chiefs, the gowns worn by the First Ladies, and famous gems such as the Hope Diamond (which Mrs. McLean gave the institution), and the Star of Asia sapphire. As time went on, it became, as a wit has dubbed it, "the nation's attic."

During my eighteen years on the board I voted with approval for the expansion of the Smithsonian under the direction of two very capable secretaries — Leonard Carmichael, the former president of Tufts College who was succeeded in 1964 by S. Dillon Ripley. It was under Carmichael that the National Museum of History and Technology was built with an appropriation from Congress, and it was Carmichael who proposed the building of the Air and Space Museum, which will house, in addition to the spacecraft, the plane which the Wright Brothers flew at Kitty Hawk, and Lindbergh's *Spirit of St. Louis.*

When the old patent office fell vacant, the Congress at Carmichael's instigation had it converted into two national art museums; Mr. Ripley in his turn was a proponent of the John F. Kennedy Center for the Performing Arts, the Woodrow Wilson International Center for Scholars, and the Hirshhorn Museum and Sculpture Garden. The National Gallery of Art, the gift of Andrew Mellon, and the Freer Gallery of Art are both technically under the aegis of the Smithsonian, although the latter has its own endowment, and the National Gallery is administered by a separate board of trustees and operates on its own budget. Today, Mr. Smithson would certainly be amazed to learn that there are eighteen museums, art galleries, and even an observatory in Cambridge, Massachusetts, within the galaxy that bears his name.

In 1965, it was my good luck to preside over the Smithsonian's bicentennial dinner, in honor of the birth of the founder. Clinton Anderson of New Mexico was the senior senatorial regent, but he was ill, and I took his place. The two speakers of the evening were Sir Patrick Deane, then the British ambassador, and my friend Thomas Boylston Adams, president of the Massachusetts Historical Society and the great-great-great-grandson of John Quincy Adams, who was President when James Smithson made his gift. Tom Adams spoke first, and for his sense of history and his wit was well applauded. I remember particularly the passage in which he said:

"In 400 years of history, for I count the history of modern America as beginning with the arrival of the fishermen in the 16th Century, the American has shown that he is capable of many things. He tends to be superlative but not subtle. He is a superlative liar — but not, usually, a very convincing one. He can be generous to the point of madness, but in the way of trade few have shown less compunction in squeezing six pennies out of a nickel. He could write the Declaration of Independence, fight the American Revolution and produce that wonderful foundation for a republic, the American Constitution. He could destroy the slave power, though in doing so he destroyed the ascendancy of his own peculiar American type, so magnificently epitomized in Abraham Lincoln. He could welcome to his shores new waves of immigration, absorb them and discover a modification of his type in the person of President Kennedy to lead him once more into the paths of intellectualism and altruism . . . .

But we have possibilities. We shall need them. As the American Revolution spread ideas far beyond the limits of this continent, so the Smithsonian Institution is founded in an idea which must conquer the whole earth. The international quality of the increase of knowledge and the power of its diffusion to level national boundaries and unite mankind in constructive endeavor was dreamed by Smithson, fought for by Adams."

The ambassador when his turn came, having paid tribute to Mr. Smithson for an innovation that brought the two nations into such happy agreement, reached back in time to those episodes such as the Boston Tea Party, when our two governments were involved in problems about which we could not agree. He spoke with a good sense of humor, and thanks to both of them it was an evening to remember.

My affiliation with the Smithsonian became even more personal when the director accepted our gift of the old Lawrence coach, a treasured possession of our family in which my grandmother, my mother, my brother, and my sister had driven from the church to their wedding receptions. Alice refused to do so when we were married in Jaffrey — she said the country roads were just too narrow for such a broad-beamed vehicle. It has a wide, handsome cabin mounted on leather springs with a place behind for a footman and a step that unfolds when the door is open. According to the original bill of sale, which I gave to the Smithsonian, it cost $1000 to build in 1855; and for some years it was on display at the Eastern States Exposition in Springfield, where it was damaged by water in the great hurricane flood of 1938. Then it was returned to us and was restored by a famous carriage maker in New Jersey, at a cost of $14,000, before it was shipped to Washington. It now stands in the carriage section side by side with General Washington's coach from Mount Vernon, and close by is a "piano-box buggy" that we Saltonstalls had long used without realizing that it too had become a rarity.

IX. "If I was of any help . . . I am glad."

There are lasting satisfactions that come to anyone who has been in Congress for nearly two decades. I think affectionately of my friendship with Dick Russell, with whom I served with such trust and understanding on the Committee on Armed Services; of my friendship with John Stennis, both in the committee room and on our travels, and of my collaboration with John Sparkman of Alabama on the problems of Small Business — on that committee John and I never failed to bring in a unanimous report. These three were all Democrats and the fact that we worked things out with such unity was a reflection of the confidence we felt for each other.

I still hear the echo of Dick Russell's exclamation in an Appropriation Committee meeting on the defense bill. "Damn it, Lev. You got just the bill you wanted when you had only a third of the votes."

Looking back, I believe I was right to have voted consistently for the larger amounts for foreign aid that the President requested. I have no regret that I voted for censure of Senator McCarthy; Senator Ferguson and I, of the four Republicans who attended the White House Tuesday meetings, were the only ones to do so. I take satisfaction in the part I played in bringing business to Massachusetts, in the establishment of the government research laboratories in Natick, and in creating the Cape Cod National Seashore Park with Senator John Kennedy. I tried to give aid to our fishing industries, but with how much success I am still not sure; as governor and as senator I had more success in helping the development of the electronics industry in New England, and as a senator helped to sustain and build our state's cranberry industry. As an amateur historian I look back with pleasure on my affiliation with Justice Holmes's bequest, the National Archives, and the Smithsonian Institution.

Perhaps the most satisfactory recollection as a senator was my bringing together in conferences opposite points of view for a compromise agreement; a timing and a method which my friends on the Appropriations Committee dubbed "the Saltonstall package." And I will never forget my associations with President Eisenhower on Tuesday mornings in the White House, with Gen. George Marshall when he was commander in chief and secretary of defense, with Gen. Omar Bradley, Admiral Nimitz and Admiral Rickover.

Civil rights was the subject of recurring debate throughout my years in the Senate, and after the Supreme Court's decision of 1954, the southern senators slowly began to compromise, although there were a number of sticky points before language acceptable to both sides was arrived at. I remember one bill involving contempt of court: the proponents argued that a jury should be established to decide when a contempt-of-court finding was justified. I voted no because I felt that any contempt of court finding should be determined by the judge alone. A day or two later, Senator Stennis, my friend from Mississippi, thanked me for my vote. But I said, "John, don't thank me. I simply did what I thought was right."

Shortly after this I had to vote on another amendment to the same bill and this time Roy Wilkins, chairman of the NAACP, went out of his way to thank me for my stand. And again I said, "Please don't thank me; I voted the way I thought was right."

It still stays in my mind that the leaders of two such opposing points of view should have been gratified by my votes on what I considered the merits of the case.

The post-war debates on appropriations frequently aroused a good deal of emotion, and this became increasingly true in the case of foreign aid. Rep. Otto Passman of Louisiana, who was chairman of the foreign aid subcommittee of the Appropriations Committee in the House, had little sympathy for granting large amounts for foreign aid and had little patience with me because I was in favor of supporting Eisenhower's program in Europe and Asia.

I remember one heated committee conference between members of the Senate and the House in which Passman made a big oration with many statistics, and then Chairman Hayden of the Senate subcommittee asked me to sound off in defense of the amount the Senate was willing to spend. There was a difference of perhaps $40 million. I pricked up my ears when at the end of several meetings I heard Rep. John Tabor of New York whisper to me that, "The House will not go below fifty-fifty of the total amount in dispute." Passman hinted that if the Senate would agree to fifty-fifty we could specify in which countries the money might be spent. I asked for a recess of a half hour, and in the interval I called Douglas Dillon, then the undersecretary of state.

It was pretty late, nearing midnight, and I think he had already gone to bed. "If I can get a fifty-fifty split of the difference between the House and the Senate on foreign aid, where do you want it to go?" Dillon, now wide awake, began to specify the countries and the amounts, and I made notes as he spoke. When the meeting was resumed, I moved that the Senate accept the split and that the amount be allocated here, here, and here. Passman and Tabor were both satisfied, and that ended the conference.

* * *

Back home perhaps the biggest controversy which took place while I was in the Senate involved the Channel 5 contest and the battle between *Herald* and *The Globe*. I was criticized by both sides in that affair, but I took no part or sides in it.

I was also criticized in 1962 at the Republican pre-primary convention when Senator Edward Brooke won the endorsement for Attorney General. I was the convention chairman, and many people felt that Elliot Richardson would have won the contest if I had not called for a second ballot.

My feeling was very simple. The fellow running the loudspeaker on the floor wasn't doing very well. People on the floor were trying to be recognized to have their district polled and I thought I would lose all control if I didn't gavel the convention for a second vote. Richardson, who was and still is a good friend of mine, was sitting behind me and wanted to protest my action, but Henry Minot, my friend and adviser, was with him and stopped him. Richardson was only a few votes away from the endorsement at the end of the first ballot and I always felt that he would have won on the initial ballot if the lady who worked for him in the United States attorney's office had withdrawn. She had about six votes and wouldn't withdraw.

In 1966, I ran into more difficulty when some Republicans thought I favored Brooke over Gov. John A. Volpe. It was at the time I announced my retirement and the Volpe people, who had heard through the grapevine that I was contemplating retirement, wanted me to let the governor know in advance about my decision. Brooke had a man at the courthouse when I announced my decision and he relayed the word to the then attorney general, who immediately announced his candidacy for my seat and got the jump on Volpe.

* * *

As I indicated previously, I always admired President Eisenhower for his nonpolitical approach to the presidency. He acted from the heart and couldn't stand the idea of making decisions based on the political results to him and his administration.

During the Tuesday meetings with Ike I got to know Richard Nixon quite well. I first met him in the Senate, and I was responsible for bringing him to Massachusetts as the main speaker at the Republican pre-primary convention in Worcester in 1952. When the convention was over, I brought him back to my home in Dover and he and I and my daughter, Susan, had dinner. We went swimming in the pond on the property and he afterwards often mentioned the good time he had at my farm. We had such an enjoyable dinner and evening that he almost missed his train back to Washington. He was most pleasant company that evening.

Throughout his eight years as Vice President, Nixon was generally very quiet, particularly at the Tuesday sessions in the President's office. He seldom took the lead in the discussions, but when he did, his advice was very good. I feel sorry for him now and the way his career came to an end. I also feel that the Woodward and Bernstein book *The Final Days* was unnecessary. Maybe the information is true, maybe it isn't. Chuck Colson says Nixon's supposed excessive drinking was not so. I have seen Mr. Nixon take a number of drinks on occasion, but I never saw him overdo it. At least not when he was Vice President. I never saw him when he was President.

Although I admired and had much to do with President Kennedy, I had relatively little contact with his brother, Robert Kennedy. Once I recall while I was in Sen. Everett Dirksen's office with Robert Kennedy, Hubert Humphrey, Hugh Scott, and others drafting the language for the civil-rights legislation of 1961, Kennedy came over to me after the meeting and shook my hand and thanked me. To this day I don't know what for. I think he was probably just trying to butter me up.

Sen. William Knowland of California was a very stubborn leader while he was in the Senate. He had a one-track mind and was very close-mouthed. He always seemed to know how everyone else was going to vote, but many of us never had any idea where he was or how he would vote. When Taft became ill and made Knowland acting leader, I was minority whip. My feelings were hurt at the time because no one in the Republican leadership discussed the move with me. Personally I don't think I had the temperament for the job, but I was hurt that it wasn't offered to me.

My relations with the late Joe Martin never were friendly. There was nothing personal in the chasm between us, but Martin just didn't want another Harvard man with connections running for high office in Massachusetts. I can still see Martin trying to get Dick Wigglesworth, a close friend of mine, to persuade me not to run for governor in 1938. As I said earlier, Martin wanted George Bates, who was a representative from Salem, to run. I told him: "Joe, let Bates run if he wants to, but I'm in it all the way." After I became governor, our relationship warmed somewhat.

* * *

No man likes to think about retirement, least of all in the exciting atmosphere of Washington. But in 1966, when I had to decide whether I should run again, I was seventy-four; Alice was agreeable to my serving one more term, but I felt I could not be sure of my strength or my usefulness when I entered my eighties. I remember how my good friend Alexander Smith of New Jersey had had to take naps and conserve his energy when he was campaigning for what proved to be his last term. After those six years, both his wife and his doctor were opposed to him running again and as the time for a final decision approached, he asked for my advice. "Lev," he said, "I want you to give me your candid opinion. What do you think I ought to do?"

"Well," I replied, "if your wife feels as seriously about it as she does, and it will be difficult for you to campaign vigorously, I think you ought to retire." Our friendship survived, but I don't think he ever quite forgave me for being so frank.

What prompted my own decision was seeing our two oldest members, Carl Hayden of Arizona, and Theodore Greene of Rhode Island, both of whom in earlier years had played such a leading part in the Senate, now close their eyes and relax in their chairs, not once, but repeatedly. This was a warning I took to myself. To step down before I was seventy-five, to return to our farm in Dover and to the family gatherings, and to renew my associations in Boston and Cambridge, was the sensible thing to do.

Most senators and congressmen, however, do not want to retire and hang on as long as the electorate will tolerate them. They are perhaps influenced by the reality of Washington politics that once a senator or representative resigns, retires, or has been defeated, he or she is really "out" in the true sense of the word. Former colleagues are always glad to see the "outs" — briefly — for only a handshake and a catch-up on the news. But that's the extent of it because the senators and representatives have much business to perform and cannot dally with their old associates. That is why when I retired and returned to Dover, I vowed that I would never return to Washington unless I had something specific to do or some person to see.

I have often been asked whether I believe there should be a limit on the number of terms senators and representatives should be allowed to serve. Such a limit of, say, six terms in the House or two in the Senate certainly is inviting, but I believe the detrimental aspects of such a limitation far outweigh the good features. Congressmen would become lame ducks, as is the case with a second-term President, and this fact would greatly curtail the outgoing congressman's ability to perform and get things passed.

* * *

During the strenuous years when I knew I would be called on to speak, I used to get help and sound advice by recalling a handful of quotations which I have for many years carried with me in my wallet. As, for instance, when Horace said: "Be brief so that the thought does not stand in its own way, hindered by words that weigh down the tired ears."

This axiom I learned from Sam Rayburn when he was Speaker of the House: "The unspoken word never defeats one . . . what one does not say does not have to be explained."

Disraeli (to a new member who had asked whether he should speak) said: "It is better to have members wonder why you don't speak rather than wonder why you do."

The much-admired Professor Santayana wrote to Chauncey Stillman, and said in part, "The greatest service which any man can render to his fellows consists not in any specific and may be rendered in any profession. It consists in the influence direct and indirect which he may exert by force of character."

Lord Francis Jeffrey said: "Good will, like a good name, is got by many actions and lost by one."

And the clear-headed statement by Walter S. Gifford that I have mentioned earlier: "Success in life is relative. In my judgment success means making the most of such ability, personality and physique as you have. Don't measure your success against others, but against your own potentialities."

These are sound truths and have always been of invaluable assistance to me over the years.

My credo in the Senate, as it was in the Massachusetts House, was to be thoroughly prepared before speaking on a subject. There is always someone present who is an expert on whatever one plans to discuss, so I made it a point to be prepared when I spoke. Dick Russell never spoke at any great length. He just made his point. Senator Byrd gave long, written speeches, but no one could hear him when he addressed the Senate so you had to read the text of his remarks later to find out exactly what he said. But Byrd always knew what he was talking about and was greatly respected by his colleagues. John Kennedy didn't speak very often when he was in the Senate. But when he did, as he did when he proposed his important amendment to the Taft-Hartley legislation, he was very well versed on the subject matter. And he usually had someone like Archibald Cox sitting next to him to assist him.

* * *

A senator's staff is predicated upon the population of his state and as Massachusetts is one of the larger, I was entitled to seventeen assistants. Three of my trusted team in Boston came down with me to Washington, Henry Minot, James Reynolds, and Russell Gerould; and when as time went on they asked to be relieved, I saw them go with sincere regret. Their places were filled by men of the younger generation: by Bradford Morse, a lawyer from Lowell, for whom I found a place in the Pentagon, and who because of his interest in national defense ultimately joined my staff and later became my administrative assistant; by Jonathan Moore, a Massachusetts boy who came to me after having seen foreign service in Africa; by Elliot Richardson of Ropes and Gray, a distinguished law firm in Boston, whose advice I sought in my search for a young assistant, only to discover that Elliot, himself, was ready to come to Washington; by Philip Allen, who was attracted by the work I was doing in the Armed Services Committee; by Charles Colson, a captain of marines, who served me loyally and was invaluable as my campaign manager in 1960 and chief administrator of my office. More recently Colson's loyalty to another led him into difficulties.

And others: Tom Winship, the son of the editor of *The Boston Globe* and more recently its editor, who helped with our public relations and correspondence; John Jackson, who was most loyal over many years and who once was badly hurt in an auto accident when he was on a mission on my behalf and later killed in another accident; and my son, Bill, who joined the force in 1954 and stayed with me until I retired. These are a few of "my alumni," to whom I am particularly grateful.

Of my secretaries, I depended on the skill and patience of Pennie Gouzoule, Betty Bryden, and Evelyn Slater, the foremost of several conscientious girls. In the summer months there were college students who joined us to see how the wheels worked, and who for a nominal salary of $60 a month were admitted to the floor of the Senate and so became my "ears" on matters that were being debated while I was engrossed in committee work. I am a strong believer in inviting college students of both sexes to become familiar not only with Congress but with the many bureaus and commissions which conduct the day-to-day business of our national government.

* * *

Perhaps the most emotional experience I ever enjoyed in a lifetime of public service came in 1970 — the 350th anniversary of the sailing of the Mayflower from Plymouth, England.

On Sept. 16, 1620, 100 men and women left Plymouth and landed at Plymouth Rock on Dec. 20, 1620. One elder had died and a baby had been born on the trip across. They arrived in

December, but by next April there were only forty survivors.

I was pleased when Governor Sargent asked me to represent him and Massachusetts, first in Leyden, where the Pilgrims embarked, only to be diverted by adverse winds to Plymouth. At Plymouth, with the lord mayor and other officials, in my cutaway and top hat I reviewed the marines and witnessed a colorful parade before some 70,000 people. As a guest of the city, I was housed in the late Nancy Astor's home, which she had given to the city. There were visits to the surrounding historic castles and to the British Navy Yard, and when I was called on to speak, I stressed the hardihood of the Pilgrims in that tiny, cold, crowded ship, and their courage.

I walked up and down the Hoe, a beautiful set of grass terraces sloping down to the harbor. In my mind I tried to picture the gala band concert and the dancing on this famous green that Lady Astor arranged for Prime Minister Winston Churchill as he came to inspect the second-worst bombing of Britain in the Blitz. Instead of tears, Lady Astor and the citizens of Plymouth greeted him with smiles and cheers and they danced on the Hoe before they began to clean up the rubble of the bombing. It made me proud of the British fortitude.

So passed for me three exciting days. Altogether, it was a mighty pleasant experience of a lifetime in public affairs, and especially so because I was invited by the Queen Mother to lunch with her. Our No. 5 in the Henley crew, Bill Middendorf, had written a little booklet concerning the crew. He had sent one to our ambassador, whose aide turned it over to me to give to the Queen Mother when I met her at luncheon. She quickly skimmed through it, and we reminisced together about that occasion which meant so much to our crew when we revisited Henley and rowed again fifty years after we had won in 1914.

The trophies that were given to me on this important anniversary in Plymouth I turned over to Governor Sargent for the archives in the State House.

* * *

One monument that is known around the world is the Bunker Hill Monument in Charlestown, which was built by subscriptions. The last large gift that helped to complete the monument came from Judah Truro of New Orleans, and this is how it happened: Gen. Resin Davis Shepard, my great-great-grandfather, saved Judah's life in the Battle of New Orleans in 1812 by placing the wounded soldier on a hay cart that hurried him to a hospital. Truro, when he learned about the need of funds to complete the monument, sent $10,000 to General Shepard to be matched here in Boston, and my forebear, I think, must have chipped in.

I told this story at a reception in Charlestown honoring one of their judges, when Sonny McDonough, the long-popular governor's councilor, was presiding. Sonny was a great humorist and very successful in the insurance business. When I finished my story and started out of the chamber, Sonny, smiling at the audience, remarked, "If the Saltonstalls helped to finance the monument, you can be sure they put a mortgage on it the next Monday." I rushed back to the microphone and countered, "If we put a mortgage on the Bunker Hill Monument, you can be sure Sonny got the insurance on that mortgage." Neither Sonny nor I have ever forgotten that exchange.

* * *

As I walk along the street, these days, people stop and say, "You look well," or as one man remarked as he shook my hand, "Glad to see you are still standing up!" I suppose what pleases me the most is the gratitude of those who stop me and say: "I've never met you before, but I do want to thank you for what you did to help me get a job in 1933." My answer always is: "If I was of any help to you, I am glad." I rarely recall what I did, but it pleases me to have them remember. I still get letters from those who see me on the MBTA or read some newspaper story that carries my name, and some are amusing. I recall a short one I received from a mother while I was governor saying, "I have just had triplets. What are you going to do about it?" I think I answered her I wasn't sure.

But, seriously, the reward of the forty-five years that I have been in politics are these personal meetings with strangers, the gratitude of those whom I have tried to assist, and the friendships that have lasted.

INDEX

www.ingramcontent.com/pod-product-compliance
Lightning Source LLC
Chambersburg PA
CBHW021713130826
49797CB00043B/191